The Unexpected Gift of Trauma

The
Unexpected
Gift of Trauma

The Path to
Posttraumatic Growth

···

DR. EDITH SHIRO

With Linda Sparrowe

HARVEST
An Imprint of WILLIAM MORROW

Posttraumatic Growth Inventory used with permission of Richard G. Tedeschi and Lawrence Calhoun from *Trauma & Transformation: Growing in the Aftermath of Suffering* (1995); permission conveyed through Copyright Clearance Center, Inc.

Posttraumatic Changes Questionnaire used with permission of Stephen Joseph from *What Doesn't Kill Us: The New Psychology of Posttraumatic Growth* (2011); permission conveyed through Copyright Clearance Center, Inc.

This book contains advice and information relating to health care. It should be used to supplement rather than replace the advice of your doctor or another trained health professional. If you know or suspect you have a health problem, it is recommended that you seek your physician's advice before embarking on any medical program or treatment. All efforts have been made to ensure the accuracy of the information contained in this book as of the date of publication. This publisher and the author disclaim liability for any medical outcomes that may occur as a result of applying the methods suggested in this book. Names and identifying details of some of the people portrayed in this book have been changed.

HarperCollins books may be purchased for educational, business, or sales promotional use. For information, please email the Special Markets Department at SPsales@harpercollins.com.

FIRST EDITION

Designed by Chloe Foster

Library of Congress Cataloging-in-Publication Data has been applied for.

ISBN 978-0-358-71366-1

22 23 24 25 26 LBC 5 4 3 2 1

To Ariel

en memoria de papi

Contents

The World Can Be a Scary Place

Trauma has always been part of the human experience.

You don't have to look very far to find suffering in the world: the news is filled with examples of genocide, hate crimes, terrorist attacks, wars, and natural disasters. Victim statistics speak to the hidden pain within our homes: one in five children are molested; one in four grew up with an alcoholic caregiver; one in four women have been physically abused by an intimate partner. Microaggressions related to racial inequality, religious intolerance, gender, and sexual orientation dominate the headlines. Fear and unrest in the streets have split communities apart; a rise in police brutality, suicides, and domestic violence have all thrown more fuel on the fire. And if that weren't enough to question the safety of our world, along came COVID-19, the worldwide pandemic that upended everything, leaving people feeling isolated and frightened.

And no wonder. Many lost their jobs, while others had jobs that put them at risk for getting sick or dying. Their daily routines stopped making sense, and they questioned whether things would ever return to normal again. Millions were isolated from their families and friends for periods of time, which compounded their distress. The pandemic has triggered deep-rooted *collective* wounds of loneliness. This collective trauma is our silent, unrecognized epidemic.

All of this is trauma. As much as we'd like it to be otherwise, trauma is an unavoidable part of what it means to be alive, to be in this world. It's the feeling that arises from an event we experience, a feeling that our lives have been shattered, that the world is a dangerous, unpredictable place, and that there's no light at the end of the proverbial tunnel. Everything we believed to be true no longer holds, and we are left with a debilitating sense of hopelessness and confusion, and often lifelong physical and mental health issues. It's no wonder that people want to know how to circumvent trauma or, at the very least, recover quickly from the pain. They want to know how to cultivate resilience so they can return as quickly as possible to where they were before tragedy struck; so they can inoculate themselves and those they love from future suffering. Later on in the book, I talk about why resilience may be an impediment to posttraumatic growth (PTG).

If trauma indeed shatters our deepest-held beliefs regarding the world and our place in it, is it even possible to grow from it? Can it really be a catalyst for positive transformation? And how is it that some people can go through a horrific experience and remain stuck in pain for years, barely able to function, while others going through *the same traumatic event* will not only survive but thrive—not in spite of their experience but because of it? That is the paradox of trauma: it has both the power to destroy and the power to transform.

This paradox has animated my work as a clinical psychologist for more than two decades. To some, it may feel disrespectful or even untrue to insist that growth and transformation can emerge from unspeakable tragedy. Yet, it can.

I have witnessed it over and over again in individuals who have suffered heartbreak and loss, domestic abuse, and catastrophic illness; in communities that have endured the worst of the worst—torture, ravages of war, global pandemics, unrelenting racism or homophobia, violence, and massive destruction from natural disasters. And, I have known it to be true long before I became a clinical psychologist.

A Personal Connection: My Lifelong Interest in Trauma

My fascination with these questions began in my childhood and is deeply personal. Every generation on both sides of my family has suffered greatly from trauma. I am the granddaughter of Holocaust survivors, who were the only members of their families to get out of the Nazi death camps alive. I'm also the granddaughter of Syrian refugees who fled their home country, traveling on foot with their six young children—from Aleppo into Israel. My grandmother, heavy with child, gave birth in the Bloudan mountains and had no choice but to keep going. I'm the daughter of Jewish immigrants, who escaped from political, religious, and social persecution and made their way to South America. I've been a minority Jewish woman in Venezuela, and, later, a minority Latina immigrant studying and working in the United States. I have experienced the impact of migration and multicultural conditions firsthand. I know what it's like to be exposed to discrimination in my own neighborhood and city. This, too, is trauma.

The experience of my maternal grandparents, whom I affectionately called Nana and Lalu since I was a child, was particularly instrumental in awakening my interest in the complexities of trauma and, eventually, my research and clinical practice. Nana and Lalu were born in Transylvania (now Romania). Nana was an only child who grew up poor in the city of Oradea. Her father was a gambler and her mother tried to make ends meet by taking in sewing and other odd jobs. Nana was very lonely, and she took comfort in reading books, listening to music, and drawing. During the war, Nana and her parents were transported to Auschwitz, where they were quickly separated from each other. She never saw them again. Nana suffered greatly in the concentration camps, enduring appalling abuse at the hands of her captors. Eventually she was able to escape and made her way on foot to a communal house where several young survivors of the camps had gathered. It was there she met my grandfather, and it was there my mother was born.

Lalu grew up in the village of Crasna. His family was more stable financially, his father was a Jewish community leader in the village, and he remembers a childhood that was relatively happy and carefree, filled with many adventures and good friends. That all changed, of course, when the soldiers came and took them all to the concentration camps. He was the only one of his family to survive the slaughter.

Communism and the continued persecution of the Jews forced Nana and Lalu to escape Romania with their two daughters and eventually make their way to Venezuela, where they joined a family member who had already settled there. My father's family, in the meantime, had left Israel and immigrated to Venezuela as well. That's where my mother and father met and where I was born, a second-generation Holocaust survivor of Syrian refugees.

Growing up among immigrant families in Venezuela, I knew people who seemed stuck in their trauma. Some were completely numb, shut down, barely able to function. Others seemed outwardly to have it together, and yet struggled with a deep depression that wore them down. My grandmother was among them.

Outwardly, Nana was beautiful; a stately, self-possessed woman with a brilliant, creative mind. She spoke several languages, spent much of her time working, writing, and reading, and loved to cook delicious meals for her family. Inwardly, however, she was suffering. She talked about the war often, the pain and fear she experienced, the horror of witnessing her family members being shot and killed, her uncanny luck of being in the right line where lives were spared, all of which I ingested with every spoonful of matzo ball soup she so lovingly prepared. Although I always felt her love for me—she was an amazing grandmother—I often felt her sadness as well, without always knowing where it came from. In many ways, the painful reminders of her past, which Nana relived in her mind and through the stories she told, kept her from truly enjoying life. Sadly, she died relatively young.

There were others in my community who were determined to keep going, not dwell on the past, and become successful in spite of all they had gone through. The more I heard their stories, the more these trauma responses made sense to me: after all, some had barely survived the atrocities of war while others struggled to adjust after being forced to leave their countries behind.

There was another group, however, that captivated me: those who enjoyed a level of happiness and well-being seemingly at odds with their gruesome past. My grandfather was one of them. In fact, to me, he epitomized what I would come to recognize as posttraumatic growth.

I loved being around Lalu. Everyone enjoyed his company. His joy was infectious. He was always up for exploring new ideas, new places. He loved to travel and often told us stories of his adventures. He had a deep appreciation for his family and his community, and it gave him great pleasure to take care of others who were struggling. He taught us to be grateful for the little things we had and to never take anything for granted.

Lalu hadn't always been so joyful. My mother tells me that it was quite difficult for him after the war. Like everyone else, he had lost so much and had suffered immensely. He became deeply depressed for a couple of years. And then something switched in him. He wrote about it in the journals he kept:

> Like so many millions more, I have learned that life and death go hand in hand. There is an old song that tells the story of a peasant who meets a mysterious man on horseback who gives him an order: "You have to get there." All my life I felt an internal voice that dictated to me that "you have to get there." In my life and in that of all of those who survived what was the terrible Second World War, many times we had to repeat with great force that internal order. Throughout my life the mysterious man on horseback was my life instinct and the impulse that made me feel what to follow. I would hear his voice blowing into my ear, "Strive and go." Even in the most extremely difficult moments, when I was hungry, frozen, sick and persecuted, I heard him say "you have to fight, you have to get there . . ."

Lalu certainly had moments of sadness, burdened by the memories of what he and his family had endured during the Holocaust. He never forgot what happened nor did he minimize the suffering of so many. But at one point, he made a choice to put the past in the past and move forward, knowing he "had to fight," he had "to get there," if not for himself, then for his family and for his community. At one point, he asked himself, *Did I really get there?* As he wrote in his journal, "The answer isn't worth thinking much about nor does it allow for philosophizing about." He said, "I now contemplate our family: my wife, my daughters, their husbands, my grandchildren, and the answer is clear: the fight was worth it . . . yes, I did arrive."

He could talk about his feelings and he could talk about the past—often from a philosophical or cultural perspective—without allowing it to intrude on the present. In fact, he chose to fully embrace the present, with curiosity and gratitude—grateful for everything he had, for being alive, for being given a second chance. He was such an inspiration to me, always encouraging us to keep our eyes and hearts open to new adventures, to new ideas, and to the fullness of life. Lalu was not only free of the suffering from his past; he had transcended it.

There were many in our community like Lalu, who believed that their experiences gave their lives more meaning and purpose and helped them to become wiser and kinder members of society. And there were those who were simply resilient and determined to succeed in spite of what they had been through. There were also many like Nana, who were tethered to their pain and their past. All of this fascinated me. I wanted to know what kept some imprisoned in their trauma, others barely touched by theirs, and still others not only healed but transformed.

My curiosity about the human experience eventually led me to pursue my doctorate in clinical psychology with an emphasis on trauma and, more specifically, posttraumatic growth. Although I was fortunate to learn from some brilliant minds whose PTG research has informed my own, most of the psychological studies in the field have focused almost exclusively on the negative consequences of trauma, overlooking its positive impacts on our lives. Some researchers believe that the growth people report from trauma is just their subjective perception, that it's nothing more than an illusion or a temporary feeling.

I don't agree. My research and clinical work have underscored what I observed growing up: the possibility of growth is no illusion; it's real, it's quantifiable, and it's possible. I've helped hundreds of individuals, families, and communities, some of whom have faced unimaginable hardships, heal from and grow beyond their traumas. The very idea of growth can seem beyond the realm of possibility—and yet it happens time and again. I don't ever want to minimize the physical, mental, and emotional effort it takes to do the work. And, at the same time, I know that it is possible if people commit fully to the process.

How We Respond to Trauma

Not everyone achieves PTG; and not everyone necessarily desires to. What I've come to realize in my years of work in this field is that very few people know that PTG exists and is even possible—and that's one of the misconceptions about trauma that I'd like to change with this book.

Throughout the book I share many inspiring stories from the lives of my patients and a few well-known public figures, to illustrate their journeys from suffering to healing. To protect their privacy, however, I have changed the names of my patients and some of the defining characteristics of their story.

Most people who have been impacted by trauma generally respond in three different ways: they either get stuck in trauma, bounce back, or leap forward.

Stuck in Trauma

Some people suffer greatly long past the initial traumatic experience. They stay stagnant in pain and loss, unable to recover or even return to some semblance of life before trauma. They're paralyzed by all they've lost and by the pain they continue to feel. They may feel overwhelmed and without the resources to recover.

Clinically, we refer to this as PTSD (posttraumatic stress disorder), and it can last for many years. It can occur as a result of any type of traumatic event—and as a reaction to it—and it cuts across all socioeconomic levels, ethnicities, and cultures. Our cultural awareness of PTSD has increased dramatically in recent decades, and it's often one of the first conditions people associate with trauma.

María is a prime example. She grew up in the Dominican Republic and when she was just nine years old her father, in a drunken state, gave her to a sexual predator. His monstrous abuse was protected under the guise of being a "sorcerer." The harm she endured at the hands of this older man nearly killed her. Somehow, she managed to escape, but the experience left her paralyzed with fear. She couldn't go to school, she couldn't relate to or trust her parents, and she contemplated suicide on more than one occasion. For many years, she stayed stuck in PTSD, unable to enter into, much less enjoy, a loving physical relationship. I'll talk more about María's journey throughout the book.

Bouncing Back

Some people are more resilient; they have a lot more tools at their disposal, such as strong family support, the ability to regulate their emotions, a spiritual awareness and connection, and certain personality traits—all of which enables them to return to their old life or at least adjust to a life similar to what they had before the trauma. It won't ever really be the same, but it'll be good enough and they will be fine right there. Much of the current research on trauma focuses on this group, as a model of healing and recovery. And, in some ways, it is.

Resilience allows people to weather the storm and stay put. They've been through war, experienced acts of cruelty, felt as though their lives have been shattered, suffered through a divorce, the death of someone they love—any traumatic event—and still find the fortitude, strength, and flexibility to function, *in spite of what they've been through*. Resilient people are often highly successful members of society, driven to excel. They may suffer from low-level depression, anxiety, have emotional setbacks, or experience traumatic memories, but they still do well in life.

Three Possible Outcomes

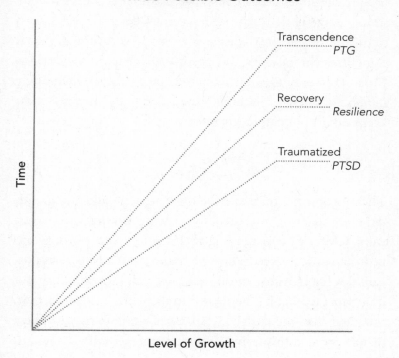

My patient Miranda is the very definition of resilience. Although she's never gotten over the intense grief she experienced after the death of her beloved mother, she hasn't let it get in her way of the life she's created. She's thrown herself into everything that has come her way with determination and focus. She became a highly regarded doctor and, at the same time, she is a wife, and a mother of four children. She's strong, tough, and adaptable, able to rebound and move forward. And, like most resilient people, she feels good about the life she's created and sees no reason to upend it.

Some traditional psychologists suggest that people who haven't developed PTSD or shown classic signs of distress are simply denying their pain, using certain defense mechanisms to push it out of their conscious awareness. Although that is sometimes the case, it's also possible that such individuals as Miranda have figured out how to cope with overwhelmingly difficult challenges without experiencing the paralysis that keeps others in debilitating pain.

Leaping Forward

These people fascinate me the most—people like my grandfather, who are committed to growing *beyond* where they were before, of transcending their trauma and moving into posttraumatic growth. They see trauma and adversity as possibilities for transformation, wisdom, and growth. They not only process what has happened to them and recover from it, but their lives are enriched *because* of the experience. These people more than survive; each one emerges with a new understanding of life, a deeper connection to community, and more awareness of their divine purpose. Such an opportunity for rebirth often gives rise to a renewed commitment to be of service and to share the gift of their wisdom with others.

The news is filled with examples of "everyday heroes" who endured childhood abuse, abject poverty, or domestic violence. People like Oprah Winfrey, Frida Kahlo, Lady Gaga, orchestra conductor Gustavo Dudamel, Nelson Mandela, and activist Malala Yousafzai have bravely chosen to name, heal, and integrate their traumatic past into their lives and use their fame as a way to ease the suffering of others.

I have countless examples of people I've worked with who

were able to go from debilitating PTSD to the freedom that posttraumatic growth offers. Alejandro, a teenager whose story I tell in these pages, was shot multiple times when a gunman opened fire at his high school. As you can imagine, as a survivor of the shooting, he endured terrible emotional and physical suffering. Over the years, he began to see that his experience—as horrific as it was—gave him a purpose in life and the strength and compassion to put it into action. He tells me all the time that he knows he survived for a reason; that his God has something more important in mind for him. He has begun speaking out to other kids about what he went through, sharing what he had learned, and vowing to be meaningful to society.

I'm not suggesting that everyone who has experienced trauma fits neatly into any of these three responses and stays there. Nor am I suggesting that posttraumatic growth is an automatic, immediate, or even linear outcome of the trauma-recovery process. Trauma is complicated. The road to posttraumatic growth is hard. It requires daily, conscious awareness of our intention to move beyond the traumatic event or situation, without dismissing or downplaying the difficulties we're going through.

In order to do that, however, we need to know that transformation is possible; that it can't be rushed; and that there's a way to get there. Research has long shown that PTG is indeed possible, but until now, hasn't delineated a clear path forward. I wrote *The Unexpected Gift of Trauma* to not only introduce posttraumatic growth, but to offer an explicit five-stage model to achieve it, which has proved successful on an individual, cultural, and systemic level.

How to Use This Book

I invite you to read this book wherever you are on your post-traumatic journey. There is no timeline to complete this book or these stages. My hope is that this book meets you where you are, provides you with what you need at this moment, and continues to support you as you make your way further along your path of healing. Because not everyone is familiar with PTG, it may help you to share what you're learning with your support network—your mentor, therapist, close friends also going through the journey with you. There is no mandate on how to read this book—I'll leave that up to you.

In Part I, I define some fundamental concepts, share some history around trauma, and get more specific about what posttraumatic growth is—and what it is not—on an individual level as well as a collective level. I introduce what I call "floating factors," which have the power to either increase the possibility of posttraumatic growth or hinder it, and give examples of the different ways that trauma can show up in our everyday lives as well as the power it has to destroy families, communities, and entire cultures. We may experience trauma born from our own adverse childhood experiences or from historic or intergenerational suffering we may not even be aware of. Posttraumatic growth allows us not only to transcend the trauma for ourselves and for the collective, but to stop the effects of the trauma from going forward to the next generation.

The idea of posttraumatic growth—deriving benefit from painful experiences—may sound counterintuitive, but I've witnessed tremendous growth in my patients over the years with my five-stage model. This approach has helped individuals and communities go from crisis to growth. I've seen this growth in those who have endured unspeakable acts of violence as well as others who have suffered through the heartbreak of a painful divorce, a debilitating accident, the shame of being bullied, or the death of a child. Once hopeless and anxious, they have emerged empowered and confident. All of this continues to inspire my belief that trauma can be a springboard for radical transformation and emotional and spiritual growth; that there is profound wisdom locked within our suffering, waiting to be revealed.

Part II presents my five-stage framework in detail; here's a snapshot of what to expect:

1. **The Stage of Awareness: Radical Acceptance.** In this first stage, you admit that you're in pain and don't have the emotional tools to deal with what's happening by yourself.
2. **The Stage of Awakening: Safety and Protection.** Seek out help and support in the form of a person you can trust, a safe space or situation.
3. **The Stage of Becoming: A New Narrative.** As you become curious about other ways of thinking and being, you begin to craft a new narrative for who you are and all the possibilities of what you can become.
4. **The Stage of Being: Integration.** Here, you can integrate the old ways of being with your new understanding of yourself and your situation. And you can enjoy a newfound sense of identity.

5. **The Stage of Transforming: Wisdom and Growth.** In this stage, you become clearer about your purpose in life, your relationships are more meaningful, you become an active member in your community, and you begin to help others in return.

My hope is that having a roadmap will help you recognize when you're stuck and what to do next to navigate the process, so you can experience a sense of renewal and rebirth, and even a spiritual awakening. My five stages provide a language to identify, define, express, and communicate the process of healing. They serve as predictable milestones to measure progress, thereby minimizing hopelessness and despair. The framework not only guides anyone experiencing the trauma, but it can be a roadmap for their expert companions—therapists, mentors, sponsors, and even family members—to offer PTG as a possibility.

Within each stage, I share specific tools and practices that facilitate the healing and growth process and explain the intrinsic and contextual factors that influence positive transformation. I also elucidate the obstacles we may encounter along the way that can impede growth or even re-traumatize us if we're not careful. And, finally, I share ways we can stay in posttraumatic growth.

A Book for Our Times

This five-stage framework was developed and grew over many years as I helped patients see their way through to the other side of trauma. It's been an invaluable tool in my practice, and a gift for my patients who have created lives they never believed were possible. I believe that *The Unexpected Gift of Trauma* is a book people need right now. It presents not only a way to transcend perpetually debilitating posttraumatic stress, but it's also a clear path to meaningful transformation. This book is for those who've experienced acute and chronic trauma and who believe (and fear) they'll never move beyond it. It's for those who carry the residue of intergenerational and historical trauma and wonder what they can do to stop it from affecting future generations. And it is for all of us who want to do whatever we can to ease the burden of others, to remember our shared humanity, and to invite us into a kinder, healthier, and more equitable world.

I

Understanding Posttraumatic Growth

Chapter 1

The Framework

I believe not only that trauma is curable, but that the healing process can be a catalyst for profound awakening.

—PETER A. LEVINE, PHD

For the past thirty years, I have been privileged to work with individuals, families, and communities who have suffered greatly from personal, cultural, and systemic traumas. I've shared many of their stories in these pages as examples of how trauma infiltrates our lives—and the lives of our families and communities. Refugees fleeing from violent, repressive regimes; women and children physically, sexually, or emotionally abused; communities reeling from the aftermath of genocide, either current or historical; victims of school shootings and their families; and hundreds of others trying to make sense of and heal from acrimonious divorces, school bullying, suicide, accidents, and premature deaths.

I feel honored they've chosen to put their trust in me, allowing me to bear witness to their pain and listen deeply to their stories. The work we do together sets them on a path to recovery, and beyond that, toward growth and wisdom. Every story they've told of lives being shattered, families torn apart, the despair and loneliness that erode their ability to function, breaks my heart open. And every story of vulnerability, courage, and determination that moves them from broken to whole, from confusion to clarity, affirms my faith in the human spirit. Over and over again, my work reminds me that growth can spring from adversity in sometimes surprising ways.

The path to posttraumatic growth is not an easy one, but there are ways to facilitate the process. I am always hopeful people will find a therapist, mentor, teacher, or companion who believes in the possibility of posttraumatic growth—or even a space, group, or organization—and can facilitate their achieving it. My five-stage model was inspired by those who came before me and pioneered the early work on PTG; it has emerged from my clinical work and what I have learned from working with countless patients, and it continues to be informed by my lifelong spiritual journey. I think of it as a path, a roadmap, or a framework that gives people a universal language and a structure they can use to make sense of their trauma, process it, and grow from it.

Just as we will discuss throughout this book, the model describes the process of healing from a unique blend of psychodynamic psychology, neurobiology, and epigenetics. It takes a holistic, mind-body-spirit approach that centers both the individual and the collective. It's informed by a relational and systemic approach; it's intergenerational and cultural.

No road to growth is a straight line. There's no such thing as a linear approach, because there's nothing linear or predictable about human emotions or experiences. It is not meant to place our experiences, feelings, or reactions neatly into boxes contained within the stages. Every feeling, every thought, every reaction is unique—and every person experiences them differently. And yet, I've observed that, over time, patterns emerge, a common language is revealed that expresses an almost universality in the ways people face their traumas and heal from them, which never ceases to amaze me. My model has codified what I've observed and gives people a framework to understand what's happening. My goal is to offer a shared language that will help us translate and make sense of what we were going through.

Previous PTG Models

The concept of posttraumatic growth has been around a lot longer than I have—and so have myriad paths to attain it. I've benefited from some amazing researchers, clinicians, and mentors who came before me, whose understanding of trauma and posttraumatic growth has informed my own, and whose models for healing have paved the way for the framework I've developed.

Psychologists and researchers Richard Tedeschi and Lawrence Calhoun, who coined the term "posttraumatic growth," use a five-step process, which entails learning from the trauma; managing distress; disclosing the trauma; creating a narrative; and finding a mission. Judith Herman, the author of *Trauma and Recovery,* uses a four-step path to recovery, which focuses on individual empowerment: creating a safe container; remembering the trauma and mourning the old self; creating a new identity; and reestablishing community. Stephen Joseph, in his book *What Doesn't Kill Us,* outlines six "signposts," that can facilitate posttraumatic growth. They include taking stock of the situation; harvesting hope; reauthoring; identifying change; valuing change; and putting change into action. Ronnie Janoff-Bulman's theory of shattered assumptions—which I talk about in later chapters—was also instrumental in my understanding of posttraumatic growth. And, finally, with the guidance and mentorship of Carl Auerbach, PhD, psychology professor at Yeshiva University, we developed the initial model out of the work we did with Cambodian refugees.* The model has continued to grow and become more sophisticated over the past twenty-five years to become what it is today.

Every model is an attempt to provide a structure, a kind of roadmap people can follow that will lead them toward healing and growth. For the most part, these approaches I've described come out of an individualistic point of view, presenting a theory of trauma that is centered in the individual experience and that looks at how trauma has prevented a person from functioning. My approach goes beyond the individual to include a cultural, contextual, and systemic focus. My model also views healing through a neuropsychological, intergenerational, and spiritual perspective and looks at how it manifests in the body, mind, and nervous system.

The Five-Stage Model of PTG

The framework I've developed begins with the understanding that committing to the process of growth requires a willingness to leap beyond one's comfort zone with mindful

---

* For more information, check out the chapter Carl Auerbach and I wrote in *Mass Trauma and Emotional Healing Around the World*, ed. Ani Kalayjian and Dominque Eugene (Praeger Press, 2010).

attention and an openness to receive the gifts of wisdom and growth.

Trauma and posttraumatic growth are always relational, always contextual. That means it's impossible to separate the individual and their experience from their family, community, culture, or heritage. Our traumas didn't happen in isolation; our healing can't either. What we have been through affects how we see ourselves, how we relate to others, and how we view the world and our place in it. This *collective* understanding—that there is no such thing as an individual and that we are a part of a larger group—is woven into the very fabric of our lives.

Second, the model is informed by neuroscience, particularly the study of epigenetics and neuroplasticity, which we talk about at length in Chapter 5. Neuroscience takes into account how our brain and nervous system process unresolved traumas not only from our childhood, but also those that have been passed down to us from previous generations. The emerging research on epigenetics has changed the way we think of trauma and the way we approach recovery.

And finally, the model has a strong mind-body-heart component. The pilgrimages and expeditions I've embarked on; the traditions I've immersed myself in; and the spiritual teachers I've studied with have opened my eyes and heart to the ways in which we are interconnected. We have the power to heal ourselves, and in doing so, to heal our family and our communities, and to protect future generations. The meditation techniques, mind-body modalities, energy work, and other practices I've learned have given me insight into the body's role in resolving traumatic residue, and have shown me the wisdom that lies within our deepest pain. It has taught

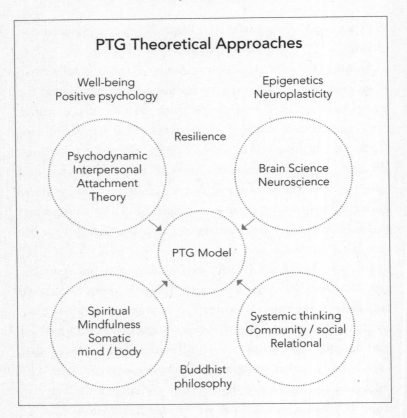

PTG Theoretical Approaches

Well-being
Positive psychology

Epigenetics
Neuroplasticity

Resilience

Psychodynamic
Interpersonal
Attachment
Theory

Brain Science
Neuroscience

PTG Model

Spiritual
Mindfulness
Somatic
mind / body

Systemic thinking
Community / social
Relational

Buddhist
philosophy

me that we are more than just this body, this mind, and these experiences. We are spiritual beings within a human experience.

The Five Stages: A Path to a New Reality

So what does the road from suffering to growth look like? How do we navigate it? First, remember, the healing process isn't linear. The stages are designed to build upon each other, but you're not marching through one stage at a time, checking off the boxes as you go. You may find you need to linger in one place for a while, until you're ready to move on. Maybe something comes up for you as you're doing the work in stage three and you need to go back to stage two and reestablish a sense of safety or ask for help. You may be ready to acknowledge one experience that's causing you pain, but not another.

The whole process begins with **Radical Acceptance,** the stage in which you admit you're in pain and you don't have the emotional tools or the physical strength to deal with what's happening by yourself. This is the moment of surrender. The self is weakened and vulnerable. You have a hard time relating to others; you feel isolated from family and friends, bewildered and overwhelmed. The world is chaotic, malevolent, and broken—unresponsive to your cries for help.

When you've accepted that your life is shattered, and you're ready to ask for or able to find help, you move into stage two, which is **Safety and Protection.** This is where you seek out a person you can trust, a safe place or a situation in which you feel protected, so that you can lay your burden down—without shame or blame—and express your true feelings. You do that by noticing and identifying the feelings, where you're carrying them in your body, and reconnecting with them. You can express them in a multitude of ways: talking, crying, moving, dancing, screaming, shaking—anything that will move the energy. You feel cared for and less alone, sheltered by the world around you. Things aren't so scary anymore. Within this safety net, you can allow yourself to feel your pain and allow others to respond to you with kindness. It's as though you can finally exhale.

The first two stages of posttraumatic growth can be

intense—it is akin to the shattering of the world as you know it. However, as the Sufi poet Rumi says, the opening of the wound is the place where the light enters, allowing you to release years of pain and suffering. This sense of spaciousness opens the doorway to the third stage: **A New Narrative**. This stage is more of a transitional and exploratory one. You permit yourself to be curious and open to other ways of thinking and being. You feel stronger within yourself, more valued within your community, and the world begins to make sense again, but in a new way. You're gathering new information, making plans, and forming a new perspective about yourself and the world—although at this point it's more theoretical; you haven't internalized anything yet. You're still trying on new identities in order to rebuild your own, and you tentatively recognize the world as accepting and intelligible.

By the fourth stage, **Integration**, you've chosen a new set of values and beliefs, and you're ready to put them into practice; to test-drive this new self out in the world. You're more self-assured and, on the whole, your relationships are healthier, and you're more in control of your life. You begin to expand upon the new narrative you've created—the new way of understanding yourself, your relationship to others, and the world—to include the whole of your experiences. You are *you* because of all you've lived through. Now that you have begun to heal from the wounds of your trauma, you see how to integrate the past event with your new narrative, the new world with the old. Integration might look something like: *I am a survivor of domestic violence and I am also a professor, a family member, and a loving friend.*

The fifth stage, which I call **Wisdom and Growth**, is at

the core of my work. This is when our trauma becomes the catalyst for transformation, and it is the stage I want everyone to reach.

In this stage, you begin to have a clear sense of identity and belonging; you feel more confident and proactive. Perhaps you've discovered your life's mission and have a new-found energy and passion because of your experiences. Your priorities shift, including toward serving others, because you now know what's truly important. Your life has meaning and purpose. You feel more spacious and have more clarity than you did before your traumatic experience. You now see there are multiple ways to do things, multiple opportunities for new possibilities to emerge. Many people at this stage feel they've grown spiritually, even acquiring higher levels of consciousness. This often leads to a desire to connect with others more compassionately, enhancing their desire to become an integral part of their communities.

Each of the five stages addresses trauma, recovery, and growth through three different, yet interlocking, lenses: our relationship to the self; our relationship to others; and our self in the world.

The self. This is the understanding of who we are, our identity. The self is about the power of personal strength. In strengthening our relationship to the self, we learn how to love the whole of ourselves—our vulnerabilities as well as our resilience, the shattered self and the confident one.

Others. This is how we are in relationships. It's about power through *connections*; that is, how we relate to others. It is how we exist beyond our individual selves; how our strength is evident in relationship with others.

The world. This is how we view the world and how we can either engage in it or withdraw from it. We sometimes call this "having agency," which can give us a sense of control over our environment. This is where we see the world as chaotic or more manageable, a world of no possibilities or a world full of possibilities. It is our individual power exerting itself in the world.

In Part II, I explain in more detail each step along the path to consciousness and growth, sharing examples from the stories I tell in these pages—and introducing some new ones, too. That way we can look at how people who have different experiences—and different reactions to those experiences— move through the stages from suffering to growth. I provide ways in which you can incorporate the stages into your own life—practices, questions to answer, and quick tips to experiment with—in order to benefit from your own journey toward healing.

NAVIGATING THE FIVE STAGES

1. **The Stage of Awareness: Radical Acceptance.** We acknowledge and accept the pain of our past experience and the hold that it has had on our lives

2. **The Stage of Awakening: Safety and Protection.** We take refuge in the safety of a therapist, a mentor, or a group of people we can trust.

3. **The Stage of Becoming: A New Narrative.** We give ourselves permission to reimagine a life replete with new possibilities and connections.

4. **The Stage of Being: Integration.** We embrace the wisdom born of our past experiences and integrate them into a new understanding of our self, our relationships, and the world.

5. **The Stage of Transforming: Wisdom and Growth.** We arrive at a place that feels like home, a place where we can nurture body and soul, independence and connection, and move toward a more conscious life, one of service and unconditional love.

Chapter 2

The Trauma of Everyday Life

You must have chaos within you in order to give birth to a dancing star.

—FRIEDRICH NIETZSCHE

The real voyage of discovery consists not in seeking new landscapes, but in having new eyes.

—MARCEL PROUST

As children, we look to our caregivers to guide us, to be nurturing and attentive; and when they are "good enough," providing a safe and nurturing environment, our world makes sense. It's safe and predictable. Unless something happens to destroy those assumptions, we maintain them as we get older. Growing up, we may subconsciously believe that good things happen to good people and, conversely, bad things *only* happen to bad or careless people. We might think to ourselves, *Since I am good and kind and hardworking—a decent human being—I'm invulnerable to tragedy and serious illness. I am strong and in control; my faith is unshakable.*

And then something happens. We have an experience so shocking it shakes us to the core, like a tragic death in the family or a terminal cancer diagnosis. Suddenly, it's as though we've been thrown into the epicenter of an earthquake; everything crumbles and shatters around us, calling into question everything we know to be true and leading us to believe we are somehow at fault. We are left feeling overwhelmed, helpless, and confused; unworthy and ashamed. If only we'd paid more attention, been kinder, worked harder, prayed more. This is a trauma response.

The trauma itself comes not from the event, but from how we interpret the event, the resources we have to deal with it, and the way we process it. Our response is connected to the meaning we make of the experience we have, but it's not necessarily proportional to the intensity of that experience. We can be in a car accident and come out of it unscathed. Someone we love dies, and we can mourn them and keep going. We lose our home to a fire or hurricane and soldier on. And then one day, we get fired from our job, or discover our partner is having an affair, or get assaulted walking home in broad daylight, and our world falls apart. What happened to us makes us question what it means to be this person, in this body. *How did this happen to me? What did I do wrong? Why am I being punished?*

When this happens, we become disconnected, dissociated from ourselves and from others. Such a rupture can destroy our connection with our support network and shatter our sense of belonging; it can sever the relationship we have with our community and cause us to lose our basic sense of self. This is particularly true when something traumatic happens in childhood and it's brought about by those very people—parents, educators, friends, and family—who are supposed to keep us safe.

Social and political psychologist Ronnie Janoff-Bulman calls this disconnect a "shattering of assumptions." David Trickey, a psychologist and codirector of the UK Trauma Council in London, calls it a "rupture in meaning-making." We all have certain assumptions that help us navigate the world, belief systems through which we process information and bring order to chaos. These are related to fundamental issues like our self-esteem, our faith in the kindness of others, our feelings of trust, security, and intimacy, even our understanding of death and loss.

My patient Alejandro's story illustrates this perfectly. Alejandro was born and raised in Venezuela, in a middle-class family with very few resources. By the time he was eleven, the political and cultural climate in Venezuela had become more unstable, and his family felt their lives were in danger. They decided to immigrate to the United States. They didn't really want to leave their home, but they said, "Okay, we're going to make the sacrifice because our lives will be better in the United States." They moved to a town in the Midwest, and Alejandro and his little brother enrolled in public school. By the time he was in high school, Alejandro had become an incredible soccer player—he lived for the sport. He already had agents approaching him and he knew for certain he would be successful as a professional player.

As they settled into their new life, Alejandro's parents often talked about how safe they felt in the United States, how the country was a predictable place, with a stable government they could count on. They believed if you worked hard and did well in school, you could be successful and happy there.

All of their assumptions changed in a single afternoon when a gunman opened fire at Alejandro's high school, killing many teenagers. Even more were injured, Alejandro included. Alejandro managed to call his father, who was with Alejandro's eighty-year-old grandfather (he was visiting from Venezuela at the time). The whole family was devastated. Everything they believed to be true was shattered. Alejandro's injuries—bullets lodged in his lungs, his legs, and his hips—destroyed his soccer dreams and with them, his identity. The family has worked hard to rebuild their lives, but they felt lost in a world that no longer felt safe or made any sense. The grandfather has never gotten over the trauma and still relives the shock of it all, the phone call, the scene at the school, the pain and suffering.

The word "trauma" comes from *trâvma,* a Greek word meaning "wound" or "injury." The *Oxford English Dictionary* describes it as "a psychic injury, especially one caused by emotional shock, the memory of which is repressed and remains unhealed." It can stem from a single event like a tragic accident, an assault, or a painful divorce, or from a repeated event such as years of abuse. It transcends socioeconomic status, age, gender, culture, ethnicity, or sexual orientation. Every single person goes through some kind of traumatic experience at some point in their lives—even being born can be traumatic. Judith Herman, MD, author of *Trauma and Recovery,* says psychological trauma is "an affliction of the powerless." With overwhelming force, it strips a victim of a "sense of control, connection, and meaning."

The Many Faces of Trauma

Trauma is often associated with major life events—like a school shooting—that people, almost without exception, agree are horrific. And rightly so. Atrocities such as war, genocide, terrorist attacks, global pandemics, and earthquakes and other natural disasters are all examples of traumatic events. We can clearly see the resulting destruction, bear witness to its power to rip apart families and communities, and empathically feel their pain.

These kinds of traumas can also play out as acts of violence leveled at individuals, and sadly, we've got plenty of examples of these as well: People being verbally or physically attacked because of their race, social class, sexual orientation, gender expression, the size and shape of their bodies, physical appearance, or their religious or spiritual beliefs. The numbers of Black men and women murdered by the police, caught on videotape so we can't deny or turn away from what happened. The murder or persecution of trans women, violence against marginalized groups like LGBTQ+, Muslims and Jews, immigrants, and Asian Americans—much of which makes its way onto the nightly news.

Trauma can also happen behind closed doors, within families or among strangers. These events are often hidden or purposely kept secret out of shame or fear. They may include domestic violence, rape, neglect, drug and alcohol addictions, dysfunctional family dynamics, and childhood physical, emotional, or sexual abuse.

Trauma can also be experienced from invisible wounds or microaggressions, leveled against those who are seen as suspect, "foreign," or different. By definition, these wounds are not always easy to identify, but they can cut like a knife. Asian men and women being taunted and blamed for causing the COVID-19 pandemic; Black men noticing people crossing the street to the other sidewalk to avoid walking by them; people with disabilities being laughed at, pitied, or treated like children—these are just a few of many examples.

I have experienced these microtraumas firsthand, as a Latina immigrant. When I first came to the United States from Venezuela, I settled in Boston. I was a clinical psychologist and had found a great job at one of the hospitals in the city, working with patients. I loved it. Outside of work, however, my life was a different story. Sometimes at a store, the salesperson would refuse to sell to me, questioning my ability to buy something because I didn't sound like I had the money. When I went to apply for a driver's license, the clerk listened to my heavy accent, frowned, and said, "You don't belong here. Why don't you go back to your own country?" Speaking Spanish with a friend on the T (Boston's subway system) would often result in stares and offhand remarks, like, "We speak English in this country." Microaggressions can be overt or subtle; for example, when a white person dismisses a Black person's experience by saying things like *You're being overly sensitive.*

Whether it's public or private, blatant or subtle, trauma is a physiological response to an event that happened suddenly and without warning. But it is not the event itself. As trauma expert and medical doctor Gabor Maté says, "Trauma is not what happened *to* you. It's what happens *inside of* you as a result of what happened to you." It's anything that overwhelms a person's ability to cope and to integrate their emotional experience. When we are unable to process the emotions around the event, they remain stuck in the body and keep us in a perpetual "state of helplessness and terror," as Bessel van der Kolk explains in his seminal book, *The Body Keeps the Score*.

Trauma Is Always Relational

Even when it feels personal, trauma is relational, cultural, and political. It's relational because humans are social beings and what happens to an individual ripples through their family and their community. It's cultural and political because an individual's experience exists within the context of the beliefs and values of their culture. Their identity—their race, citizenship, gender, sexual orientation, social class, or religion—and how it's valued within their culture and political climate shapes their experience. In other words, trauma is contextual.

For example, when a woman suffers domestic abuse, it is not only a personal trauma; it is connected to her family and to a cultural and political system that would give a man power and control over his wife and children. In the case of María, when her father sold her to the old sorcerer who raped and tortured her, he did so with impunity. He was the head of a household within a culture that never questioned a father's or husband's authority. When individuals succumb to alcohol or drug addiction, what lies underneath may be a history of childhood abuse or neglect, or a life of poverty and violence. A woman who is attacked or raped in a country that institutionalizes gender inequality and discriminates against women may face unthinkable consequences for reporting her abuser or attempting to get medical help. A woman in a more egalitarian country often has more resources available to her.

Even within the same culture, people can have similar experiences with radically different outcomes. Those whose lives are valued the least suffer the most. Racial and gender inequities often determine consequences. A white college student at an Ivy League university may have many resources available to her—a rape crisis center, therapists, and legal advice, whereas an immigrant woman of color living in the same city may struggle to get help or find anyone who believes her when she talks about the pain she feels. A young girl who comes from a very religious family may be too ashamed to seek help and fearful that her family will blame her and kick her out of the house, so she cannot access resources that might otherwise help her.

Every culture has its own trauma. For many people in marginalized communities, trauma is not only connected to a specific action or event, it can also arise from the *fear* of the event happening. Even something as seemingly mundane as driving, for example, can invoke this in Black people who rightfully fear being racially profiled, pulled over by the police, arrested, or worse. Latinos and other immigrants fear being detained and deported, even when they were born in the United States or have their immigration papers in order.

Judith Herman says that victims of any kind of trauma need a social context to affirm their experience and protect them from further psychological harm. Individuals can turn to their families, partners, friends, and maybe their religious communities for support. In the case of large-scale cultural violence, she says, the social context is "created by political movements that give voice to the disempowered." Without social context, individual and collective traumas are often met with silence and denial, repression and dissociation. We see many examples of this, such as the "disappeared" in Argentina, slavery in the United States, or the Armenian genocide. Those afflicted can only begin to heal when they are acknowledged and validated in a social context.

Long Before It Was Called PTSD

Trauma was not officially recognized as a psychological disorder until it appeared in the third edition of the DSM (the *Diagnostic and Statistical Manual of Mental Disorders*) in 1980. However, its physical and psychological effects during combat were well established hundreds, if not thousands of years before. In biblical times, for example, those who suffered from "faintheartedness" in battle were sent home, lest their fear become contagious and affect those around them. Historically, any adverse psychological or emotional response to war was seen as a character flaw or a moral weakness. During the American Civil War, many young soldiers returned home with "nostalgia" or a "soldier's heart," because of the stress of combat. World War I soldiers came back with "shell shock," thought to be the physiological effect of enduring heavy explosives. The soldier was blamed for being too mentally and emotionally weak to stay and fight. In World War II, soldiers suffered from "combat fatigue." Psychiatrists often gave them time off to rest and recuperate before insisting they return to the battlefield—because the prevailing wisdom back then was that men felt better when they were with their comrades.

But few in the medical field focused on the long-lasting

psychological anguish experienced by those coming back from the war and attempting to reintegrate into their old life. That is, according to Herman, until the anti-war movement of the 1960s and '70s. After witnessing the vast number of soldiers returning from the Vietnam War struggling to reintegrate into civilian life and battling suicidal feelings, drug or alcohol addiction, and debilitating flashbacks, protesters urged politicians, the Veterans Administration, and the medical profession to take postwar trauma seriously. Finally, the term "posttraumatic stress disorder" was coined to describe what had happened to them. Formally, PTSD is defined as a mental health disorder or a debilitating stress response that occurs as a result of experiencing or witnessing an overwhelmingly traumatic event. And, slowly, as a result, regulations were put into place to protect veterans and their families.[1]

PTSD and Beyond

Sigmund Freud tried to give trauma a social context as early as the late nineteenth century, when he made a startling discovery about its origins. He had been a student of Jean-Martin Charcot, a French neuroscientist and well-known anticlerical, who used rigorous scientific methods to understand the neurological symptoms of hysteria, a condition caused by a "roving uterus" (*hysterika* in Greek means "uterus"). Charcot concluded that it affected a woman's nervous system and yet he also noted its symptoms—amnesia, temporary blindness, epilepsy, anxiety, and uterine pain—were psychological and could be alleviated through hypnosis. Freud and two other prominent psychiatrists, Pierre Janet and Josef Breuer, however, discovered something much more sinister:

hysteria was the psychological effect of repressed traumatic memories.

The psychiatrists decided to listen to their female patients—a pretty radical decision at the time—and were amazed that they not only freely spoke about their experiences, but they felt better afterward. The doctors had given their patients a place within which to safely tell their stories. It was the beginning of what Freud termed "psychoanalysis" and Janet called "psychological analysis." Janet's work, which still holds true today, centered on the *symptoms* of trauma, most particularly dissociation and depression. Freud, on the other hand, wanted to know the *cause* of those symptoms. He was shocked to discover experiences of early childhood sexual abuse and incest hidden within the repressed memories of his female patients. Every single one of them. Over time, he came to believe that all "hysterical" symptoms had their origins in sexual trauma. The early work of both these psychiatrists was surprisingly prescient, but Freud's theory almost immediately caused some backlash.

Freud could not wait to introduce his seduction theory to the world. However, this theory of repressed memories was not well received among his colleagues, who almost exclusively were male and decidedly uncomfortable with his discovery. They even accused him of being insane. He was forced to retract his diagnosis in 1905, and, instead, declared that women's traumatic memories were mere fantasies and expressions of repressed sexual *desires,* not abuses.

It took another hundred years before women's trauma experiences were taken seriously and Freud's theory of sexual repression began to lose its prominence in psychological circles as well as in society.[2] Just as it took time for society to recognize

Symptoms of PTSD

INTRUSION	PHYSICAL	REACTIVITY	COGNITIVE	BEHAVIORAL
Invasive thoughts	Fatigue	Irritability	Difficulty focusing	Avoidance of triggering people, places, or situations
Nightmares	Insomnia	Angry outbursts	Difficulty making decisions	
Flashbacks	Headaches	Reckless or self-destructive behavior		Social withdrawal and isolation
Repeated, involuntary memories	Loss of appetite		Difficulty remembering important aspects of trauma event	
	Hyperactivity	Hypervigilance		Substance abuse
Distressing dreams	Muscle tension	Concentration difficulties		
	Racing heart		Confusion	Self-destructive behavior
		Sleep disturbances	Dissociation	
			Negative thoughts and feelings	Agitation, irritability, or hostility
			Distorted beliefs about oneself and others	

the traumatizing effects of war, so it took time for society to admit that sexual violence against women and girls was a serious problem. As Herman points out in *Trauma and Recovery*, this change began in the 1970s, when women organized and protested to force societal change. In the 2010s, the #MeToo movement, along with women's rights organizations, took up the mantle and demanded further protections against rape, coercion, and sexual harassment. As a result, rape, once defined as nonconsensual sex, was redefined as an act of violence that could be committed by domestic partners as well as strangers.

It has taken us a long time to recognize that underneath all these misconceptions, diagnoses, symptoms, and behaviors lies a traumatic experience, which is what explains the suffering in a person's life. Unfortunately, we still have a long way to go.

The Subjective Experience of Trauma

We've made great strides in how we define and approach trauma since the time of Freud. These days trauma is pretty clearly defined. It is an emotional response that happens when an event we experience exceeds our ability to handle it; when it "overwhelms our nervous system and alters the way we process and recall memories," according to Dr. van der Kolk. He writes that trauma "is not the story of something that happened back then, but the current imprint of that pain, horror, and fear living inside of us." The effects of trauma live in the body and in our cells and can show up in multiple ways, such as chronic muscle and joint pains, headaches, stomach problems, agitation, anxiety, or dissociation, among other symptoms and behaviors. It affects our brain chemistry as well as our nervous system. It influences and changes our genetics, which we inherit from our parents, a process we'll examine in more detail in Chapter 5.

Although it's easy to associate trauma with major life events, I also see the small ways it affects people's lives all the time in my practice. We often call these everyday adversities or disturbances "the little t" traumas, and the catastrophic ones "the Big T" traumas. But the fact is, we have no way of judging someone else's experience, and their experience is not ours to judge. From the outside looking in, we may think what they're going through looks like no big deal, but to the person going through it, it *is* a big deal. Consider divorce. One person's experience can be devastating, leaving them overwhelmed and fearful. They're not worthy of love; they'll never find it again; they'll be alone forever. For another person, divorce might not feel that great, but in the grand scheme of things . . . it's fine.

I recently had a new patient, Lana, who told me that something awful had happened to her a few weeks before at a family gathering. In the middle of the party, she said, her husband got drunk. It was the first time she had ever seen him like that—and she began to get angrier and angrier, as she watched him make a fool of himself. I wondered if there might be something else going on that had caused her to feel so shaken up. So, I encouraged her to tell me more. She revealed that her father had been an alcoholic. Her father-in-law, too—but her husband never or rarely drank. Not only that, but in our session, she recalled being molested when she was young. It was by an older man, and he had clearly been drinking. So, while the incident with her husband might not have been *life* shattering on its own—and anyone else with other life experiences might have perceived it differently—it triggered traumatic memories for her.

One characteristic that makes an event traumatic is that the experience is perceived to be overwhelming and, therefore, more difficult to handle. In familiar situations, people may use the resources and coping strategies they have, but when events are disproportionately big, these resources may not work. In addition, if such life events are prolonged, they are likely to cause more chronic problems and significant psychological distress.

Lana's husband's behavior consumed her. She could not stop thinking about it. How could she trust him again? Someone else might have chalked it up to a lapse in judgment and let it go. But she could not.

Getting fired from a job can be potentially another "Big T" trauma or little "t trauma," depending on the person. When my patient Felipe lost his job on Wall Street, he was crushed. He couldn't believe it. His job had been a dream come true; it meant everything to him. He defined himself by the work he did, the title he had. He spent long hours at the office, and he was friends with many of his colleagues. He told me he felt blindsided by the company's decision to fire him. Coming from a very traditional Filipino family himself, he took great pride in supporting his own. When he could no longer do that, he felt emasculated, confused, and ashamed. The whole experience made him question his identity and his capabilities as a husband and father, so much so that for a long time he couldn't bring himself to apply for another job. On the other hand, I have another patient who also lost a job she loved. Although she was surprised and disappointed at first, she took it in stride and found another job soon after.

Any major life event—divorce, kids leaving home, job loss, moving to a new town—can be interpreted differently depending on the person, their particular circumstances, and how they process it.

Trauma in Disguise

Emotional trauma is the root cause of human suffering. It disguises itself as mental health disorders, destructive behaviors, and chronic health issues. It can linger over time, remaining hidden from our conscious awareness for generations, or even be normalized by the culture or society in which we live. Trauma can be a reaction to something that recently happened or that happened years ago and yet shapes and informs the present. It is felt at the individual level, as unprocessed emotions stored in our bodies. It is also felt within the familial, societal, political, and cultural climate in which the individual lives.

There are many types of trauma, which I'll be talking more about in the chapters that follow; for now, I'll just briefly describe the most common ones.

- **Acute:** A single event, such as date rape, a home invasion, or a dreadful accident.
- **Chronic:** Prolonged exposure to experiences, such as war or combat situations, racism, domestic violence, or even regular treatments for an illness, such as chemotherapy, radiation, or dialysis.
- **Complex:** A series of events in which we're harmed repeatedly, and the harm is cumulative, such as exploitation, neglect or abandonment, or repeated sexual abuse.
- **Collective:** A response by a particular group of people, a community, or an entire culture that has experienced a traumatic event or series of events, such as genocide, war, natural disaster, forced displacement, global pandemic, earthquake, mass shooting, plane crashes, or terrorist attacks. The recent pandemic is a good example of a collective trauma.

- **Historical:** The emotional and psychological wounding over a person's lifespan—and even across generations—that comes from a massive group trauma, such as slavery, genocide, colonialism (e.g., First Nations in residential schools in Canada), and internment (e.g., Japanese living in the United States during World War II).

- **Intergenerational:** The effects people experience second- or third-hand, which have been passed down from one generation to the next, without anyone necessarily being aware of the transmission. These can include repetitive behaviors resulting from domestic violence, alcoholism, war, torture, chronic depression, or other symptoms of physical or emotional trauma. Ways of coping and adaptive behaviors developed in response to trauma can also be passed from one generation to the next.

- **Vicarious or secondary:** The way someone who was not an immediate witness to a traumatic experience absorbs and integrates aspects of it into their own lives, functioning as though they had in fact experienced it themselves. This happens sometimes to therapists, close friends or family members, or within a group setting.

- **Developmental:** Repetitive or ongoing exposure to harmful experiences that happen at vulnerable times in our lives—in infancy, early childhood, adolescence, or even in our elderly years—and within the relationships between children and their caregivers.[3] Similar to complex trauma, developmental trauma can include neglect or abandonment; physical, emotional, or sexual abuse or assault; coercion or betrayal; or even *witnessing* domestic abuse, violence, or death. It often occurs within the child's primary parenting system and interferes with healthy attachment and development.

I'm often asked how long it takes to heal from trauma and whether one trauma response is harder to recover from than another. My answer: it depends. It could take you weeks, years, or even decades. Everyone's response to trauma is different; there's no time limit on recovery. Generally speaking, however, healing from historical trauma can be particularly rough because historical trauma is much more than what happened in the past; it's what *continues* to happen—so there is no closure.

Developmental trauma can also be tricky to heal from for several reasons, not the least of which is that childhood abuse and neglect can cause neurological changes, making it harder to control our intense emotional reactions, according to a 2015 article in *Psychology Today* by Dr. David Sack.[4] It's important to note, however, that none of these challenges prevents the possibility of posttraumatic growth.

Trauma and Attachment Styles

The way we bond to our parents at a very early age—our attachment style—determines how we face trauma and process it. Depending on the quality of that bond, it can protect us against adversity, or it can be the source of a traumatic experience. Here are four attachment styles that have been thoroughly researched over the years, along with several "I" statements to consider for each one:

- **Secure:** If you grew up with parents (or caregivers) who took care of you, who responded to your needs, and made sure you felt loved and safe, chances are that, as an adult, you feel secure and loved in your primary relationships. You're able to connect easily and also enjoy a level of interdependence and trust within your relationships.

  I feel comfortable with closeness.
  I trust that I am valuable and worthy of love.
  I communicate openly and honestly.
  I can depend on my partner and be independent at the same time.

- **Avoidant:** People with this attachment style tend to be emotionally unavailable, proud of the fact that they don't need anyone. If this feels familiar, you may have grown up with parents who were disconnected, absent, or emotionally distant a good part of the time. You may have had a mother who had difficulties with drugs or alcohol, or who chose other relationships over being with you. Other adults in your life whom you thought you could rely on also proved unreliable. The behaviors you witnessed and learned as a child will almost ensure that you have a complicated relationship with your partner and quite probably a detached one with your children. Interpersonal relationships won't be easy for you unless you commit to going through some kind of transformation.

> *I have a hard time knowing my feelings or even knowing if I have them.*
> *I want a relationship, but closeness can feel awkward and mysterious.*
> *I deal with emotional problems with reason and logic.*
> *I avoid conflict at all costs.*
> *I don't depend on anyone or anything.*

- **Anxious:** This attachment style is sometimes called "emotional hunger." In this attachment style, you may have grown up with parents who were inconsistent in demonstrating their love and care. Sometimes they were kind and loving; other times, they were emotionally abusive, pushed you away, or allowed you to cry instead of comforting you. Their mixed signals made it difficult for you to know what to expect and how to act. Entering into adulthood, it may be hard to have a healthy, loving relationship; you may crave emotional connection—even when the relationship doesn't warrant such a commitment—feel anxious or jealous, needy or clingy.

> *I fear rejection and abandonment.*
> *I need reaffirmation, but I find it hard to believe.*
> *I take care of others, but I often feel resentful.*
> *I need to be heard and validated.*

- **Disorganized:** This attachment style is one rooted in fear and is considered the most difficult or insecure attachment. Your source of safety, as a child, became instead a source of fear and neglect. If you grew up in a household in which care was inconsistent and unpredictable, you may have feared for your safety. Often the fear stems from being in a volatile home situation, one in which you have either been a witness to or a victim of domestic violence. This attachment style makes it hard to have healthy relationships as an adult, particularly with your partner and your children. Although you crave intimacy and love, you fear that the very people you want that from will harm you.

> *My inner experience is sometimes chaotic and confusing.*
> *I come closer . . . then I move away.*
> *I accept you . . . then I reject you.*
> *I have a negative self-image.*
> *My parents were unpredictable and abusive.*
> *I am afraid.*

Out of all of these attachment styles, a secure attachment is a strong protective factor in the face of adversity. It can provide resources and resilience to deal with the traumatic experience. On the other hand, a disorganized attachment can be a traumatic attachment, and can leave us more vulnerable to its effects throughout our lives. Working through any of these attachment styles can result in posttraumatic growth. (I go into more details about how these attachment styles protect or hinder our growth in Chapter 4.)

Ambiguous Loss and Trauma

Although all trauma involves some kind of loss—a death of someone we're close to, loss of our home from a fire or natural disaster, loss of a job—it almost always involves some kind of resolution. But what about the losses we experience that have no chance of closure? Pauline Boss, a researcher and professor emeritus at the University of Minnesota, calls this type of trauma "ambiguous loss," which, she says, is the worst kind of loss. The author of several books, including *Loss, Trauma, and Resilience,* Dr. Boss defines ambiguous loss as "any loss that's unclear and lacks a resolution." As Dr. Boss says, they are "losses minus the facts."

There are two types of ambiguous loss: physically absent but emotionally present and emotionally present but physically absent.

PHYSICALLY ABSENT
(BUT PSYCHOLOGICALLY PRESENT)

This happens when someone leaves without saying goodbye. As Dr. Boss describes it, the person is physically absent but psychologically still present. Examples may include an absent parent in a divorce; an absent biological parent in an adoption; babies given up for adoption; or a family split apart during immigration and unsure if they'll ever be reunited. A person can go missing in war, drowning, kidnapping, terrorist attack, or a natural disaster, where there is no way of knowing whether they are alive or dead. Do we hold out hope that they'll be found—and for how long? Or do we decide they're dead—and how soon?[5]

When New York City's Twin Towers fell on 9/11, for example, thousands experienced ambiguous loss. I was fortunate, as a young clinical psychologist, to work alongside Dr. Boss to help the families of the immigrants who had been lost in the attack. Many of these people were undocumented or didn't speak English. They weren't recognized as family. And there was no collective acknowledgment or recognition of their loss, which made it particularly difficult.

The COVID-19 pandemic is another example of an event that brought on significant ambiguous loss. Thousands of people died quarantined in hospitals with their families unable to say good-bye, and thousands more were stranded in cities or countries unable to reunite with their families.

PHYSICALLY PRESENT
(BUT PSYCHOLOGICALLY ABSENT)

This is when people say good-bye without actually leaving. Ambiguous loss can happen when someone is still physically present in our lives yet has checked out emotionally or psychologically. This type of ambiguous loss can include an aging parent who has had a stroke, is in a coma, or suffers from Alzheimer's or dementia; a child with a traumatic brain injury or a spouse or a teenager with chronic depression or addiction to drugs, alcohol, or technology; a family member preoccupied with work or with heartbreak. This type of ambiguous loss makes it difficult for members of a family to stay present with one another. When this happens, Dr. Boss explains, roles can get muddy; no one quite knows how to act or what to do.

A LITTLE OF BOTH

There are times when the two types of ambiguous loss can overlap and cause even more suffering. I've seen that happen after a particularly contentious divorce, for example, when the children feel abandoned by *both* parents—the one who physically left and the one left behind, who has fallen into a depression and has essentially checked out.

Just like other types of trauma, ambiguous loss is relational and can be healed only by establishing connections with others—either therapists, expert companions, or others who have also experienced such catastrophic losses.[6]

Confusing Stress with Trauma

Clearly, trauma is stressful no matter what kind we're experiencing or what we call it. But stress is not the same as trauma.

We experience stress every single day. We often think of stress as a negative—we are constantly trying to alleviate it—but stress doesn't have to be that way. According to Stanford psychologist Kelly McGonigal, author of *The Upside of Stress,* if we learn how to embrace stress, it can actually help us grow and learn from our experiences.[7] Stress is what allows us to act decisively, have difficult conversations, start a challenging project, or even enter into new relationships. When we encounter adversity or any kind of challenges in our lives, we have the courage—the mental, emotional, and physical capacity—to face them, deal with them, and overcome them. We notice and react to whatever is happening in the moment and then, when it's over, we rest, restore, and reboot. That's the upside of stress.

The problem with stress, however, is not that we have it; it's that we don't know how to come down from it, and it can become chronic. When we're panicked or stressed and unable to calm ourselves, our nervous system gets stuck on high alert, and we can become paralyzed. We become overwhelmed, we can't function, and everything becomes too much. When this continues unabated, it can destabilize the nervous system and cause serious mental and physical problems—often for years.

What's Happening Inside

We are relational beings, which means that everything we experience we experience in relationship to others. The inner workings of the body are no exception. Without even having to think about it, our brain and nervous system are busy working together, scanning our body, facilitating communication between our mind and our body, between us and our environment, attuning to the emotional states of the people around us in an attempt to keep us healthy and safe. According to Stephen Porges, PhD, father of the Polyvagal Theory, it does this through the actions of the vagus nerve, an integral part of the autonomic nervous system. The vagus or "wandering" nerve (*vagus* means "wander" in Latin) is the longest nerve in the body—and the master connector. It connects the brain with all our major internal systems. Beginning at the base of the skull, it travels down the neck, into the upper and lower chest, through the diaphragm, and into the abdominal cavity. Along the way, it "visits" and activates various structures and the majority of the organs in our body. It scans for cues of danger as well as safety; it responds with a sense of calm when we feel connected to others around us, and it mobilizes the body's resources when it perceives peril in order to keep us safe.

When we feel threatened, either physically or psychologically, our nervous system automatically reacts without our consciously doing anything. When our lives are in danger, when we feel emotionally threatened, when we don't feel safe, we respond in one of four ways to protect ourselves—fight, flight, freeze, fawn. These responses are natural defense mechanisms that we use for our physical and emotional survival.

Fight or Flight. When something happens to frighten you, this fight-or-flight response allows you to gather your strength, concentration, and speed to either stay and fight the threat or run away from it. Your body directs as much energy as possible to make this happen. Your adrenaline soars, your blood pressure rises, and your heart feels like it's about to leap out of your chest. All of your senses are heightened, and you are hyperaware of your surroundings. In fight, psychologically you may find yourself quick to anger and feeling out of control. In flight, on the other hand, you want to get as far from the conflict as you can. You don't want to hear about it and you don't want to know about it. You'll do anything to avoid the pain.

Freeze. When you feel so threatened there is nothing you can do except surrender, your body goes into the freeze state, an indication that your parasympathetic response is in defensive mode. You become immobilized, paralyzed with fright. The dorsal (or back) side of the vagus nerve shuts everything down—your heart rate drops and your bowels literally empty. Psychologically, the freeze state paralyzes you and you are unable to make decisions or take action. As a survival mechanism, it buys you some time to figure out the next steps. The freeze state is a state of dissociation, one in which you numb out, play "dead" by sleeping, disconnecting from the experience, from your physical sensations, from your thoughts and emotions, and from others. In other words, dissociating from the pain.

Fawn. This is the "please and appease" response, a way of avoiding conflict and not calling attention to yourself. Sometimes being overly nice is the only way to survive a potentially violent or traumatizing event. A fawn response can sometimes help you placate or calm someone down who is angry or acting in a threatening manner, such as during a robbery, kidnapping, or sexual assault, or when interacting with a narcissistic partner or parent.

Returning to stasis. In a healthy survival response, when the threat has passed, we return to balance. Our system recalibrates, and the parasympathetic response takes over. We rest, allowing our heart rate to return to normal and our breathing to slow down again, enabling us to reflect on what just occurred. And then it's over.

If we stay stuck in fight-flight-freeze-fawn, problems arise. The trauma residue of our experience remains lodged in the body long after the initial event has passed, and the nervous system is unable to distinguish between what happened before and what is happening right now. Our body's natural survival response becomes a chronic trauma response, which can have serious physiological and emotional effects. Here's an example: A young woman I know was nearly hit by a train as she drove her car across the tracks, which had no warning lights or gates. Her car got stuck on the tracks and she was able to get out and run to safety just before the train crashed into and demolished her car. Her flight response saved her from danger. The problem is, every time she hears train whistles or has to drive across the railroad tracks, she panics. Ob-

Trauma Responses

FIGHT	Aggresive, angry outburst, irritable, controlling, demanding, impulsive decision making, "acts tough," "bully," critical
FLIGHT	Avoids conflict, distracted, always on the go, staying busy, overworking, perfectionist, overachiever
FREEZE	Cautious, stuckness, difficulty making decisions, isolation, lack of motivation, numbed, shut down, immobilization, collapse, scared stiff, feeling dead inside
FAWN	People pleaser, hard time saying no, lack of boundaries, defers to others, avoids conflict, prioritzes others' needs, overwhelmed, loss of self, codependent, obsessed with fitting in

viously, all it takes is an experience, a sound, a smell, a taste of something, or even a phrase—anything that in some way triggers a memory of the original experience—for the body to react all over again. In her case, she was on her way to an appointment and as she drove across the railroad tracks, the bells began to ring, and the lights began to flash. As soon as she got to the other side, she pulled over and began to hyperventilate and shake uncontrollably. She was reliving the accident as though it were happening in that moment.

When we don't naturally recover from a traumatic event and our defense mechanisms become chronic, it can turn into a posttraumatic stress disorder (PTSD) diagnosis. Some of the typical symptoms of PTSD include hyperarousal, intrusion, dissociation or avoidance, and negative cognition.

Hyperarousal. Everything is suspect in hyperarousal—loud noises, an angry voice, a sudden move. The mind sees the potential for danger everywhere—even when there is none—and often reacts irritably, irrationally, and even aggressively. Your body startles at the slightest sound, touch, or movement. Sleep can be disrupted, and safety feels elusive. You don't feel at home in your body, and you don't trust anyone, even those closest to you. Exaggerated, startled responses and abrupt mood swings are symptoms of hyperarousal.

Intrusion. This is when our past trauma continues to intrude on our life; nothing feels safe, we can't let it go, and we can't move on. It is unpredictable and can appear at any moment without warning. Our past traumas come in the form of nightmares, night terrors or distressing dreams, flashbacks, and reactions in which we act as if the traumatic event were happening—in the present moment. We are flooded with memories of our trauma, which literally trespass from another area of the brain (the amygdala) and make it impossible to create new, explicit memories in real time (in the hippocampus). The amygdala is where emotional or unconscious memories (often called "implicit memories") are stored. These amygdala neurons feed on fear—not only real fear, but also the *memory* of fear. According to Rick Hanson, PhD, chronic stress and trauma strengthen and increase these neurons and keep the memories alive, making it harder to form new, present-moment memories.

Dissociation/Avoidance. This happens when the fear or

the pain becomes too much to handle, and the mind dissociates, or checks out. When we feel powerless or overwhelmed in the face of a terrifying experience, the parasympathetic nervous system steps in to protect us from pain. It produces an altered state of consciousness that allows us to escape from our situation—by leaving our body. In other words, by numbing out and shutting down. It can also show up when we're triggered, becoming our go-to response and can appear in many forms: dissociation, denial, avoidance of any external reminders of the original distressing event, phobias, and detachment. In the extreme, it can manifest as depersonalization and derealization. In other words, we become an outside observer of ourselves and see the world around us in an unreal, dreamlike, distant state.

From Trauma into Growth

It can be hard to imagine that people can heal and grow from the types of trauma I've defined here. And yet, they do. It's not an easy road, to be clear; the steps can at times feel impossible. What I do know to be true, without a doubt, is this: when we are willing to do the work and show up fully committed, posttraumatic growth offers a way to a richer, more connected life—not in spite of what we've gone through, but because of it. In the next chapter, I'll talk more about what posttraumatic growth is—and equally important, what it is not.

Chapter 3

What Is Posttraumatic Growth?

We delight in the beauty of the butterfly but rarely admit the changes it has gone through to achieve that beauty.

——MAYA ANGELOU

The wound is the place where the light enters you.

——RUMI

When a traumatic experience shatters our world and we're left to pick up the pieces, the idea that we can heal, and actually transform as a result of the suffering, can feel impossible. It's hard enough to put what happened behind us in order to deal with the day-to-day realities of life, let alone move on. But the fact is, by embracing adversity and working through the pain we *can* derive meaning from our experience. We *can* grow from our traumas, and even more than that, we can completely transform. That is what posttraumatic growth is all about.

People talk about transformation all the time. They often say that they've been transformed, and describe being "changed for the better," feeling stronger and more resilient, even becoming a nicer, more mindful version of themselves. Which is wonderful. It truly is. When I talk about the transformation that happens as a result of posttraumatic growth, however, I'm talking about something different. Think about a caterpillar. To become a butterfly, this little creature (formally called a "larva") must lose all of its "caterpillar-ness." It must decompose; be stripped of everything—its shape, its ecosystem, its way of inching through the world. Everything. In fact, if you were to look inside the chrysalis midway through its metamorphosis, you wouldn't see a partially formed butterfly or a partially decomposed larva. All you'd see is what wildlife biologist Lindsay VanSomeren calls "pink goo," a nutrient-rich soup. No trace of the caterpillar remains. In other words, it had to die in order to be reborn as something completely new. At the same time—and this is important—the butterfly would never be what it is without its caterpillar-ness, without the enzymes, nervous system, and breathing tubes provided by the larva, VanSomeren says. The caterpillar even has what are called "imaginal disks," which are "small clusters of cells that match up with the structures they'll need as adults,"[1] such as wings, eyes, antennae, and so forth. Moreover, the butterfly's emergence into the world cannot be interrupted or assisted. The winged creature must be allowed to push its way out fully formed or it will die. It's a brilliant and quite dramatic example of transformation in nature.

When it comes to human transformation, I have long held the image of *kintsugi*, or "golden joinery," an ancient Japanese artform of mending broken pottery, as the perfect symbol of posttraumatic growth. Kintsugi comes out of *wabi-sabi*, the Japanese worldview that honors the beauty within imperfection and impermanence. In repairing cracks in a ceramic bowl, for example, or putting the broken pieces back together again, the goal isn't to hide the imperfections but to use lacquer mixed with powdered gold (or sometimes sterling silver) to enhance them and integrate them into something unique and often more beautiful than the original.

We all have broken pieces within us, wounds that remind us of experiences we would rather forget. But our wounds are the cracks, as singer-songwriter Leonard Cohen famously wrote, where the light gets in, where wisdom and connection and compassion can enter us. The lacquer represents the value of our wounds. Wabi-sabi invites us to acknowledge the beauty in our imperfections, to celebrate our uniqueness and our brokenness. As Ernest Hemingway once wrote, "The world breaks everyone and afterward many are strong in the broken places." This is what posttraumatic growth is all about.

Posttraumatic growth allows us to hold the trauma *and* the healing simultaneously—both are true. I was broken, now I'm whole. But this wholeness *includes* the broken pieces, which have been put back together in a totally different way, one that is more sustainable, more beautiful, and can ultimately be of service. It's important to note, however, that in posttraumatic growth, as in kintsugi, we're not simply repairing what's broken—that's only part of the process. We are reimagining, reinventing, and recreating a whole new story for ourselves. One that doesn't deny our wounds from the past but seasons the story with their own "nutrient soup."

As a clinical psychologist specializing in trauma, I've placed PTG at the core of my work for almost thirty years. During this time, I've raised these kinds of questions: *What if it's possible for someone to go beyond healing after experiencing trauma? What if, after bouncing back to health, they could leap forward and transform?* In fact, it's not only possible, it's achievable. PTG is the stage where true transformation happens, but to reach PTG requires an often difficult journey. My five-stage model is the process to get us there. It's the blueprint that takes us from trauma to wisdom and growth. The five stages—which I will discuss at length throughout the book—move from radically accepting the trauma to seeking safety, experiencing a shift in perspective, being able to integrate the old ways of being with a new understanding, and finally, growing and becoming wiser.

THE FIVE STAGES OF POSTTRAUMATIC GROWTH

1. **The Stage of Awareness:** Radical Acceptance

2. **The Stage of Awakening:** Safety and Protection

3. **The Stage of Becoming:** A New Narrative

4. **The Stage of Being:** Integration

5. **The Stage of Transforming:** Wisdom and Growth

I love providing space for the *process* as much as being able to bear witness to the *outcome* with countless patients; it's a privilege I take very seriously. I have many stories of unbelievable transformation, which I will share throughout the book—individuals, families, and even whole communities that have endured horrific atrocities, as well as those who have experienced heartbreak and adversity in their everyday lives. Before we dive into these examples, let's put the concept of posttraumatic growth into its historical context.

A Definition

I did not invent posttraumatic growth—it's been part of the human experience since ancient times. It often shows up in mythology, glorified as a hero's journey of transformation. Countless films portray a protagonist who suffers from trauma and, driven by this personal experience, goes on to become a hero. Luke Skywalker and Princess Leia in *Star Wars,* Bruce Wayne in *Batman,* Diana in *Wonder Woman,* T'Challa in *Black Panther,* and the Harry Potter series all come to mind. There are other, timeless and historical examples, too. Classic tales such as *The Odyssey;* indigenous stories that center animals or children of the gods; religious parables, such as that of Siddhartha, who lost his mother at birth and got enlightened as Buddha; and plenty of biblical stories. Often trauma is a requirement for becoming a hero or attaining enlightenment.

Generally, either in a story or in real life, a hero is called upon to leave the familiar and venture into the unknown, where they must face their challenges head-on and summon the courage to slay their demons or tame their dragons. Joseph Campbell, the well-known expert on comparative mythology, says the journey is one of transformation, a "rite of spiritual passage" during which the hero must die in order to be reborn.

As a psychological concept, PTG was coined by psychologists Richard Tedeschi and Lawrence Calhoun, at the University of North Carolina in the mid-nineties. Through their research and clinical practice, they show that PTG is a way of describing both the positive changes people experience as a result of horrific events and the process they go through to get there.[2]

Through PTG, Tedeschi writes, a person may discover new capacities for relating to others, trusting themselves, and appreciating life. He says that these "are capacities that weren't there before the traumatic experience or they were present, but the person wasn't aware of them." Through the process of PTG, the person begins to see the wisdom and the beauty hidden within their wounds as gifts that completely change the way they see the world and how they participate in it.

The transformation people experience as a result of doing the work brings with it many gifts: a new meaning of life; a sense of internal peace; deeper connections to others and to a higher power; and a stronger sense of self. PTG is a way of finding purpose from the suffering and creating a life beyond the struggle trauma brings. It describes the experience of people who not only bounce back from trauma, but also use it as a springboard for further growth. It's rarely linear and it requires a willingness to move beyond one's comfort zone with mindful attention and an openness to receive the gifts that await—the gifts of wisdom and growth. That's why I sometimes refer to the process of posttraumatic growth as being akin to a butterfly emerging from a chrysalis. As Rupi

Kaur wrote, "You don't just become the butterfly. Growth is a process." We must be willing to let go of being a caterpillar in order to become a butterfly; its transformation doesn't happen overnight. Nor does ours. It takes patience and struggle in order to set ourselves free, in order to finally emerge from the darkness into the light more beautiful than we could ever imagine with the wings we need to take flight.

I see examples of PTG everywhere, even in people who have never heard of it or don't have the words to express what is happening. In describing his own growth after trauma, for example, psychotherapist Ralph De La Rosa, author of *Don't Tell Me to Relax*, gave an honest, heartfelt assessment of the process without ever naming it:

> I thought the point was to heal my trauma—that's what was eating at me, after all. And it did heal. It was the hardest work I've ever done. It felt like it would go on forever. But it didn't. And while I was doing the work of healing, something else entirely was happening. I was becoming who I was meant to be all along. Going into my wounding at one time felt like some burden I had to bear because life had been so cruel to me. But it turned into the deepest spiritual work I could've ever engaged in. And not some path that someone taught me, per se, not some religious fantasy handed down from authority. Honest, genuine, spontaneous, creative spiritual presence came alive. I am eternally grateful to all the wounds, to all the people who hurt me and dismissed me. They gave me the material that alchemized into something truly beautiful.[3]

Posttraumatic growth can come out of many kinds of traumas. These traumas can be physical, such as a chronic illness, disability, a cancer diagnosis, or heart attack, as well as from the difficulty of coping with medical challenges of parents or children. They can also result from unexpected or violent circumstances, such as house fires, flooding, car crashes, rape and sexual abuse, teen pregnancy, the plight of refugees, combat, and kidnapping, among others.

Gloria is an amazing example of someone moving from extreme trauma and suffering to growth. She grew up in the countryside, on the outskirts of Buenos Aires, in a poor family with very few resources. She always wanted to study engineering, so at a young age, she managed to work and save enough money to move to New York City, where she hoped to attend university. While adjusting to a new city in a new country, Gloria finds a job in an agency that, unbeknown to her, has been engaging in illegal practices. Although she has no idea what's happening, she gets set up, eventually arrested and taken to prison at Rikers Island, where she is repeatedly gang-raped by prisoners and jail administrators alike, facilitated by a female jailer. She's denied food, beaten, and left to endure unbearable conditions. By the time she leaves prison, she is nearly catatonic. She enters a psychiatric clinic where she's unable to speak or participate in any of the therapy programs until she finds art as a form of self-expression.

When she gets out of the clinic, she decides to embark on a slow, deliberate journey toward healing. As part of that experience, she learns to express herself even more through her art and, with a supportive environment and plenty of guidance, she begins to understand what has happened to her and channels the pain of her deep trauma into her paintings. Eventually she grows increasingly stronger physically, emotionally, and spiritually. Along the way she develops a new identity and healthier relationships; her life becomes more meaningful; and she feels she has discovered a clear life purpose. Because of what happened to her, Gloria now advocates for incarcerated women and works with groups that agitate for the closing of Rikers Island. She's also an inventor and an artist, living a life she could never have imagined.

Gloria's story illustrates how someone can come out of a major, life-altering trauma and emerge stronger on the other side. But it's not only the major atrocities that open us up to growth, but also all sorts of common, everyday traumas, such as losing a job, struggling in school, being left out of your social circle, being bullied, getting divorced, or moving to a new home or city. Amanda Gorman, America's first Youth Poet Laureate, who read her poem "The Hill We Climb" in front of thousands at President Joe Biden's inauguration in 2020, is an inspiring example of someone who has turned difficulty into triumph. Amanda has struggled with an auditory sensory disorder since she was a child, which made it difficult for her to process speech. She also had a speech impediment that made certain sounds hard to enunciate. Instead of seeing it as a disability or a weakness, she grew to embrace it as her superpower. In an interview with Oprah, Amanda said she felt her experience made her a much stronger writer. "When you are learning through poetry how to speak English, it leads to a great understanding of sound, of pitch, of pronunciation, so I think of my speech impediment not as a weakness or a disability, but as one of my greatest strengths." The very thing that had been her vulnerability—her inability to articulate— became her greatest talent. Indeed, she went on to speak in front of millions and to inspire others to speak out against injustice.

Collective Growth

As we discussed, trauma can be an individual or a collective experience. Posttraumatic growth works the same way. Couples, families, and entire communities can experience posttraumatic growth collectively, tapping into the depth of pain and healing together. "There can be a determination by communities to address tragedy by attempting to create positive outcomes," Tedeschi says. Even cities or countries can share in growth. This is called "collective posttraumatic growth." In other words, those who share in the pain, who suffer together, can also come together and share in the healing.

Consider what happened in New Orleans after Hurricane Katrina. Cynthia Mitchell, a retired schoolteacher, recounts in an email her experience living in a neighborhood hard hit by the hurricane. She had been working as an intensive case manager for the NO/AIDS Task Force where she helped secure permanent supportive housing for the chronically unhoused. In her spare time as a photographer and storyteller, she would often drive from neighborhood to neighborhood, interviewing residents. After Katrina hit, she helped friends renovate their homes, and bought and renovated a home herself in a neighborhood nearly destroyed by the hurricane. This is what she says:

> In my work in New Orleans post-Katrina, I witnessed numerous individuals coming to the aid of others, whether neighbor, friend, relative, or stranger, to help ease the collective loss. It seemed that all boundaries of class, race, age, and lifestyle were dropped in place of what mattered most—people. More than sharing generators, showers,

and meals, people shared company, well-wishing, a helping hand, stories of their own struggles and survival. Contrary to what was portrayed in the media right after the crisis, average citizens and residents came together in most cases to do what they could to help. They were common everyday heroes.

Remember, trauma is not about the event itself; it's the emotional and psychological effect the event has on those who witnessed it or suffered because of it. Any event that deeply challenges your core belief can cause you to question how the world works, what kind of person you are, what kind of life you're living, and what future you have. It can give you the opportunity to grow and change. The same goes for a family, a community, or a nation. I've seen this countless times with the communities I've helped over the years.

In doing this work, I've witnessed how people rally around one another, protest together to demand systemic change, and pool their resources to help their neighbors. They tell me how the experience has healed fractures within their communities and helped them grow together.

Vicarious Posttraumatic Growth

The amazing thing about growth after trauma is that even people who have not experienced trauma themselves, but have witnessed it firsthand, can report personal growth. This phenomenon is called "vicarious posttraumatic growth." By being close to someone who is going through the process of growth, we often end up growing as well—psychologically, emotionally, and spiritually. This includes, among others, the children and spouses of cancer survivors, families of combat veterans and those battling drug and alcohol addiction; healthcare workers and trauma therapists; and friends or partners of people who have experienced rape, bullying, racism, or other forms of discrimination. In other words, the caregivers of trauma survivors.

When 9/11 happened, I was living in Manhattan, working as a psychologist with refugees and marginalized people within the five boroughs of New York City. I witnessed unbelievable suffering and trauma in the aftermath of the World Trade Center attacks—and unbelievable growth. As a refugee and an immigrant myself, I was part of that community; as a psychologist, I was part of the therapy community as well. I lived in the city and felt the horror as the Twin Towers came down. I was connected to what was happening and committed to doing whatever I could to support those on the margins who were deeply affected by the destruction and loss. Bearing witness to the strength and fortitude that so many people exhibited—and the incredible transformation that occurred post-9/11—transformed me as well.

Dispelling the Myths

Before we talk more about what posttraumatic growth *is,* let's look at what it is not. First and foremost, PTG is not an automatic or immediate outcome that arises from trauma; it requires time and intention to overcome adversity and achieve growth. For anyone working with individuals processing their trauma, it's important to remember that PTG is a process that cannot be rushed without running the risk of the person becoming retraumatized. If the person gets pushed to face their trauma too quickly or forcefully, they won't have the coping mechanisms to handle what is coming up and they may end up reliving their traumatic experience all over again.

I learned this personally in 2001. In the days following the collapse of the Twin Towers, the Red Cross reached out to a group of psychologists in the city, asking us to assist the survivors. Along with many others, I spent the following days and weeks with the victims, debriefing them and encouraging them to retell their stories. As the days went by, we realized that this intervention was not helpful. It was causing them to *relive* the experience all over again, instead of creating an opportunity for them to heal from it. It was retraumatizing them more than supporting them. The process was much too soon—they were still *in the trauma.*

Here are a few of the most common myths surrounding posttraumatic growth.

Myth No. 1: Trauma is the same for everyone. No two people experience trauma in the same way, nor do they recover in the same way. Trauma and its recovery are subjective: Everyone has their own individual responses to facing adversity, to coping, and to healing. The path to growth is unique to each experience and must be honored and followed.

Myth No. 2: No good can ever come out of trauma. This misconception comes from a medical model that is based only on the symptoms and the negative consequences of trauma. It focuses on what's missing and what's lacking. This model sees all trauma as a disorder that should be managed exclusively through medication, intense therapies, and often hospitalization. In doing so, it dismisses both the anecdotal evidence and the longitudinal data that, over and over again, suggest that people who experience trauma are also able to experience wisdom and growth after trauma. PTG is something that therapists who believe it's possible see all the time in our work with individuals, families, and communities.

Myth No. 3: Time heals all wounds. This common phrase makes me shake my head every time I hear it. It's a saying that hides and perpetuates a false idea about healing. It's not *time* that heals wounds or that alleviates pain and suffering. There is nothing magical about time. Just letting time go by is not enough. It's what you *do* during the time you have that makes all the difference. It's how you move through the process that takes you from pain to healing to growth.

Myth No. 4: PTG is a natural next step. Not necessarily. Nor is it an easy one. It requires intention and determination and a commitment of time and effort. And don't forget, it has its own timeline and cannot be rushed. Healing takes courage, vulnerability, and a certain level of faith in the process—a surrender in which one gives up control of one's life, either by default, by chance, or because there are no other options.

Myth No. 5: PTG is an illusion. Some people believe that growth after trauma is just subjective; that it is merely the perception of the person who has gone through the traumatic experience. In truth, abundant evidence exists that proves posttraumatic growth really occurs. PTG is not a way of masking trauma by changing our behavior or asserting that the symptoms are gone by shoving them underground. Growing from trauma is not the same as denying our trauma or dissociating from the suffering it created in our life. That is avoidance and denial, which represent the antithesis of transformation. Growth requires that we meet the trauma head-on and enter into a relationship with it.

Myth No. 6: PTG is just a positive reframe of trauma. There are schools of psychological thought that want to make everything positive. *Trauma is so great! It really helps us grow!* PTG takes a willingness to reevaluate our life within a new context that we create for ourselves, which includes examining and exploring the traumatic event and then integrating it into our new life. It is difficult, painful, and often requires that we hit bottom before we begin to surface anew.

Myth No. 7: PTG gets rid of PTSD. Not always. PTG isn't necessarily a permanent state. It requires ongoing maintenance. In fact, as Tedeschi says, although it may seem counterintuitive, you can experience PTSD and PTG at the same time. It is the struggle with distress that leads to growth. Posttraumatic growth is possible in increments. For example, you could be working to heal the trauma in your romantic relationship and come out of that with a deeper understanding and with healthier boundaries and a more loving connection with your partner. And yet, in other areas of your life, like your relationships at work or conflicts with your parents, you may have a lot more work to do. PTG is not a linear path.

Myth No. 8: PTG is the same as resilience. Not at all. It's become very popular to talk about resilience as a way of overcoming trauma. However, resilience doesn't help us *grow* from adversity, it helps us *cope* with it. Resilience is the capacity to bounce back to your original state after a stressful event. It's a coping mechanism developed to manage these events more effectively. PTG, on the other hand, is the opportunity to grow and expand beyond where you were to begin with, not in spite of the trauma, but *because* of it. It goes beyond psychology to also encompass neuroscience, spiritu-

Resilience vs. PTG

Resilience	Posttraumatic Growth
• BOUNCING BACK	• BOUNCING FORWARD
• Can be a personality trait	• Develops as a consequence of trauma
• Does not require profound changes	• Can redefine the personality of an individual
• Does not necessarily require having experienced trauma	• Requires being exposed to intense stress at some point
• Doesn't mean beliefs are shaken to the core	• Shakes beliefs to the core and shifts priorities
• Doesn't require a person to seek a new belief system, a new paradigm	• Requires a paradigm shift
• Doesn't necessarily ensure growth will happen	• Results in positive psychological development in the face of hardship or adversity
• Assumes an ability to cope with life after adversity	• Allows for new behaviors and attitudes that were not present before
	• May not occur without some level of discomfort, but distress diminishes over time

ality, holistic healing, and compassion. In fact, sometimes resilience actually hinders the possibility of achieving PTG—something I'll talk more about in the next chapter—because resilient people seem minimally affected by their trauma.

However, those who go through the process of growth after trauma can develop resilience along the way to healing and transformation.

Myth No. 9: PTG allows us to see the world through rose-colored glasses. Although many people tell me they believe their experience was, in retrospect, the "best thing that ever happened" to them, and even express their gratitude, it's important to remember that they are in no way implying that the tragedy and loss weren't painful. When his beloved son Aaron died at fourteen years old, Rabbi Harold Kushner, author of *When Bad Things Happen to Good People,* admitted he became a more sympathetic counselor, a more compassionate rabbi, and a more loving person because of his son's death. But he also said, "I would give up all of those gains in a second if I could have my son back. I would forgo all the spiritual growth and depth which has come my way because of our experiences and be what I was fifteen years ago . . . the father of a bright, happy boy. But I cannot choose."[4]

Another dramatic example of this comes from several of the Cambodian refugees I've worked with, who fled the violence and genocide of the Pol Pot regime that ruled their country from 1975 to 1979. These were people who had survived traumas few of us can even imagine: starvation, disease, constant threats of torture and death, and the loss of family members, their culture, and their homeland. Most of the refugees I spoke to were very clear about what they had endured and the transformation they had experienced as a result. As S.L. told me, "I would not have chosen to go through the trauma, but now that I did, I am glad. Otherwise, I would not have been who I am today."

Myth No. 10: PTG is a solitary journey. Although we must believe in the possibility and our capacity for new growth after trauma, healing is not something we can do alone. We need someone to guide us, to provide a container in which we can feel safe and secure. Our trauma is relational, systemic, and cultural; it is a result of a disconnection from ourselves, others, and the world. Therefore, our healing and transformation must involve reconnecting, finding a sense of belonging. To grow from trauma we must allow ourselves to receive the support from others—our family, friends, and even within the larger cultural context.

Growth from Trauma: The Paradox

How is it possible that anything positive can come out of something so dire as trauma? How can we find strength when what we've gone through has completely destroyed us? From loss comes gain, from illness comes health, out of weakness we find strength; isolation leads to connection, and our distress brings growth. We may go through the dark night of the soul before we see the light, be desperately lost before we can be found. This is the paradox of posttraumatic growth. As Peter Levine, a trauma expert, author of *Waking the Tiger,* and the founder of Somatic Experiencing, says, trauma has the power to destroy and the power to transform. Within the seeds of darkness and despair lives the potential for life to bloom into the light.

I can best explain the paradox by sharing the story of my patient Bill. A firefighter who was part of a squad in lower Manhattan, Bill was passionate about his job and loved being part of a close-knit team. He was right at the pinnacle of his career when, on September 11, 2001, the World Trade Center collapsed. Bill joined the scores of first responders—firefighters, police officers, Red Cross volunteers, and other professionals—who rushed into the area in hopes of saving the lives of thousands trapped in the towers. He witnessed horrific scenes of people jumping out of windows to their death, bodies strewn all over what became known as Ground Zero; many of his friends and colleagues were killed in their attempts to rescue others. He was completely traumatized by the experience, which made him feel even more alone. He became emotionally distant from his wife and kids and his friends, whom he felt could never understand what he had gone through. He barely spoke to anyone and couldn't handle being touched. It was all too overwhelming. He began to drink heavily and hated going to work. When others voiced their concerns, he insisted everything was fine. He was fine. Nothing had changed.

And then one day he found himself standing on the George Washington Bridge. He wanted to die. He had no strength left, his life had no meaning, and he prepared to jump. And yet . . . he didn't jump. Something stopped him long enough for him to realize he needed help.

Paradoxically, what had nearly destroyed him ultimately saved him. Through our work together he slowly, painstakingly worked his way through the five stages of posttraumatic growth, and he began to see that his healing depended on reestablishing a connection to his community, rather than separating himself from it, that his individual healing was bound to the collective healing of that community. He chose

PTG: from Trauma to Growth

FROM	TO
Guilt	Self-compassion
Shame	Vulnerability and acceptance
Loss	Gain
Suffering	Having both joy and pain
A FIXED, closed mindset	A GROWTH, open mindset
Rigid	Flexible
One way of looking at the trauma	Multiple points of view and perspectives
Criticizing the SELF and others	Radical acceptance of SELF and others; SELF-LOVE
Dismissing and denying	Validating and SELF-SOOTHING
Reacting	Acting and making conscious decisions
Repeating	Repairing
Repeating cycles; repeating compulsively; repeating maladaptive coping mechanisms	Repair; creating new behaviors, new beliefs, new paradigms
Carrying and repeating past trauma, ancestral, generational traumas	Becoming a transitional character; break the cycle of trauma; stop the cycle

Create new stories, new identities, new pathways

Break free from trauma reactions, have more freedom in the response, based on true meaningful values to reach out to other firefighters and first responders who had gone through the same trauma he had. He began to trust that he could overcome the pain once he experienced the support and understanding from his fellow first responders. Eventually the process led him to create an expanded downtown community of support for all those professionals and neighborhoods that had lived through the horrors of 9/11. Through his own growth and transformation, Bill was able to help transform the pain and suffering of the people around him. He had found renewed strength and purpose in being able to help others.

The Dimensions of Posttraumatic Growth

I believe anyone can go through the stages of posttraumatic growth and emerge with a sense of personal strength, more deeply connected to themselves, to others, and to the world around them. It may not be an easy road to navigate, but it can be done. It takes knowing that PTG is possible in the first place; working with a trauma-informed therapist, facilitator, or mentor who understands and offers a path to PTG; having the support of family, friends, and community; and, of course, being willing to dive into the fire, burn away the wounds of the trauma, and be reborn.

So, what does posttraumatic growth look like? Back in the 1990s, Tedeschi and Calhoun identified five "domains of growth," which include appreciation of life, personal strength, relationships with others, new possibilities, and spiritual change. These still ring true today, and I see evidence of such growth in my practice all the time. Let's take a look at these domains through the lens of my own research and clinical experience.

APPRECIATION OF LIFE

In the *Pirkei Avot,* a book of Jewish ethical teachings, there is a saying that translates as: *Who is the rich one? He who rejoices in his portion.* In other words, someone who is happy with what they have. Who has a deep appreciation for life. After living through a traumatic event and coming out the other side, everything looks brighter and more inviting. People often experience a heightened sense of gratitude, joy, and play and a renewed commitment to making the most of their life. They're so grateful even for the things they've previously taken for granted—like breathing, eating, and hanging out with friends. Little everyday challenges don't seem to be such a big deal anymore. They find it easier to experience pleasure and to stay in the present moment. They have more confidence and clarity and, because they've survived their trauma, they know they can handle anything that comes their way, even future traumas.

PERSONAL STRENGTH

Interestingly, the world becomes a less scary place when someone has experienced growth after trauma. I've heard clients say, "If I survived that, I can survive anything!" or "I had no idea I was that strong! Nothing can stop me now!" These sentiments are not that unusual for people who have been through a personal hell and survived. It's like the old adage *What doesn't kill you makes you stronger.*

We've all heard about superhuman feats of strength and

fortitude from people in crisis—the famous image of a parent lifting up the back end of a car when a child has been trapped underneath. I work with parents with ill or high-risk children who tell me they're surprised by how strong they are, physically and emotionally, and how they are able to deal with their difficulties with equanimity. Those fleeing from war zones, those who have fought off an intruder, or those who have survived a devastating fire often report they have no idea how they were able to do what they did. But they now have faith in their ability to do what needs to be done. The strength they're experiencing is no ordinary, everyday power; it is their superpower, a kind of strength that surfaces when it's needed the most.

Even in daily life, survivors may feel they finally have the strength to stand up for themselves or their family and take control of their life. Some people find they're more willing to admit their vulnerability and their softheartedness after experiencing PTG. They've learned that always trying to be the strong one, the unbreakable one, no longer serves them. Their experiences have taught them that there's strength in vulnerability and in the ability to admit we all have insecurities and that we need each other.

RELATIONSHIP WITH OTHERS

Trauma often helps people recognize their own vulnerability and see the same in others. I like to think of this as empathy training, which will allow us to become more comfortable with intimacy and make it easier to connect with others on a deeper, more conscious level.

Remember, when we're in trauma we are disconnected,

dissociated from ourselves and others. In posttraumatic growth, on the other hand, we have a new (or renewed) sense of belonging and we're more sensitized to other people's feelings and needs, more connected to the people we love. On the other hand, superficial relationships may no longer interest us, even as we begin to enjoy being around people again. We've evolved, and we feel the need to shed old friendships that no longer serve a purpose, no longer bring us joy or feel good. This doesn't always happen right away, of course, but it's not unusual to surround ourselves with a whole new set of friends.

Empathy isn't necessarily limited to people we know. We may find that we are more sensitive to the struggles of others and recognize the importance of acknowledging their suffering. We become more compassionate—less judgmental or critical—when we encounter someone on the street or when we interact with shopkeepers or essential workers. We begin to realize that other people may be going through their own traumas or are reacting a certain way because of something that has happened to them.

When working with young men and women who have been through painful experiences, I'm struck by how important it is, after the trauma, to share honestly and compassionately with others in their lives. To express more openly what it means to be friends or to be in a committed relationship.

Sometimes when we've been through our own struggles, we may be motivated to share our experiences with others as a way of helping them through similar circumstances. These interactions can form the basis for mutual support programs, community work, or even larger movements.

NEW POSSIBILITIES

Growth is not about how much money we make or how much recognition we get for the success we achieve. It's about transforming our relationship to ourself, to our community, and to the world. It's about quality of life, being at peace with who we are as a human being, and who we are in relation to those around us. We may be open to new opportunities—in our personal life as well as professionally—and see more clearly the possibilities that lie ahead. Being open allows us to change the trajectory of our life—because our life is no longer the same, *we* are not the same. After what we've been through, we now feel that *anything* is attainable, that no hurdle is too big to leap over. We see opportunities instead of roadblocks; a sense of excitement replaces anxiety, and fear gives way to creativity and joy. We are expanding our vision of what is possible.

After we've been through posttraumatic growth, the definition of who we are changes. We're eager to consider new possibilities, different ones that are more aligned with our priorities. They feel more authentic, more like us. We're through wasting our life on things that don't truly matter.

SPIRITUAL CHANGE

Trauma often stirs fundamental questions about the meaning of life and the importance of spiritual awakening. When we've been through adversity, survival can feel like we've been graced with a second chance, another opportunity to grow and transform. When people go through the stages that lead to posttraumatic growth, they inevitably experience some sort of opening into a newer and higher connection of life. They begin to understand they are part of something much bigger than themselves. That they are connected to everything around them and have acquired a more spiritual perspective that moves beyond material comforts.

In my practice, I see many examples of posttraumatic spiritual awakening, which brings people into a more conscious, loving, and connected relationship to their body, mind, and spirit, to others in their lives, and to the world. Sometimes when people experience an awakening they return to the religion of their childhood or explore a new faith; others seek new spiritual connections by turning inward through meditation or prayer or being in community with fellow seekers; still others are drawn to selfless service, eager to share their wisdom with a wider community. This wisdom often allows people to derive meaning from—and even become enriched by—their past experiences so that they can take what they have learned about life and pass it on to others.

The Path to Growth

Although I firmly believe that with enough support and determination—and by fully committing to the process—anyone can achieve posttraumatic growth, I also know that it's not an automatic step and it can be a long, arduous journey. What facilitates the process, what inhibits it and makes it less probable to happen? What makes it so difficult for some and not for others? What gets in the way and what can we do to increase our ability to move from trauma to growth? In the next chapter, we'll explore several variables—what I call "floating factors"—that can either enhance or hinder our ability to move into posttraumatic growth.

Chapter 4

Floating Factors

And the day came when the risk to remain tight in a bud
was more painful than the risk it took to blossom.

—ANAÏS NIN

As I talked about in the last chapter, growth after trauma
is not automatic; it takes time, effort, and a sustained commitment. The journey from trauma through posttraumatic
growth takes us from the known to the unknown, from psychological death to rebirth, until we return home completely
transformed. The process of PTG is an invitation to truly
look at our early traumas, and other stressful experiences, not
as symptoms of illness or as disorders but as a way to become
conscious and aware.

Not everyone is ready or even interested in going through
all the discomfort and challenges PTG requires, and that's
fine. I get that. Some people want to put their traumatic experience behind them and get on with their lives. Some are
more interested in increasing their resilience. There are certain
variables that can enhance the likelihood of PTG happening,
and some that diminish it. What I'm talking about here are
the variables that improve or impair the chances of moving

fully into transformation, into posttraumatic growth. I call them "floating factors," because sometimes they do facilitate growth, sometimes they don't; sometimes they combine with other factors to make them more protective or, conversely, get tangled up with others to make them more of a hindrance.

Many of these variables have been studied for years. In the early 1980s, American behavioral scientist Norman Garmezy, whose work centered on childhood trauma, came up with what he called a set of "protective factors," which he believed influence the outcome of trauma. He grouped these factors into three categories: those inherent in the individual; those available in the family; and those present in the larger community. Although most of his research focused on childhood trauma, these factors can impact people at any age and appear to transcend ethnic, social class, and geographic boundaries. Although nothing can safeguard anyone from future traumas—trauma is part of the human experience—some variables may help us meet whatever befalls us in a healthier way. It's important to remember that trauma is relational and contextual—and so is the healing process. In fact, one of the protective factors is family and social support. When we feel cared for, when we can trust those who are supposed to keep us safe, when we experience a secure attachment, we have a certain buffer against the outside world, a cushion that can soften the blow or create a gentler landing. It's like being wrapped in the arms of a caregiver or being loved and watched over by the community, not having to "go it alone."

Certain personality traits work in our favor as well, especially in childhood, such as being resilient, extroverted, curious, able to self-regulate emotionally, willing to ask for help, and open to new experiences. A strong sense of belonging, as well as good interpersonal relationships and social support systems outside the family unit, have also been shown to be beneficial. We'll touch on many of these floating factors in this chapter. But let's start with resilience first, a concept most people are familiar with.

Resilience: A Double-Edged Sword

When the world appears to be a dangerous, unpredictable place, people naturally want to know what they can do to survive. They want to develop grit, learn to choose happiness, and cultivate resilience. Resilience—the capacity to recover quickly from difficulties—is what can help us weather the storm caused by a traumatic experience and give us the coping skills we need to resume our lives. The paradox, however, is that it can also block us from entering the process of post-traumatic growth. So, which is it? Does resilience enhance or diminish our ability to heal our trauma and transform? Like most things having to do with human nature, it depends.

Anita and Dalia are two sisters who came to see me after a very stressful event happened in their family. They saw their father as unstable and self-centered, who physically and emotionally abused their mother, and repeatedly cheated on her with other women. Finally he was caught in several illegal business transactions and was deported back to his country. Their mother, abused and demoralized, was completely codependent on her husband and on her own parents. She didn't take any responsibility for her actions or emotions; in many ways she was very childlike.

After their father was deported, their mother decided she needed to take care of herself and abandoned Anita and

Dalia, who were eighteen and twenty, respectively, leaving them to figure things out for themselves. Although they both came out of a highly disorganized family dynamic, their responses were vastly different.

At eighteen years old, Anita feels responsible for her father. She travels to visit him as often as she can and works tirelessly with lawyers to get him back into the United States. He repeatedly calls her, whining that he's lonely, he needs her to visit him, he doesn't like to be alone. Within six months, Anita has a psychotic break. All the trauma, the responsibilities, and the demands from her father have put her over the edge. She has all the symptoms of a breakdown—she's angry, rebellious, can't control her actions, fights with everyone, including her father and even her sister. She ends up hospitalized and medicated. She goes from therapist to therapist looking for help, but each one diagnoses her as mentally ill. By the time she comes to see me, it's clear to me she's traumatized. But she's not psychotic; she's not mentally ill. She's broken by the unrelenting trauma in her life. Anita is completely in touch with her emotions—she feels *everything*—but has no tools with which to process them. Very slowly, she is beginning to enter the first stage of posttraumatic growth—scared but hopeful.

In the meantime, Dalia is doing fine; for the most part, she's resilient and is able to cope. She tried for a while to help Anita, but she prefers to focus on her own life. She told me she recognizes that her father is unstable and absent, and that her mother is unavailable. She accepts their limitations, and she can handle that. She doesn't really think much about either of them. She stays in her lane and doesn't get involved. She has plenty of friends and a new boyfriend she's hoping to marry soon: she's incredibly resilient and doesn't really see much reason to dwell on her family's dysfunction. She's moved on. Anita fears Dalia will fall apart once she gets married. That's certainly possible—or she could keep on keeping on and be fine.

Resilience undeniably plays a crucial role in trauma recovery, and I don't want to minimize that. It often protects people from becoming immobilized by their anxiety and chronic stress, and prevents them from slipping back into depression or self-destructive behaviors or getting stuck in PTSD. Resilient individuals are capable of coping successfully with formidable demands without experiencing the impairment that is typical for other people facing similar challenges. Families, communities, and cultures can also be resilient. Such resilience gives them the means and the tools to support one another, strengthen leadership, foster greater stability, and stay focused on their core purpose and future goals. I certainly witnessed this ability firsthand in my immigrant community in Venezuela.

It seems like everyone is talking about resilience these days. Books have been written about it; workshops and TEDx talks created around the theme. All of this tells us that resilience is good. And it absolutely can be. Resilience has many benefits. Does that mean resilience is *required* for posttraumatic growth? Not necessarily. I'll explain, but first let's begin by defining the term.

First and foremost: Resilience is *not the same as posttraumatic growth*. Resilience is bouncing back; PTG is catapulting forward, soaring beyond the pre-trauma state. Resilience is a skill we develop, not something we go through. It's the ability to recover quickly from adversity, to be tough in the face of trauma, hardships, and significant difficulties. It's a skill set that comes from a combination of biological, psychological, and social factors, which can reduce the effects of acute or chronic stress and encourage ways in which we can adapt to life's challenges. When people have strong, positive relationships and good self-esteem, they are less likely to dwell on their past, blame others for their own shortcomings, or see themselves as helpless victims. I've witnessed this happen countless times in working with patients as a clinical psychologist and trauma therapist.

Several years ago, I started working with Miranda, the young woman I mentioned in the Introduction. Her mother had died about a year after she got married. But she didn't come to therapy to talk about her mother. She came to talk about her marital problems. She and her husband, she said, were having a rough time communicating, made harder by the fact they had four young children. She talked about her anxiety, the panic attacks she would sometimes have, and she wanted advice on what to do when she couldn't soothe her nerves.

After a few sessions, she mentions her mother had died, almost like an afterthought. And yet she talks about their close relationship, the suddenness of her death, and how it has affected her. She tells me she's always been very attached to her mother. She was a big presence in her life, so much so that it sometimes feels like she's in the room with us. She talks about her mother, recalling things she would say, ways in which she thought about life, and what she would do in any given situation. Everyone in her family loved her mother, and they are all deeply shaken by her death.

In spite of the intensity of her loss, Miranda has thrown herself into everything in her life with full passion and presence—without allowing herself to fall apart. She's become a highly regarded doctor, like her father, and a mother of young children. Coming from a conservative family, she takes care of everything—the cooking, cleaning, childcare, and scheduling. She sometimes jokes that her husband, so helpless in the day-to-day tasks, is more like her fifth child. She is able to be present, in very practical ways, for her patients, for her family—and even for herself. She is solution-driven and really can deal with anything—no problem feels too big for her to handle. And when her anxiety gets the better of her, she isn't so interested in exploring where it all came from. Instead, she wants me to suggest helpful ways she can manage her emotions and get back on track. In many aspects she feels she's made progress—she's better able to acknowledge and share her feelings—so she doesn't see the purpose of shaking things up by diving too deeply into her past. She'd rather focus on the present and look toward the future.

Miranda is what I would call resilient. She is, in some ways, the personification of resilience, which comes from the Latin *resilire*, meaning "to recoil, rebound, spring back." She has certainly demonstrated an ability to bounce back from adversity. She shows "strength of character, toughness, and adaptability," all common synonyms for resilience, and she feels good about the life she's created.

Resilience allows us to endure a tragedy and stay put. It helps us find balance in our lives and can keep distress at bay. In that regard, resilience is indeed a positive factor for dealing with trauma. Like Miranda, resilient people are often highly successful members of society, driven to excel and convinced their trauma is either a distant memory or was healed long ago. They may suffer from low-level depression and anxiety, have emotional setbacks, or experience traumatic memories, but none of that gets in their way of doing well in life. Resilience is hugely important in our ability to recover from trauma, live a normal life, and not get stuck in the suffering of PTSD.

The Paradox of Resilience

As important as resilience is in trauma recovery, it can be a hindrance to transformation. It can actually stop us from moving into posttraumatic growth. Why? Because resilient people are adaptable and can adjust to adversity; they have good coping skills. Resilience allows us to return to homeostasis, to return to where we were *before* tragedy struck. It's a way to inoculate ourselves and those we love from future suffering. Make no mistake, being resilient has helped many people cope with adversity and get on with their lives— which is a good thing. What resilience doesn't do is allow for the opportunity to *grow* from our experiences, to transform and even thrive *because* of what we've been through. To become stronger than ever, to make our pain matter, to facilitate and promote greater meaning and purpose, and to grow both emotionally and spiritually. In other words, to experience *posttraumatic growth*.

Oftentimes resilient people get through the first two stages of my PTG model—accepting that they're in pain and benefiting from therapy or other forms of support—and then are able to go back to normal quickly. Positive psychology and social expectations encourage people to do just that.

But that's not how posttraumatic growth works. The process asks us to do something really radical, and often quite traumatic. People who go through the PTG process start out feeling broken and unable to bounce back easily. Beginning with the very first step of the healing process, posttraumatic growth requires that we break down the barriers that prevent us from acknowledging our suffering, and radically accept our pain. People don't start to grow and transform until they fall apart; until they've been shaken to the core. The very definition of resilience—"the ability to bounce back, adapt, and be tough yet flexible, sturdy and strong"—doesn't allow for such soul-shaking psychological earthquakes. Resilience craves order; transformation is messy. Feelings are disorganized, chaotic, and confusing; expressing or even naming them doesn't come easy. But when we don't allow the emotions to rise to the surface, we stunt or block the very experiences we're having, and don't allow for sadness, fear, or depression to be expressed. Transformation requires the shattering of what used to be in order to reimagine what is possible, a commitment to grow *through* the suffering and emerge reborn. But it cannot happen unless we consciously and radically accept our pain.

Although resilient people are often able to continue functioning at a fairly high level after trauma, their trauma can remain buried and unresolved, which means it could show up again—maybe even years later—until it is brought to light and dealt with. Sometimes it can reemerge when you least expect it, when something seemingly unrelated to the initial event triggers the buried trauma and puts you over the edge. It could happen when you have a child or when you travel somewhere that takes you back to a time when you were young; or when you hear a song you used to listen to that's attached to a memory.

This happened to my patient Isabel, an incredibly resilient

and capable woman in her early forties, who came to see me soon after the birth of her second child. She was super depressed and, in her words, "an anxious mess." As she shared her story, it became clear to both of us that she wasn't suffering from postpartum depression, as she thought, but from a trauma response connected to a long-forgotten childhood experience.

Isabel told me that she had immigrated to the United States fifteen years ago, without her family, barely knowing the language, and enrolled in university where she studied economics. She had had a complicated relationship with her mother, a woman who was emotionally unavailable, but she put all of that behind her when she left. She loved her life in her adopted country. She found a great job soon after graduating, and even met the man she ended up marrying. After struggling at first to start a family, Isabel gave birth to a little girl, Daniela, and both she and her husband worked hard to create a stable, loving family. When Daniela was five years old, Isabel got pregnant again—just as the pandemic began. As her due date got closer, she realized she would need extra help taking care of Daniela. She reached out to her mother and offered to pay her way to the United States if she would help her, but her mother didn't respond. Isabel begged her to come at least until after the baby was born, but as usual, she refused to make Isabel's request a priority and after a lot of back and forth, never showed up.

Isabel admitted that the birth of her baby Jessie—and her mother's refusal to come—had plunged her into depression and anxiety. She was having trouble holding Jessie, she felt awkward touching her naked body, and even breastfeeding felt uncomfortable, which had never happened with Daniela.

And then one afternoon, as she was preparing to breastfeed, she had an unsettling flashback. Images of a man; her as a little girl, maybe four or five years old; a playroom at the home of a family friend; the man coming into the room and touching her all over. She said she didn't remember anything else about that day. When she tried to talk to her mother about it, her mother shut down and refused to discuss it. As she began putting all the pieces together, she realized she needed help. She told me she was ready to do whatever she had to do to heal her trauma so her depression wouldn't affect her ability to care for her children, and her response to her childhood memories wouldn't lead to their suffering, too.

Posttraumatic growth requires us to bring everything into the light, including our traumas that have been buried deep inside. In doing so, it not only changes the way we relate to our trauma, it transforms us. Ironically, the least resilient, those who are the most traumatized, are often the most likely to experience posttraumatic growth. They may feel they have nothing to lose, that their lives have become unbearable, and something *has* to change. As psychologist Richard Tedeschi says, "Remember, it's the struggle with distress that leads to growth, not the traumatic event itself."

Resilience is beneficial in early childhood and it also can be an outcome or a by-product in the process of posttraumatic growth. It is through the process of PTG that we can become more resilient to the stress and struggles of everyday life.

Within the floating factors, resilience and coping mechanisms can either facilitate or paradoxically hinder posttraumatic growth; other factors can also enhance our ability to grow and transform—or keep us stuck. Let's look at a few of those with that in mind from a relational standpoint: the self (personality traits and attributes), the other (interpersonal relationships), and the world (cultural context).

The Self

Personality traits and attributes. Our personality characteristics influence the way we face life events and our ability to bounce back from adversity or leap forward into growth. And research bears that out. Norman Garmezy's model of protective factors shows that hardiness, autonomy, sociability, and positive self-esteem all contribute to childhood resilience. Beginning in the mid-1950s in a longitudinal study on the island of Kauai, researchers Drs. Emmy Werner and Ruth Smith also looked at protective factors in children at risk. One of the most important things they found was that children who were sociable, curious, naturally optimistic, open, and extroverted, and who developed strong bonds with their caregivers, were better able to face adversity.[1]

Other studies also noted that children who are more assertive, have autonomy and a positive self-regard, and believe that they have agency—what psychologists call "an internal locus of control"—have an easier time *recovering* from traumatic experiences. Internal control, a sense of achievement, and optimism can protect them from the stressful aftermath of a traumatic event and build resilience. These personality traits appear to be protective throughout adulthood.

In my clinical experience, I have seen how some of these factors can either facilitate or hinder posttraumatic growth. Let's take optimism, for example. "Realistic" optimism can keep us believing we can get through the turmoil we're facing. *With the confidence, brains, and support I have, I know I can do this.* However, too much positivity can also mask how we truly feel—*No, really, I'm great!*—and keep us from getting the support we need: *Wow, look at you; you're so resilient! You bounced back so quickly!*

All of these traits can give us confidence in our own strength and in our ability to face adversity and recover. Being extroverted and goal-oriented can also strongly support growth. When we direct our energy and resources outward, we can focus on what needs to get done, how we can make stuff happen, and who needs our attention. A bit of caution, however: All of this outward-directed energy can sometimes keep us from looking inward, which can limit our ability to ask for help and see the possibility of growth. It can cause us to gloss over, ignore, or not even notice what's really going on inside.

Cognitive skills. It appears that cognitive processing—the ability to take in information and use it effectively—helps us understand what's happening in our own mind and body, interact with others intelligently, and operate day-to-day in the world. Cognitive processing, as a way into posttraumatic growth, can happen when we are distressed enough to want to figure out what is going on, find meaning within the suffering, and learn from it. Let's look at two examples of cognitive floating factors here.

- **Growth vs. Fixed Mindset:** Studies tell us that children and adults who have a growth mindset, as opposed to a fixed mindset, are better able to imagine a way out of struggle. Carol Dweck, a Stanford University psychology professor who coined the term, says that a growth mindset is more critical for success than a high IQ or a particular talent. A growth mindset sees possibilities instead of doomsday scenarios; a fixed mindset sees only failure: *I'll never be able to do anything right. I'm a loser. Nothing positive can come out of this experience.* People with a fixed mindset believe they'll never be any different from how they are right now—that their intelligence and abilities are fixed, and if they could change, they would have. Those with a growth mindset believe they can learn from their mistakes, do anything they set their mind to if they work hard enough—in other words, they can grow from their experience.[4]

It's important, however, for therapists, mentors, or any expert companions not to force the growth mindset too soon or impose a change of perspective the person may not be ready to make. Otherwise, it could have the opposite effect, and the person could be retraumatized.

- **Intrusive vs. Deliberate Rumination:** You don't need to go through a harrowing or traumatic event to understand what it feels like to get stuck in obsessive thinking. Who hasn't mulled something over, trying to understand what happened? What they'd done? "Ruminate" literally means to turn something over in your mind, to chew on something. Although it sounds like it would automatically be detrimental to posttraumatic growth, that's not always true. Rumination is actually a way the mind processes and attempts to make meaning out of an event. There are two types of rumination—intrusive and deliberate—both of which are important factors in meaning-making. Intrusive (or obsessive) rumination is an unintentional process that happens when we can't stop thinking about a traumatic event. We overthink things by replaying the event in our head, dissecting every aspect of the story, focusing on the negative emotions and details, all of which can bring about substantial emotional distress, according to numerous studies.[2] It can feel as though we have no control over the thoughts and images that surface. Intrusive rumination keeps us stuck in the past and can lead to PTSD or a chronic stress response.[3] Deliberate (or constructive) rumination, on the other hand, is a conscious effort to understand and derive meaning from the experience. It's purposeful self-examination that leads to self-realization, a way of studying the past in order to inform the present and stop the effects of the trauma going forward. *How did this happen? What can I learn from it?* From deliberate rumination we strive to discover the positive aspects of our experience, the wisdom within the wound, both of which can support us in moving toward growth.

As with all the floating factors, neither type of rumination can be said to hinder or enhance growth 100 percent of the time. So much depends on the timing and the intensity of the threat. It may not be possible, for example, to deliberately ruminate right after something awful happens, when we're still reeling from the horror of it all. It's too soon. So intrusive rumination can be a coping mechanism

and a survival strategy, a way of sitting with and acknowledging what happened, and can be as important as deliberate rumination in making meaning of
the experience early on. All of this is to say that both
intrusive and deliberate rumination play vital roles
in the possibility of posttraumatic growth.

The Other

How we relate to others and what types of support are available to us—especially in childhood—can influence how we
process trauma as adults, how likely it is we can heal from
it, and how likely we are to grow because of it. Pre-trauma
resources can often determine how we face whatever comes
our way.

Interpersonal relationships. Because trauma is relational,
it almost goes without saying that we need support and love
and constancy from those who are supposed to care for us so
we can develop clear expectations about the world and our
place in it. As Dr. van der Kolk says, "How loved you felt as
a child is a great predictor of how you manage all kinds of
difficult situations later in life." That love and support don't
always come from our parents—nor do they have to. We may
have been able to connect with grandparents or another caregiver or a teacher, coach, mentor, or even the parents of a
close friend whose support made a difference in our young
lives.

Those who were naturally outgoing and sociable as children may have an easier time connecting with others as
adults, which may help them manage difficult circumstances.

On the other hand, those who were withdrawn as young kids, who often felt anxious or powerless, were more vulnerable to the effects of traumatic situations or chronic adversity. These individuals may be less likely to grow into well-adjusted adults and more likely to experience mental health issues later on in life.

Of course, the factors of resilience or vulnerability, connection or isolation, and sociability or inhibition may be predictive but they're not absolute, even in childhood. Growing up with strong family or community ties; being confident and outgoing, and knowing when to ask for help may give us the tools we need to effectively bounce back from trauma as adults, but not necessarily the impetus to work toward PTG. For those who grew up in a chaotic or disorganized household, who were most vulnerable as children, their history of posttraumatic stress can become "the engine of transformation," as psychologist Stephen Joseph calls it in *What Doesn't Kill Us*, which sets them upon the path of posttraumatic growth later on in life,

Because I work so often with marginalized communities and people who have endured unspeakable atrocities, I have seen this contradiction many times. For example, you may remember my dear friend María Trusa from the Dominican Republic; she had very few, if any, resources—either internal or external—growing up in a chaotic family, and she suffered greatly at the hands of an abuser. And yet, as an adult, she chose posttraumatic growth, determined to make sense of her experiences and to transform her pain into purpose.

Attachment styles. So much of what we learn about ourselves, our relationship with others and about the world, we learn in childhood—from the people who are charged with caring for us. Most often these people are our parents or grandparents, but they could have been a trusted teacher or coach, a mentor, or a spiritual leader. As children we learn by listening, watching, and mimicking the words, actions, and reactions of those closest to us. We learn what it means to be in relationships by watching others and mirroring their behavior. We get messages about our own bodies by noticing how others treat and talk about theirs. Our self-esteem and self-worth are intimately connected to how we're treated by our family and people closest to us. All of this gets stored in our body.

As discussed in Chapter 2, the relationship we have with our primary caregivers in childhood—what psychologists call our "attachment style"—becomes the foundation of our relationships in adulthood, particularly with our life partners and our own children. It can also determine how we respond to traumatic events. You may have had a secure attachment as a child, with warm, loving parents, or an insecure one, in which you grew up with parents or caregivers who were emotionally unavailable (avoidant style); inconsistent in showing or withholding their love (anxious style); or who created a volatile, unstable environment in which you feared for your safety (disorganized style). Those with such insecure, disorganized, or chaotic attachments in childhood are generally more vulnerable in the face of adversity *and* at the same time, possibly more likely to go through the process of growth as adults. Those with a secure attachment are generally more protected from becoming overwhelmed by a traumatic event *and* are not necessarily likely to go through posttraumatic growth. Let's see why.

Say that when you were growing up, you had a warm, loving relationship with your mother, had good friends your age and great relationships with other adults in your life. You felt confident and happy. Most probably, you have (or will have) a healthy relationship with your life partner and with your children as well. You may have an easier time trusting others, reaching out for support when you need it, being affectionate and receiving affection, and balancing the desire for connection and independence—both for you and your partner and children. Research shows that a secure attachment style gives you the most protection from the adverse effects of trauma during childhood and later on in life. You feel you can face whatever comes your way.

It can also happen, however, that an event is so traumatic it shatters your confidence and sense of security and you fall apart. You are traumatized. Only then does the possibility of posttraumatic growth surface. This was Julian's experience as a young kid growing up in Colombia. He was surrounded by love. He was the youngest of six siblings who all adored their little brother. His parents were affectionate and protective yet encouraged the kids to be independent and creative. Everyone in their small town and at the school he went to seemed to know Julian and delight in his company. But the political climate was very unstable, and as violence escalated and robberies and kidnappings became more commonplace, Julian's parents became concerned. They took the family to Miami, where they made plans to seek asylum. When they told Julian and his siblings they were not going back, Julian couldn't believe it. Why didn't anyone tell him, he wanted to know. He didn't get to say good-bye to his friends, to his teachers, to the janitor at the school, whom he liked so much. *They'll be so worried. They'll think I left without saying good-bye on purpose.*

Julian became depressed. He refused to learn English, he didn't want to make friends, he cried everyday—*I just want to go home.* His suffering threw the whole family into despair; they were so worried about him—he had always been the positive, happy one. And now, he was traumatized. Finally, a year later, when the family was able to return to Colombia to pack up their belongings, Julian was able to properly say good-bye. Because his family was patient and supportive— and Julian agreed to therapy—he was able to recover and find his place in Miami. These days he's doing so well; he's found a way to express his emotions through his art, and he has close friends he hangs out with.

Sense of belonging. This is a factor that seems so obvious, doesn't it? When we are disconnected from ourselves, from one another, and from the larger culture, we suffer. When we belong to something bigger than ourselves, when we feel we fit in somewhere, we have the strength to deal with whatever comes up more easily. We're not alone. In childhood, of course, a sense of belonging is intimately tied to healthy attachment to our parents or others whose job it is to keep us safe, nourished, and loved. As adults, we often organize our lives around belonging to and identifying with particular groups. For example, you may be a member of a work group or volunteer organization or part of a close circle of friends. Some people feel comfortable in small, intimate groups. Others derive meaning by belonging to a much larger circle, such as a political group, a social justice organization, a group that supports and honors their sexual orientation or ethnicity, or a certain religious or spiritual community.

According to Dan Siegel, clinical professor of psychiatry at UCLA School of Medicine and director of the Mindsight Institute, connectedness is the key to transformation and "a factor underlying recovery of mental illness." He says that disconnection is not only a source of addiction and depression, it's a form of trauma because "we are built to belong."[5] A feeling of belonging can serve as a protective factor for difficulties with mental health issues and in the face of trauma and adversity.

In her book *Trauma and Recovery*, Judith Herman writes:

> The solidarity of a group provides the strongest protection against terror and despair, and the strongest antidote to traumatic experience. Trauma isolates; the group re-creates a sense of belonging. Trauma shames and stigmatizes; the group bears witness and affirms. Trauma degrades the victim; the group exalts her. Trauma dehumanizes the victim; the group restores her humanity.

She goes on to say that there comes a time when a sense of connection is restored by another person's simple act of generosity. The sense of belonging, then, provides a sense of safety for a person who has endured trauma, and it can set in motion the process of posttraumatic growth.

Trauma can keep us isolated from others and prevent us from feeling like we belong. *I feel lonely even when I'm with people. I feel like an outsider with nothing to contribute. I don't want others to know how broken I feel.* This need to belong can lead someone toward posttraumatic growth. For example, when I was working with Alejandro, whose life was shattered by the school shooting that took the lives of seventeen people, he admitted that he often felt disconnected partly because he had been through horrors that others could never even imagine. He often shared with me that he felt isolated and alone.

Although having a sense of belonging can help us feel connected to others, it can also keep us separate from ourselves. While belonging is part of the process of posttraumatic growth, it can also hinder or prevent growth. How? By keeping us in our "comfort zone." We feel protected enough, our needs are being met to a certain extent, and we don't want to risk letting go of any of it. Also, while our sense of belonging gives us an identity, which is important, it can also inhibit our individuality and prevent us from differentiating or distinguishing ourselves from the group as a whole. That in itself can be confining and traumatic. A great example of this is in the television series *Unorthodox,* based on a true story of a young girl in a tight-knit Hasidic Jewish community in Brooklyn, New York. Forced to conform to the demands of her culture, she married unwillingly at nineteen and submitted to the expectations put on her as a married woman, which included having many babies right away. Unable to become pregnant after a year, she flees Brooklyn and ends up in Berlin, where she slowly builds a new life on her own, free from the restrictions she felt within her community.

The World

Cultural and environmental context. As we all know by now, trauma doesn't happen in a vacuum, nor does posttraumatic growth. There are many factors that influence whether we can meet our trauma and transcend it or whether we'll succumb to a debilitating posttraumatic stress response. Some of these floating factors include: the type of trauma (acute or chronic); the timing and the severity of it; the age we were when the initial trauma happened; the culture we come from and the beliefs it holds about the trauma we experienced; and our social class, as well as our ethnicity, gender, religious affiliation, and sexual orientation. Let's look at how a couple of these floating factors affects the possibility of posttraumatic growth.

- **Age, timing, and severity:** Most researchers agree that the younger we are when we experience a traumatic event, the longer the trauma remains in our body and the harder it is to heal and grow from it. While I generally believe that to be true, I have also had clients who told me what they witnessed during combat, for example, or what they went through when they lost their child to violence, is beyond anything they ever experienced in childhood. They may not have been able to heal from their past traumas, but they say that the severity of the new experience pushed them over the edge, traumatizing them even more and, eventually, led them to choose the path toward posttraumatic growth. Sometimes the timing of an event, the stage of life we're in, may elevate it from annoying or manageable to catastrophic—the proverbial straw that broke the camel's back. The timing can also influence whether someone is ready and willing to do the hard work to transform the pain into wisdom or whether it's beyond their capacity at that moment.
- **Cultural beliefs:** The culture in which we live— and the beliefs of that culture—can determine the

probability that the trauma we're going through
will be acknowledged, that the possibility of healing will be available to help us make meaning of
our pain. In other words, some communities are
more open and more supportive to the healing
process than others. The cultural systems within
which we live give us a set of rules, a language to
understand the values, beliefs, and expectations
of how society operates. For most people, there's
a certain level of comfort and security in that. After all, when you feel welcomed and a part of a
larger community, you can derive strength from
that. When there are services and organizations designed to ensure the right of citizens to be happy,
healthy, and free, individuals and communities can
thrive. When cultures have trauma-informed systems in place—in other words, they recognize and
respond to trauma—they are willing to respond to
the unique needs of their diverse populations. I see
how this happens successfully on a cultural level
whenever I go to Bhutan, a country that values the
collective happiness of its citizens above all else.
Bhutan's Gross National Happiness, which is part
of the country's constitution, centers psychological
well-being, health, cultural and ecological diversity
and resilience, education, and community vitality,
among others, as essential human rights.

Cultural factors can also contribute to the suffering of certain groups within a society, groups whose
identities aren't valued, or when a society or culture
has not recognized or processed its own trauma.

When that happens, the rules society has imposed can actually cause harm—and prevent access to healing and growth. For example, in a culture that doesn't honor women's rights and has imposed laws that restrict women's autonomy and independence, a woman may fear repercussions if she were to report she'd been raped, so she stays silent. As a result, she remains imprisoned by her trauma, alone and ostracized from family and community support. In other, more inclusive cultures, the chances of her having access to posttraumatic growth therapy are much higher. Whole communities may enjoy certain freedoms that aren't available to other, more marginalized communities within the same society because of their religious affiliation, race, sexual orientation, or immigration status. Refugees who have fled violence in their home countries may end up living in difficult conditions with no immediate way out. Others, who are fortunate to land in a culture that makes room for them, may benefit from organizations and services that focus on their mental health as well as their physical needs. For example, during my clinical work at the Bellevue Program for Survivors of Torture in New York City, we supported refugees from all over the world by providing psychological, social, and physical services, which eventually helped them thrive within the community. They had a better chance of healing from the trauma they'd endured in their homelands and from the trauma of settling in a foreign country.

As you can see, all of these factors in some way contribute to our post-trauma experience—either by blocking access to growth or by opening the door to transformation. No one factor leads to or inhibits posttraumatic growth; there are a variety of factors at play, along with individual will and determination.

Now that you understand the floating factors, let's take a broader look at trauma. Up until now, we've focused mostly on the challenging events that happen to individuals, and the source of the trauma is very clear. That may be an obvious kind of trauma, but it's not the only one. Traumas can also be ancestral, passed down through generations. They can remain hidden, unprocessed and buried within us so deeply that we don't even realize there's a reason for our suffering. Our job is to unearth them, bring them to light so that they can be healed and so the cycle of intergenerational trauma can be stopped. In the next chapter, I'll explore how they came to live within us in the first place, how we can derive wisdom from them, and how to release them.

Chapter 5

The Intergenerational
Legacy of Trauma

In the history of the collective, as in the history of the individual, everything depends on the development of consciousness.

—CARL JUNG

The trauma experiences of those who came before us are embedded in the culture in which we live and can make the process (and outcome) of posttraumatic growth more challenging. This intergenerational trauma comes from our parents, grandparents, great-grandparents, and back through our ancestral lineage. These preexisting traumas get passed on physiologically, psychologically, and socially, and can determine how we deal with life's struggles and how we face adversity.

My patient Paula and her daughter Guadalupe are good examples of this. Paula was sexually abused from the time she was three years old until she was thirteen by seven men in her family, including cousins and uncles. She told me in our first session together that she grew up feeling guilty, ashamed, and worthless, filled with anxiety and depression—and, understandably, a deep-seated suspicion of men. She needed help, she said, because she was afraid she had passed all of this along to her daughter, Guadalupe, even though she'd never told her anything about her past experiences. Guadalupe now has the same fears as her mother, without having had any major traumatic experiences herself. As an adult, Guadalupe has a visceral reaction against—or seemingly irrational distrust of—men; she struggles with self-confidence and self-worth and has unconsciously entered into relationships that are harmful, without knowing why any of this is happening. The trauma she inherited from her mother becomes entangled with—and indistinguishable from—any future experiences. Similarly, the men who abused Paula may very well have been repeating abusive behaviors they had experienced in childhood. Thus, they also passed along the pattern of abuse from previous generations. Every perpetrator is also a victim.

Research and clinical experience confirm that people like Guadalupe, whose family members or ancestors suffered from trauma, have a tendency to be more prone to trauma themselves. Certain beliefs, values, and principles we hold may have been unknowingly passed on from generation to generation, and they shape the way we understand the world and our place in that world, the way we function in relationships, and how we make decisions.

It's also important to understand, of course, that trauma isn't the only thing that can get passed on. We can inherit all kinds of beliefs and experiences from our ancestors, including their resilience, strength, joy, and wisdom. In this chapter, I will explain more about how current and intergenerational transmission happen from a psychological, neurological, and emotional perspective.

Trauma Is Contagious: The Ripple Effect

This tendency to repeat traumas from generation to generation within a family or within a group of people makes traumas highly contagious. I know that sounds implausible. How could you become affected by an experience that happened to someone else years before? An experience you weren't even part of (or that happened long before you were born)? And how could you unwittingly pass it along to the next generation yourself? Even more inconceivable, perhaps, is the possibility that you could "catch" someone else's trauma just by hearing about it or witnessing it in person or even on the nightly news. The fact is, both of these scenarios are true.

We see evidence of trauma's contagion from a neurological, cultural, and cellular perspective. The contagion can be a horizontal transmission; that is, we are impacted by directly engaging with survivors of trauma or witnessing or hearing about atrocities. The contagion can also be a vertical transmission; that is, we can genetically inherit trauma through the DNA of our parents, grandparents, great-grandparents, and on down the ancestral line.

HORIZONTAL TRANSMISSION

Neurological. Let's begin with the simplest explanation—humans are naturally empathic beings; we feel each other's joys and sorrows. Trauma is contagious in the same way that laughter is contagious. Have you ever been with a baby who is laughing and find yourself laughing, too, even when you have no idea what's so funny? Her delight is contagious! Or perhaps you read about or talked with someone who is anxious or sad or going through something traumatic and felt those feelings yourself—as though you were the one having the experience. Their pain is also contagious. It appears the more empathic we are, the more we are affected by other people's feelings and experiences. An article published in *Scientific American* cites research that suggests that "10 to 20 percent of people closely involved with those who have PTSD 'catch' the condition themselves—with the numbers varying depending on the study and the group being investigated (such as therapists, social workers or family members)."[1] That is called "vicarious" or "secondary trauma."

How is that possible? It appears that the brain doesn't necessarily distinguish between an actual experience and an imagined one. According to psychologist Judith Daniels of the University of Groningen in the Netherlands, our brain can still register the trauma even when "there is no *direct* input from the sensory organs that might be saved in memory in the brain." It does that, she explains, because the "regions of the brain that process visual imagery have a very strong overlap with regions that process imagined visual experience." In other words, it doesn't seem to matter whether the information comes directly from the senses or from our imagination.[2]

The biological explanation for trauma's contagion can be found in brain cells called "mirror neurons," which are located at the center of the brain. These "emotional" neurons get activated when we experience something traumatic and, even more to the point, when we hear of or experience someone else being traumatized. They work, says psychologist Daniel Goleman, by tracking "the emotional flow, movement and even intentions of the person we are with, and replicating this sensed state in our own brain by stirring in our brain the same areas active in the other person."[3] It's not just that we are affected by other people's traumas; we become traumatized ourselves.

Cultural. Another type of horizontal transmission happens through "mimetic desire," a form of vicarious learning. Vicarious learning is something that happens all the time; it's an important way we learn from the experience of others—by watching, listening to, and empathizing with what they're doing and paying attention to how others are reacting to those actions. René Girard, the French philosopher and historian who coined the term "mimetic desire" in the mid-twentieth century, believed that human desire is highly imitative; in other words, we learn what we desire by mimicking the desires of others we look up to—and of the culture we live in. He also thought there was a downside to mimetic desire: he believed it could lead to violence. We see examples of this all the time in our culture. A young kid or a teenager may be interested in becoming friends with another student, but notices other kids are making fun of that person, maybe even harassing or threatening him. Watching their behavior can cause the kid to change their mind and maybe even join in the bullying.

We've seen worst-case scenarios of this form of mimetic desire far too often in school shootings. Following the first massive school shooting at Columbine High School in Colorado, an entire subculture of young people obsessed with the shooters sprung up on social media. Many of them glorified the murderers as standing up for the little guy and getting rid of the bullies. Research shows that the majority of perpetrators were themselves victims of sometimes extreme bullying;

even more serious, many of those committing atrocities admit to being influenced by the infamy and notoriety of the
Columbine shooters.[4]

There has been plenty of debate about whether violent
movies or video games normalize violence, especially when
children are exposed to them on a regular basis. A study conducted in 2017 looking at 17,000 children from ages nine to
nineteen showed a strong correlation between playing violent
video games and exhibiting aggressive behavior.

VERTICAL TRANSMISSION

Trauma can also be contagious from generation to generation. This is how it works: the generations that came before
us passed their trauma on to us, and then we unconsciously
pass it along to our children—and on and on through our
family lineage, our community, and the culture. But it isn't
only the big, traumatic experiences from our past, the residue
of which gets imprinted in our cellular memory. It truly can
be anything.

Here's a simple example. Many years before Leon was born,
his grandmother nearly drowned in a neighborhood pool,
even though there was a lifeguard on duty. She was obviously
traumatized, and she repeatedly impressed upon Leon's mom
and her siblings that pools were horrible, dangerous places.
The children were forbidden to go swimming; not only were
pools off-limits, but so were creeks, lakes, and oceans. As a
result, they all grew up terrified of water, and passed their fear
onto their own kids.

By the time Leon became a father, his fears, which he had
inherited from his grandmother and his mother, had grown
to encompass much more than swimming pools and lake wa-

ter. He had somehow internalized the message that life itself was dangerous. He, of course, kept his children away from the water, but he also refused to allow them to bike, to play sports, or to venture outdoors very much. It was much safer to stay indoors, which he preferred to do. Both Leon and his mother were affected by the trauma his grandmother experienced. And that experience became encoded in their bodies. Leon especially began to function from that fear; looking at the world and life through a traumatic lens, which then got passed along to his children.

Unfortunately, there are more extreme examples of intergenerational trauma that is contagious and can affect multiple generations. In 2017, Anne Marks, executive director of the nonprofit, Youth ALIVE!, spoke to a congressional committee about violence as one example of how trauma can spread. In her talk she said, "It's not just the condition of the wounded person that makes violence a health issue. It's the ripple effects of violence; it's the spread of trauma that an act of violence instigates."[5] She went on to say that violence may be the disease, but trauma is the virus that spreads it "from incident to person to family, street, neighborhood, community, and city." And she's right. Trauma is never confined to a single person's response to an event. While it does move inward, affecting an individual's physical and emotional health, it's also busy infiltrating the lives of that person's family members, the people they love, those they give birth to, and those with whom they share cultural and historical ancestry. As research shows, it can spread from past generations to family and from family to future generations; from ancient cultures to their modern equivalents. Indeed, trauma can have far-reaching consequences for individuals, families, and communities.

Violence has a clear connection with trauma, and often happens at the hands of those who suffered acts of violence themselves. According to the National Institute of Justice, child abuse and neglect "increased the odds of future delinquency and adult criminality" by almost 30 percent. In a more recent study, 75 percent of youth offenders reported they were physically abused during their childhood. And 56 percent of kids who were maltreated as children committed further acts of violence.

On top of that, the likelihood that the victims of sexual abuse and domestic violence will put themselves in situations where they will continue to be abused is troublingly high. When we're traumatized, it's not uncommon to fall into compulsive repetitive patterns of behavior that reenact the trauma, which becomes a contagious pattern of abuse, violence, victimization, or addiction. Studies bear this out. Among the most fascinating research, I think, comes from my mentor and colleague Kenneth Hardy, whose book *Teens Who Hurt* and seminal article "Healing the Hidden Wounds of Racial Trauma," shed light on how racial injustice contributes to the recurring cycle of trauma.[6] We also see evidence of this in adults who have been physically or sexually abused in childhood.

This is most apparent in relationships, particularly those that are dysfunctional. I see examples of this all the time—women who have suffered at the hands of their fathers or grandfathers gravitate toward men who are also abusers. And, as my patient Paula's story demonstrates, often these men were repeatedly abused themselves by a violent family member and go on to abuse their own children, who then abuse theirs. The players are different, but the game itself is essentially the same. A single event in one person's life can impact many others along the way. Fortunately, there are ways to break the cycle. Even a single person's healing can heal past and future generations, as I will discuss in subsequent chapters. Trauma has far-reaching consequences not only in individuals and families, but also historically within communities and cultures.

Historical trauma. Intergenerational trauma happens not only at the individual and family level, but also at the community level, contributing historically to the suffering of a whole group of people. Thomas Hübl, contemporary mystic, spiritual teacher, and author of *Healing Collective Trauma*, adds to that definition in a way that particularly resonates with me:

> When the people of a particular culture or tradition have been torn from their homes and lands, when their libraries, burial places, religious centers, or sacred sites have been desecrated or denied them, when their language, rituals, or customs have been banned, forbidden, or forgotten, when they and their people have been separated, humiliated, brutalized, tortured, or murdered, a traumatic wound cleaves the collective psyche—scarring both persecuted and persecutor—and will be carried and transmitted for many generations.

Although it was originally coined to describe the experience of children of Holocaust survivors, and children of Japanese interned in camps during World War II, "historical trauma" refers to the experience of any group of people who share a history of oppression, victimization, or an exposure to a massive group trauma. But, of course, it's much more than that, because it isn't just encoded in the bodies of those who initially experienced the atrocities. As Dr. Maria Yellow Horse Brave Heart, a Native American social worker, associate professor, and mental health expert, says, historical trauma is a "cumulative emotional and psychological wounding *across generations, including the lifespan* [emphasis mine], which emanates from massive group trauma."

Just to give you an idea of how prevalent historical trauma is, here are a few examples: the Jews who survived the Holocaust, the Armenians who suffered genocide in Turkey, the Cambodians at the hands of the Khmer Rouge, and the torture and murder of "the disappeared" in Argentina's Dirty War; the effects of colonization on indigenous peoples in North and South America, Australia, and elsewhere; the millions of Kosovar Albanians who suffered from ethnic cleansing or were forcibly displaced by the Serbians in the 1990s; the slave trade in North America and Europe; and Black Americans and people of color who continue to experience racism and blatant discrimination in the United States.

Whatever the group, the reaction to such wounding—which Dr. Brave Heart calls a "historical trauma response," and psychologist and researcher Eduardo Duran calls a soul wound—is the same, creating a profound demoralizing effect on the psyche and the collective consciousness of the community. Such symptoms often include a higher incidence of drug and alcohol abuse, depression, anxiety, posttraumatic stress responses, physical ailments, suicidal ideation, and a sense of worthlessness. Duran, who is also the author of the book *Healing the Soul Wound*, believes this wound must be healed by subsequent generations, which we talk more about in Chapter 6. Thomas Hübl echoes Duran's beliefs so beautifully when he writes:

> What can you do when you carry scars not on your body but within your soul? And what happens when those spiritual wounds exist not just in you, but in everyone in your life? Whether or not we have experienced personal trauma, we are all—in very real ways—impacted by the legacy of familial and cultural suffering. Recent research has shown that trauma affects groups just as acutely as it does individuals; it bridges families, generations, communities, and borders.

Systemic trauma. Many of the cultural and ethnic groups that experience historic or collective traumas find their suffering prolonged by institutions—laws, policies, and cultural prejudices—designed to keep them powerless and deny them their rights. This increases posttraumatic stress within the community. Systemic trauma perpetuates injustice and oppression; targets, exploits, and marginalizes specific groups of people; and enacts laws to codify, justify, and maintain inequity. Systemic trauma can include forced displacement, isolation, food insecurity, inadequate healthcare, environmental injustice, and unequal opportunities in early childhood education and employment.

One stark example of this is the experience of Black people in the United States. The threat of racial hatred and police brutality looms over their communities, often instilling fear and anxiety in parents for their children, especially their sons, whenever they leave the house. Although slavery has been outlawed since 1865, its legacy continues to play out in multiple ways in the culture. According to Ibram X. Kendi, humanities professor at Boston University and a prolific author, Black people have been led to believe that systemic racism is somehow their fault—that there is something inherently wrong with their attitudes and behaviors, which is why they're "enslaved, segregated, and mass incarcerated." He says it's critically important that Black people know there's *nothing* wrong with them, that Black people as a group do not need to be *healed* from racist trauma. All they need is to be *freed* from racist trauma.[7]

Inherited Patterns of Behavior

Being a second-generation Holocaust survivor, I am not surprised by the research findings on trauma transmission that has centered on first-, second-, and third-generation survivors. Several studies, such as those conducted by Rachel Yehuda, show that, as children, we can be affected by the shame, fear, and guilt of our parents, grandparents, or great-grandparents, without necessarily being aware of the cause of such inheritance.[8] Another 2019 study on the consequences of the Holocaust on offspring suggested that having two survivor parents contributed to children developing traumatic psychological symptoms and genetic changes—a clear indication one person's life experience can affect subsequent generations.[9] The intergenerational transmission of the traumatic experiences doesn't always mean that we are destined to suffer from trauma ourselves. Such transmission can also serve as a source of resilience and strength—even as the studies make note of our vulnerability. For example, two studies showed that the offspring of survivors who have served as caregivers for their aging parents and grandparents have a greater commitment to that care than those whose parents did not experience the Holocaust; *and* they show more anxiety about their parents' condition.[10]

I particularly resonate with the work of Irit Felsen, a clinical psychologist who specializes in the trauma of Holocaust survivors, whom I heard speak at a conference a few years ago. She talked about how children of survivors are acutely aware of the inhumanity and the potential aggressor in others, which is understandable given the atrocities their ancestors faced leading up to and during World War II. Because of this, she says, children of survivors often show a profound need and capacity to humanize every interaction, to reach everyone in a way that goes beyond the average and expected behavior, as a coping mechanism. For example, you become "best friends" with the clerk in the grocery store or you are overly affectionate with your professor. This, Felsen says, "can sometimes manifest in being unusually personable, by using humor, offering compliments and small gifts, and sometimes by inappropriate means, such as compulsively sexualizing interactions. A strategy for feeling greater safety with the stranger, as it elicits a personal connection."

During the war, many Jews suffered from, at best, a shortage of food and, at worst, extreme hunger and starvation, often resulting in an anxious relationship with food. In a small study published in *Journal of Nutrition Education and Behavior* researchers Amy Sindler, Nancy Wellman, and Oren Baruch Stier discovered several specific ways in which this was true: Survivors had difficulty throwing away food (even after it spoiled); they tended to stash excess food; they had difficulty standing in line to buy food; and they became anxious when food wasn't readily available.[11] That scarcity mentality has been passed on so now, two generations later, their children and grandchildren appear to have an unconscious need to keep their pantries stocked with food, to ensure there will always be enough to eat, and often serving food to others as a way to show their love. I can personally attest to this happening to me in my own family and in so many other Jewish families I grew up with. According to Dr. Felsen, offspring of Holocaust survivors had a particularly difficult time during the COVID-19 pandemic. Potentially losing access to healthcare and the fear of not having enough food and supplies triggered memories of what their parents had gone through during the Holocaust.[12]

Children, grandchildren, and even great-grandchildren of Holocaust survivors often feel as though they have absorbed the anxiety and sorrow of their parents or grandparents. Some recall a sense of foreboding—a blanket of worry, fear, or unease—that comes along with the fierce loyalty and love they feel toward their elders. One way these emotions are expressed is by becoming what Dr. Felsen calls "trained empathic helpers," acutely attuned to the emotional state of their parents. Unfortunately, they're not so good at tending to—or even recognizing—their own emotional needs out of fear that centering their own needs will hurt their parents. This often spills over to the way they relate to other people in their lives; they can be extremely empathic to other people's suffering—so much so that they often have difficulty differentiating themselves from the other's pain. They can be either overly involved or completely detached.

Many children of survivors also report they have had flashbacks of events they never lived through in the first place, feelings that don't belong to them, that they have somehow absorbed. I know that experience well. I was very close to both Nana and Lalu, my beloved maternal grandparents, who were the only members of their families to survive the Nazi death camps. They suffered greatly during the war. And although I've never personally experienced war, I feel I have an intimate knowledge of it. I sometimes have dreams in which I get a strong sense of being persecuted, a felt sense of being at war. I can taste it, smell it, feel its energy in my body—the fear and anxiety associated with combat, the need to flee. Some of my cousins have had similar experiences.

Our Ancestral Legacy

So how is it that I can know war without ever experiencing anything remotely like it? I inherited the residue of trauma from my Nana and Lalu, which I carry with me and which has informed my own view of the world and my place within it. The intergenerational trauma I experienced was played out in the overt and subliminal messages I received from my grandparents while they were still alive. Through the stories they told, the pain they felt, and the wisdom they imparted, they made sure that the trauma they suffered, and the genocide they witnessed, would never be forgotten. As a loving granddaughter, the feelings behind their stories stayed with me long after they were gone. Some of the stories were hard to bear; others were full of the wisdom and joy that emerged from the hardships. All of this has lived within me all my life.

In her book *Wounds into Wisdom*, psychotherapist and Rabbi Tirzah Firestone writes that, as children, our psychic borders are highly permeable. When a family member experiences a traumatic event and has not been able to integrate it or heal from it, they can inadvertently pass it on, depositing it into "the developing self of the child, who then becomes a reservoir for the adult's trauma images, which can then shape the child's life."[13] All of this is an unconscious, and often silent, process.

When a child grows up in a household, for example, in which the father is violent when he drinks, it becomes impossible for her to trust the predictability of life. She learns she cannot rely on others to keep her safe or to always love her, because things can be really, really good when her father is sober and turn really, really ugly when he's drunk. And there's no way for her to predict what will happen when. But here's the thing: Not only does this child adapt her behaviors in order to survive an unsafe environment, but she unconsciously internalizes what she's experiencing. It may eventually affect the way she parents her own children and how she passes on not only the adaptive behaviors that kept her safe, but also the unresolved emotions she still carries from the trauma.

As a result of her unconscious traumatic response, her children may exhibit all sorts of emotional and behavioral symptoms themselves that seemingly come out of nowhere, without ever experiencing a particular trauma themselves. That can often result in being labeled with a mental illness and reduced to a psychiatric diagnosis—such as chronic depression, borderline personality disorder, and others—when it actually can be the effects of unresolved historical or intergenerational trauma. Dr. Gabor Maté, a Hungarian Canadian physician and addiction expert, agrees. He says that most mental illness is a "normal response to the abnormalities of the society in which we live"; that most mental health conditions "originate from unresolved childhood trauma."[14]

Maté's statement resonates with what I believe to be true and is born out of my own clinical experience: that most mental illness is, in fact, unresolved trauma, which can get passed on from generation to generation.

The Discovery of Epigenetics

For a long time, scientists believed that what we inherit genetically could not be altered. That whatever was written into our genetic code determined our behavior, our health, and our way of operating in the world. For example, if you're shy or socially anxious, just like your mother or your father, you will always be that way. It's encoded in your DNA; it is who you are. If you come from a long line of alcoholics, you have a much higher risk of becoming one yourself—and you will have to fight against that tendency to stay healthy. But then, over the last several years, research has uncovered something rather startling: that you're not who you are solely because of the genes you've inherited; external and environmental factors also play a role. And, you actually have the ability to alter the information expressed in your genes—the fate you've been dealt—by modifying your behavior.

This good news was corroborated by Richard Davidson, professor of psychiatry and psychology at the University of Wisconsin–Madison and founder of the Center for Healthy Minds. He set out to prove that inheriting shyness was not a life sentence. He and his research team used Robie the Robot to ascertain whether a child's "genetic predisposition toward shyness" could be changed as the result of their environment. They discovered that shy kids became more outgoing later in life as a result of their interactions with Robie the Robot.[15]

Davidson, in his book with cowriter Daniel Goleman, *Altered Traits,* goes on to show our minds can transform our brain and enhance our ability to change our personality traits long term.[16]

All this happens through a process called epigenetics, which is the study of how behaviors and the environment can cause changes in gene expression. According to the CDC, epigenetics (which literally means "above genetics") is an additional layer of instructions that lie on top of our DNA, which chemically change the shape, function, and expression of those genes without altering the information in the DNA sequence itself. In other words, epigenetic changes are reversible and, while they do not change the DNA sequence, they do change the way our body reads and expresses it. In other words, our environment or lifestyle choices—such as environmental toxins, our diet, our exercise habits, our stress levels, and so on—can affect which genes get turned on or turned off, without changing our DNA. And these changes can be passed on to the next generation. The most well-known explanation of epigenetics comes from Mother Nature—more specifically, from honeybees. Worker bees and the queen bee have the same DNA, but they have different diets. According to Paul Hurd, the lead researcher of a 2018 study of honeybee larva, the only reason the queen becomes the queen is because of the way genes are switched on or off in response to the specific diet.[17] What that shows, essentially, is that behavior can modify gene expression—without changing the DNA.

To apply this to human beings and to trauma, if someone was sexually abused as a child but has since done work to heal their trauma, it is possible for them to turn off the genetic expression of that trauma (its "molecular scar"). When that happens, they are no longer passing the trauma on to future generations; they are passing along the healing. When we heal our own traumas, we heal others; when others are healed, the world can begin to heal.

Rachel Yehuda, professor of psychiatry and neuroscience, and the director of Trauma Stress Studies at Mount Sinai School of Medicine in New York City, is an expert in the field of epigenetics and PTSD. She studied children of Holocaust survivors who were born after World War II and discovered that, in spite of their resilience and coping strategies, they were more vulnerable to depression and anxiety than those whose parents were not affected by the Holocaust.[18] She also found that the children had the same stress hormone imbalances that were present in the survivors themselves, without ever directly experiencing the trauma.[19]

Much research has been done on the children of women who had suffered a traumatic experience while pregnant, including a study Yehuda conducted with women who had to evacuate the World Trade Center on 9/11. The research has consistently demonstrated that those children suffered from multiple physical, emotional, and behavioral issues—especially when the maternal trauma occurred in the third trimester. Let's say a woman is pregnant and forced to migrate to another country where she does not know the language or the culture. She has left so much behind, and she is unsure of what her resources will be. She may be in an environment that doesn't feel safe, she doesn't feel protected enough, and she goes through extreme moments of distress, which obviously affect her health. The anxiety and depression she is experiencing will be transmitted to her baby in utero in such a way that it can change the information in the baby's genes and the expression of those genes as well. Because of the mother's distress, because of the trauma, and because of the difficulty in the womb, the baby will be born with survival reactions. The baby has absorbed the anxiety from her mother into her own nervous system, internalized the knowledge that her environment is not safe. According to several longitudinal studies, there's a strong possibility she will experience anxiety and depression herself as she grows up.[20]

I saw evidence of this in a slightly different way with several of the women I worked with soon after 9/11. Lucia is a good example. After the buildings collapsed, she came all the way from Honduras frantically searching for her husband, who had been working at Windows on the World, a restaurant on the 107th floor of the World Trade Center, when it collapsed. Lucia was seven months pregnant when she arrived in Manhattan. She spoke no English; she had no idea where to go or whom to talk to. By the time she got help, her extreme anxiety and fear had begun to affect her health. She gave birth soon afterward and the baby exhibited signs of dysregulation, including an increased startle response, chronic irritability, with an inability to be soothed, and a harder time latching on during nursing. All of these symptoms showed that the baby was probably traumatized in utero. Both Lucia and her baby needed psychological support in order to heal from the trauma.

The good news is if the mother is able to adapt to her situation and provide a loving and secure environment for herself and her child, she may have a better chance of shifting the information in her little one's genes, make systematic adjustments, and therefore change the beliefs and experiences she has going forward in life. Providing a secure attachment with her child may decrease the likelihood that her child will suffer later in life.

Although the research is still relatively young, epigenetics offers great promise for those suffering from trauma. If we can indeed modify genetic information without disturbing our DNA, that means our trauma does not need to be an automatic life sentence. That means we aren't destined to experience its repercussions forever. Although trauma affects us physically, mentally, and emotionally, we have the capacity to change the outcome ourselves—the power not only to heal from it at the genetic level, but to stop its transmission to future generations.

The Hope of Neuroplasticity

One related concept I really like, because it too is filled with hope, is neuroplasticity, which refers to the brain's ability to repair itself through growth, reorganization, and rewiring. The brain has a capacity to form new synaptic connections, based on our experiences and the way we respond to learning or injury. While trauma can adversely affect our whole being, we have the ability to reverse the damage. Things we once thought were fixed or permanent—our genetics and our brain wiring—are more mutable than we realized. Just as trauma lives in our body, so we must look to the inherent wisdom of the body to help us break the transgenerational cycle of pain and heal not only our own physical, emotional, and spiritual wounds, but also those of our families, our communities, and the planet.

Imagining Intergenerational Growth

To go from trauma to posttraumatic growth, we have to become conscious of the intergenerational and historic transmission of our trauma; we have to be willing to transform the automatic unconscious reactions, beliefs, and decisions we've inherited. At the same time, it's pretty hard to heal from intergenerational trauma without committing to the process of posttraumatic growth. And yet, being weighed down by the suffering of our ancestors can often make the journey to posttraumatic growth more difficult. Once the suffering from intergenerational trauma becomes unbearable—feeling stuck, repeating unhealthy behaviors, struggling with anxiety and depression—we may be open to starting the PTG process.

In working with individuals affected by intergenerational trauma and helping them get to the other side of healing, I find that they get through the first stage, the Stage of Awareness, and even the second, the Stage of Awakening. But the third stage, the Stage of Becoming, can be tricky, because that is when they're invited to consider new ways of seeing themselves and understanding the world. They're asked to get creative, be curious about and open to different perspectives. This is where they often get stuck. They've been working from a fixed mindset with the same repetitive beliefs that have been part of their family's DNA for generations. These beliefs and ways of being are so ingrained that it can feel impossible to see the world in any other way. Once they can do that, they can move into the fourth stage, the Stage of Being, and later, into the Stage of Transforming.

If we don't address our historical trauma, psychologically and genetically, we will stay stuck in our pain, and it may be harder to consider a new perspective of the world and our place in it. Many Holocaust survivors and their descendants, for example, find it quite difficult to get beyond the narrative they've told themselves their whole lives: *I am a victim of the Holocaust. I am a survivor of the war. I am a Jew who is being persecuted.* Whatever narrative we've grown up with, that's the information that lives in our body and defines us. That's what can make it hard for us to see beyond the perception we have of ourselves and to envision something different.

And yet, the only way to begin to stop the cycle of trauma, the compulsive repetition of suffering, is to become aware of our own wounds. That happens when we commit to the process of posttraumatic growth. It isn't easy, but it helps to remember that we're not just doing this for ourselves, we're doing this for our descendants. We can stop the transmission of our inherited suffering, and pass along the wisdom without the pain attached. That's the beauty of epigenetics—and the promise of posttraumatic growth.

The example I often share with my patients is the story of Moses leading the Jews out of Egypt and into the Promised Land. By the time Moses rescued the Jews and led them to freedom, they had been enslaved for more than four hundred years. As the rabbinical teachings go, the walk through the desert and into Israel, the Promised Land, was a very short distance that could have easily taken a week. Instead it took them forty years. Why? The sages illuminate this from a psychological and spiritual perspective: they weren't ready. The Jews wandered in the desert, literally walked in circles, until the older generation, those who had been slaves in Egypt, died. The new generation, which was born anew in the desert, did not have the same slave mentality as their elders; they were born free. The old generation couldn't enter the Promised Land, because they weren't ready to let go of their old life. They whined, *Give us food. We don't believe we can get there. We don't have water. Give us water. Let us go back to Egypt. We were safe there. Life was easier.* They could not start a new nation carrying traumas and fears from their suffering in Egypt. The younger generation, however, transformed. They were ready to embrace freedom. They were open to new perspectives, they integrated the old with the new, and they were ready.

As I tell my patients, in order to enter the Promised Land, in order to acquire growth, wisdom, and consciousness, the fifth stage of posttraumatic growth, we must do the work of shedding our limiting beliefs. We must experience the emotional death and subsequent rebirth that is necessary for transformation to happen. Hopefully it won't take forty years. But, even if it feels like it does, remember that those forty years in the desert allowed the travelers to take the many steps necessary to release all that was untrue and limiting on their journey to personal growth and spiritual freedom. The path to the Promised Land truly takes time, commitment, and effort.

Chapter 6

From Collective Trauma to Collective Growth

Never doubt that a small group of thoughtful, committed citizens can change the world. Indeed, it's the only thing that ever has.

—MARGARET MEAD

As we talked about in Chapter 1, the stages of trauma recovery and growth succeed not only at the individual level but also at the collective level. Collective trauma requires collective healing, and from collective healing comes collective growth. Collective trauma—be it 9/11, the COVID-19 pandemic, natural disasters, genocide, or racial injustice—can end up connecting us in ways that make us stronger, more empathic, and compassionate and can force us to grow *as a community*. We can come out of the experience with a greater sense of purpose and with our priorities reorganized. Reconnecting with another person, or a group of people, reaching out for help or offering it to others gives us an opportunity to grow as a community.

Although we talked a lot about individual experiences

of trauma, it's important to remember trauma is always relational—even those experiences that feel deeply personal—and that means it can only be healed relationally. Looking at it from a systemic perspective, we find there's no separation between the individual and the system, so what affects one person affects everyone, whether we're dealing on a familial, communal, or cultural level. Trauma is a "violation of human connection," as Judith Herman says, a disruption of basic trust in our relationships, so to heal and transform, we must restore that connection.

Collective trauma is not so different from personal trauma—it just happens on a more massive scale. Although individuals within a given group may have very different reactions to the same traumatic event, collective trauma centers the *group* experience, its shared ethos. The group is more than a gathering of individuals; it is a collective consciousness with its own identity.

So, what is collective trauma? Collective trauma is usually defined as any catastrophic event or major disruption that brings about unimaginable suffering to individuals, families, communities, or cultures, and they have no coping mechanisms or resources to deal with it. It can be a singular event that causes a major disruption, or a chronic, ongoing injustice that a community or culture endures collectively.

Unfortunately, we don't have to think very hard to come up with plenty of historical and recent examples. Here are a few of the most obvious ones: the COVID-19 pandemic and New York City's 9/11; Hurricane Katrina and other natural disasters that have devastated cities, states, and whole countries; the AIDS epidemic; the climate crisis; the Holocaust and other genocides; the forced migration of those seeking asylum; and acts of violence perpetrated by a multitude of isms and phobias, including racism, sexism, ableism, classism, and xenophobia, as well as trans- and homophobia. The number of examples can feel endless and overwhelming.

While individual trauma is considered a blow to the psyche, as sociologist Kai Erikson suggests in his book *A New Species of Trouble: The Human Experience of Modern Disasters,* collective trauma is a blow to our basic sense of belonging, ripping asunder the idea that community is a place of safety and support. While individual trauma is a *rupture in meaning* that shatters our own assumptions about the world and our place in it, collective trauma is a *crisis of meaning* that calls into question the identity and belief system of an entire group of people. While individual trauma is unprocessed emotions stored in the body from our own past, collective trauma is the fragmentation of our *shared* collective history, causing division and isolation and the disintegration of the very fabric of the culture. In order to heal, we must reconcile our shared past so it can be integrated fully into the present, and we can break the cycle of transgenerational trauma.

The COVID-19 pandemic is a perfect example of a shared trauma, one that has touched nearly everyone in every part of the world. I don't think it's an exaggeration to say that this pandemic has shattered our collective assumption that the world is a safe and equitable place, that systems exist to protect us from harm or, at the very least, that experts have the know-how to fix what's broken and stop the spread of such a contagious disease. I remember in early 2020, staring in disbelief at an email that told me my flight to Europe—to speak at the World Happiness Fest—had been canceled, along with thousands of other flights coming into and going out of the United States. And furthermore, New York City was on lockdown. Not only was I not going to Europe, I wasn't even going to the bodega down the street.

As weeks became months and months turned into years, it became obvious that the normal we all longed for wasn't coming back. That the control we thought we had over our lives was limited at best, if not an illusion all along. Not surprisingly, calls to mental health hotlines skyrocketed; my own patient load increased threefold; and, as the death toll rose, more people than usual complained of increased anxiety and depression (upward of a 40 percent increase, as of early 2021). Schools and playgrounds, churches and shopping centers, neighbors' homes and even those of family members were no longer safe havens; they were all potential breeding grounds for the virus.

People responded in a variety of ways. When the first infection was reported in New Zealand, the people quarantined fully, until it was deemed safe enough to venture out. People in other countries, like the United States, struggled to reconcile their fiercely independent nature with the need to follow strict protocols. Fear, anxiety, and skepticism pitted neighbor against neighbor, sometimes even family members against each other. The pandemic brought into sharp focus the disparities between white and Black citizens, between the rich and the poor, between "developed" countries and emerging ones. Essential workers, such as grocery clerks, sanitation workers, public transportation employees, those in postal and packaging services—as well as doctors, nurses, and hospital staff—had no shelter-at-home option and put themselves at risk every day. Black and brown Americans sickened and died at twice the rate of white Americans, and millions all over the world were left grieving and struggling to stay afloat.

As I write this, the pandemic is far from over, and it's too soon to tell what sort of growth will arise out of the trauma and despair. What we do know so far, however, is that light has begun to crack through the hard shell of the collective wound. That it sometimes takes a tragedy, an almost unbearable collective experience, to awaken a sense of empathy and the desire to create more interconnection of the human condition. We've already seen so many examples of acts of kindness: teachers going above and beyond to make sure their students—especially those who come from struggling families—get the help and resources they need. Townspeople ordering food and products from local businesses to help them stay afloat. Neighbors sharing resources (for example, the #pandemicoflove movement), sometimes anonymously delivering extra food, diapers, clothing, medicine, or books and games to those who are confined to their homes. Millions committing to wearing masks and keeping their distance, as an act of kindness, not only to protect themselves, but also to protect those they come into contact with.

Microaggressions, Invisible Wounds, and Moral Injuries

Not all collective trauma is as obvious as a pandemic, terrorist attack, or natural disaster, however. Trauma can also be invisible and insidious. It can show up in the form of microaggressions delivered by a dominant culture toward certain groups of people to keep them "in their place," separated from the larger community. Kevin Nadal, a professor at John Jay College of Criminal Justice, has been speaking on and writing about microaggressions for years. He defines them as "everyday, subtle, intentional—and oftentimes unintentional—interactions or behaviors that communicate some sort of bias toward historically marginalized groups." The difference between microaggressions and overt discriminatory acts of bias or violence, he says, is that people who commit microaggressions might not even be conscious they're doing anything harmful.

Microaggressions can be anything from repeated, subtle acts of bullying a child in school to the covert discrimination that happens on an everyday basis to Black, brown, and indigenous peoples, immigrants, people with disabilities, women, and those who identify as LGBTQ+. These often include verbal and nonverbal slights, assaults, exclusions, and systemic aggressions. Some common examples include:

- A white person locking their car doors when stopped at a traffic light next to a car driven by a Black man.
- Telling a Latina in the United States that they speak really good English, believing they weren't born there.
- A salesclerk following two Black women in a department store, because she believes either that the women are stealing something or they can't possibly afford to shop there.
- Touching someone's wheelchair without asking permission.
- Assuming a disabled person needs help without asking.

- Asking invasive questions about a queer or trans person's body or sex life.
- Harassing a woman on the street by making lewd comments about her body and the way she dresses.

While microaggressions are subtle and often part of everyday life, invisible wounds are common in individuals and within groups that have endured or witnessed terrible atrocities. War veterans, refugees fleeing from violent regimes, and people who have suffered from domestic violence are often plagued by injuries (both physiological and psychological) that aren't obvious to anyone else. These can include PTSD and traumatic brain injuries, as well as shame, despair, anger, guilt, regret, and the inability to connect with others.

The first time I heard the term "moral injury" was from my dear friend and colleague Jack Saul, a psychologist and visual artist who has worked with war reporters and photographers, human rights workers, and veterans, bearing witness, as he says, "to the moral struggles that accompany war." He defines moral injury as the "unfair distribution of moral pain and moral distress." Clinical psychiatrist Jonathan Shay, who originally coined the term, says moral injury is "a betrayal of what is right by someone who holds legitimate authority in a high-stakes situation."[1] In other words, it's a moral judgment that challenges our deepest ethical code and our ability to trust in others and ourselves. The harm may be caused by something a person did, something that was done to that person, or something the person witnessed that goes against everything they believe to be right and just. Journalist Diane

Silver calls it "a deep soul wound that pierces a person's identity, sense of morality, and relationship to society."[2]

Many soldiers return from war with, as someone said, "blood on their hands and shame in their hearts." Following orders that went against their own moral code (and went against what they believed was their country's code of ethics) resulted in PTSD and moral injury. I remember having a conversation with a veteran of the war in Afghanistan, who told me his own suffering was compounded by the lack of acknowledgment from the American public when he and his fellow soldiers returned. They believed they had fought for freedom and their efforts went unrecognized.

In her book *Wounds into Wisdom,* Tirzah Firestone recounts the story of Avner, a young Israeli soldier who committed grave acts of violence, along with other members of his unit, toward families in a Palestinian village. He tells Firestone he was the sergeant in charge of a sniper team, who would take over the houses of the people in the village and torment them. One night he and another soldier heard a piercing scream from inside one of the houses. They smashed the windows with the guns and looked inside to see an old woman, who apparently had fallen from her bed, lying in agony on the floor. He goes on to say:

"We are peering in with our guns, with our helmets on. Then at the end of the hallway, we see the heads of her family members sticking out. They are petrified. They are scared of us. *Of me.*" Realizing the situation was really messed up, the soldiers left. Avner just stood there saying to himself, *What the hell am I doing? Who am I doing this for?* He told Firestone his moral dilemma only got worse throughout his service, but he managed to fulfill his duties. His moral injury continued and only began to heal when he joined a group of veterans who had experienced similar psychological trauma.[3]

Moral injury can include any act that inflicts harm, including rape, racial violence, bullying, or ostracizing. Both perpetrators and witnesses of such acts can suffer from the guilt, shame, and outrage of inflicting pain on someone else or watching it happen and either doing nothing or being powerless to stop it. We've seen examples of this in young college men in a fraternity who chose to look away or remain silent when others were hazing or otherwise abusing new fraternity "brothers."

In an article she wrote for the American Public Health Association, Oxiris Barbot, MD, describes the collective wound perpetrated on the Black community by the murder of George Floyd at the knee of a white police officer. She says:

> As a woman of color leading the country's largest public health agency, Mr. Floyd's death feels different [to me] because it represents a cumulative injury on top of the sustained acuity of health inequities playing out in horrifying details through the COVID-19 pandemic. This accumulation pays cruel dividends to communities of color. Our data predict these outcomes but cannot undo them. It's like watching a preventable collision in slow motion that we're powerless to stop. The wreckage haunts us.[4]

Moral injury can only be healed by moral repair, not by individual therapy alone. Self-forgiveness is not enough. Those suffering from the shame and guilt that such injury brings need the validation, acknowledgment, and recognition from the collective in order to find their values again and reclaim their humanity.

Moving from Trauma to Healing

No matter what kind of trauma we suffer from, the path toward healing involves acknowledging (*I hear what you're saying and I am truly listening*), validating (*I see things from your perspective, even if I don't share it*), and recognizing (*I accept the truth of what you're telling me, even if I disagree*). All three must come not only from within ourselves and our communities, but also from the outside world, particularly from a person or a group of people who can do something about it. We must be seen, we must be heard, and the pain of our suffering must be witnessed. As is the case with individuals, cultures and communities can also remain in suffering and victimization mode because there has been no validation and acknowledgment of the experienced trauma. For growth to occur, these traumas need to be brought into the light.

For example, the Armenian people suffered terribly from genocide inflicted by the Turkish government in the early part of the twentieth century. Although the Armenians can and do acknowledge the pain they endured, they cannot truly begin to heal until the Turkish government says: *We validate and acknowledge the genocide. We know it happened and we take responsibility.*

Trauma isolates, community heals. Silence increases suffering; sharing our stories brings healing. A community can be as small as a family unit or as large as a nation, or any group of people who, in some ways, have a shared history of trauma. In order to heal, we must reconcile that shared past so it can be integrated fully into the present. When that happens, we can move into the future unencumbered by the pain of our past and able to free future generations from the cycle of trauma.

Validation, acknowledgment, and recognition. My patients Eva and Emilio came to see me shortly after they immigrated with their children to the United States from Spain. They are part of a large, intense family of siblings, parents, grandparents, aunts, uncles, all of whom expected them to participate in everything the family did—community events, dinners, celebrations, travel. In Spain, the children were expected to visit the grandparents' house every other day. The first time we met they told me that they had been "forced" to leave the country; they hadn't wanted to move to Miami, but they had to because, just a few months before, they had suspected that the grandfather had sexually abused two of their children.

The story of the abuse spread quickly throughout the city in which they lived, and they felt they had to leave to protect their children from further harm. The grandfather denied everything. Slowly more people began to share their own stories and it came out that he had possibly abused others. By the time we started our therapy sessions, the grandfather was being prosecuted and was later sent to prison.

Although they worked hard over the last five years to acknowledge and radically accept (at least to themselves) that their lives had been shattered, something was missing that was preventing true healing and posttraumatic growth to happen. As Eva explained to me, she recorded one of the kids describing the abuse he'd endured; in it, he mentioned that the grandfather's wife had been a witness to it. *She had seen it happen.* Eva was horrified. She told me, "I want to show her this recording. I want her to listen to it. I want her to acknowledge that she was complicit in the abuse of my child. All I want is for her to say, yes, I admit, I knew this was going on." Eva wanted this woman to validate and recognize what had happened.

Although the acknowledgment never came, Eva and Emilio and their family began to look toward their community for support. They connected with others—rabbis, community leaders, other families and friends—who provided comfort and deeply listened to them relay their experience. They felt like their new extended community acknowledged and believed their story, validated their reactions and symptoms, and responded to them with understanding, love, and acceptance.

Validation, acknowledgment, and recognition are critical for healing to occur on a systemic level as well. Tirzah Firestone reminds us of the importance of global recognition. She writes "Something deep in the psyche shifts when we know we are not alone. Without human eyes and ears to share our reality, our suffering becomes meaningless and unbearable." Those who have suffered from terrorist attacks, genocide, and other atrocities feel a responsibility to tell their stories, to testify to what they witnessed, so that the world can recognize the horrors inflicted upon their people—and as Firestone suggests, "reverse the process of genocide's inhumanity." Those who recognize such acts "are the eyes that have the power to restore humanity."

In December 1999, German chancellor Angela Merkel gave a stirring speech at the Auschwitz-Birkenau Memorial, in which she expressed a "deep sense of shame for the barbaric crimes that were here committed by Germans." Following such acknowledgment, which validated and recognized the experience of millions of Jews, many restitution and compensation programs went into effect.

Connecting through shared experience. Collective trauma is characterized by fragmentation, isolation, and division, whether that shows up at a social, political, cultural, or religious level. And it can only be healed through collective experience. The importance of the collective for marginalized people, in particular, cannot be overstated. Queer and transgender people, for example, say they never feel completely safe. Even in communities and cultures in which they enjoy some legal protection, no place seems to be free of machismo, sexism, or gender binary prejudices. This lack of safety, of course, is intensified if they live in a nation or culture where they are targeted, vilified, and tortured. But even in more outwardly accepting cultures, LGBTQ+ individuals say they're often in a state of hypervigilance, never quite knowing how they'll be accepted or when an experience might turn awkward or even violent.

I work with refugee and immigrant communities—and am an immigrant myself—and their plight is similar. Those who have come into countries illegally must often work in subpar, demeaning conditions and endure multiple acts of abuse with no means of fighting back. Whether they're in the country illegally or not, many immigrants face prejudice and racism, and the very real threat of deportation, often daily. Like the LGBTQ+ community, they live in a constant state of hypervigilance, fearing for themselves and their families. That can sometimes make gathering together a challenge, creating fear that "outing" themselves will give a signal to authorities or vigilantes and put them at further risk of harm. Nonetheless, for marginalized and oppressed people, finding community is a critical first step to having their own experience validated, by telling their stories and hearing the stories of others, which often speak to a shared experience. This newfound sense of belonging offers them hope, feelings of joy, and a sense of power and purpose.

Collective grieving. When a group of people has been deeply affected by a traumatic event, such as a natural disaster, a terrorist attack, or the death of someone beloved in their community, coming together in grief can help them heal. Being in community with people who understand what others are going through allows us to share our stories, empathize with one another, and acknowledge our own pain and theirs. I heard this repeatedly from patients in a group therapy program I was running in the Bronx for those who'd lost their family members to chronic illnesses, such as cancer and diabetes. They told me they could find solace only in the group setting, and that they could be held and understood only by one another because of their shared unique experience. They felt validated and healed within the group.

When a traumatic event happens, it can begin to unlock months, years, even generations of suffering from the collective traumas of family, community, and culture. We grieve for what we've lost, what we've never had or been given; for the harm inflicted on us (and our ancestors) by the culture in which we live—or, for those in the dominant culture, the harm we or our ancestors have inflicted on others. The grieving often comes when we are able to name the oppression, share our stories, and freely express our emotions. However, just as grief can bring people together, it can also pull people apart.

Grief isolates. Although people who have experienced a horrific tragedy together are bound in sorrow, they can also be separated by their grief. Why? Because people feel so lonely in their experience and often are unable to articulate their feelings, even when they know everyone else in the group is experiencing the same thing. Remember, trauma can isolate, fragment, and divide. We don't always understand one another's grieving process—and no doubt we may fear no one can possibly understand ours either. As a result, trauma can split families and communities apart.

Grief is unique. Everyone grieves differently. Because everyone grieves in their own isolated world, in their own unique way, they sometimes cannot build a bridge to connect with each other. The COVID-19 pandemic is an obvious illustration of this. Every member of a family in confinement dealt with the loss, uncertainty, and unpredictability in their own way, sometimes at odds with each other. Some needed to stay connected and social while others wanted to keep to themselves. Some were optimistic; others were negative and fearful.

I have found when couples or families are grieving, they can't always understand or even tolerate one another's process. One parent may grieve openly, full of emotions and barely able to function through the pain, while the other parent doesn't want to talk about it; they feel numb and force themselves to keep going. Other families, however, work consciously and deliberately to support each other and can even end up being stronger together because of their pain.

I also saw evidence of this firsthand after the collapse of

the beachfront building in Surfside, a small neighborhood in Miami, killing nearly one hundred people and displacing countless others. I've been working with the families of the victims and with the survivors, the majority of whom are Jews and Latinos who immigrated to the United States from Latin America.

The community as a whole has been going through enormous grief. Some wail against the injustice of what happened. *How can I live without my children, my partner, my parents? Why did this happen? I want the towers to fall on me, I want to die.* Others collapse under the weight of their own pain. Still others are numb, seemingly indifferent, in collective denial. *We're fine. We don't need a support group.*

I had the opportunity to meet President Joe Biden during the early days of the tragedy, when he came to pay his respects to the community, and his words really made an impact on me. Speaking from his own experience of loss and grieving, he encouraged the families of the victims, and the survivors of the collapse, to be tolerant of each other's process, to support one another and to not criticize or judge another person's process. And to remember that everyone will grieve differently.

What President Biden said is very important. Every single person has their own timing, their own style, and even their own understanding of what grief is. I had people in Surfside who wanted to go all in. They wanted to talk about the loss in minute detail, see the autopsy reports, the photos, talk to the forensic doctors and the first responders who found the human remains. Others wanted to be in front of the media, talking about it to the press and on TV. They wanted to voice their anger and push for legal representation and reparations. Still others didn't want to think about it or discuss it; they didn't want to know any details and they refused to visit the site. And finally, there were those who quit their jobs, canceled their wedding or vacation plans, and prepared to move out of the state and even out of the country. They wanted to stop remembering; they wanted to start over. All of this is grieving.

Grief as unexpressed love. One reason some people can't let go of their grieving is because it keeps them connected to what they've lost. It's like a loyalty bond in some ways. Subconsciously, they may fear if they stop grieving, it means they don't care anymore, they've already forgotten the person or the situation. If you're an immigrant, for example, and you no longer grieve what you've left behind—your country, sometimes your family, your friends, your culture—then you've disconnected from your roots. Again, after the Surfside collapse, some people said they didn't want to stop feeling the pain because that would mean they no longer loved their family member who was killed in the rubble; they needed to keep feeding the pain. They felt like if they smiled, or enjoyed something, they had betrayed their loved one.

The Roadblocks to Healing

Healing from trauma has its own timeline unique to the individual or the community suffering from the aftermath of a tragic event. Posttraumatic growth—the desire to derive meaning from our pain and transform because of it—is a nonlinear path toward liberation that takes time and determination, patience and compassion—especially when working within the collective. Growth comes out of the healing process when individuals and groups have made the physical, emotional, and spiritual commitment to make that happen. But sometimes things get in the way.

I. TOO MUCH, TOO SOON

The eagerness to find the wisdom and growth from a collective trauma can push a group to begin too soon. As I discovered after September 11, posttraumatic growth cannot be rushed. I was in the middle of Manhattan, watching as the Twin Towers came crashing down. The whole city was in chaos, confusion, and deep collective trauma. So, the same night the towers fell, the Red Cross reached out to a group of psychologists and trauma specialists, asking us to provide support to the surviving victims. By then I had already done several research studies with war refugees, torture survivors, immigrants, and the politically persecuted on trauma and resilience; I had even written about the transformative power of trauma and posttraumatic growth; and, of course, I had facilitated the process with many of my private clients and patients. I was ready. We worked day and night that first week—I didn't even go home and barely slept. And here's what happened. Almost nothing. Very little we did made a difference. We succeeded only in retraumatizing many of the people we tried to help. Why? How could that be the case? Because you can't begin to heal from something you're right in the middle of experiencing—and they were still in the middle of the trauma.

2. SUSPICION OF THE "OTHER"

Days and weeks after 9/11, we witnessed beautiful examples of the citizens of New York supporting one another in solidarity, a community bonded through a shared experience and a feeling of strength and resilience. People gathered together and helped their neighbors, created nonprofits, and came up with creative ways to change, vowing never to be caught off-guard again. Healing was happening. And then, fear got in the way.

As Jack Saul explains in his book *Collective Trauma, Collective Healing,* occasionally the aftermath of a traumatic event can cause more harm than the event itself. In the case of 9/11, fear of "other" set in and thousands of Arabs and Muslims in the United States were discriminated against even though they were deeply affected by the same tragedy. Dr. Saul says, "Their voices were pushed out of the collective narrative and their experiences deemed invalid as a result." We've seen the same thing happen during the COVID-19 pandemic: the rumor that the virus began in a laboratory in China marked all Asian Americans as suspect and gave rise to an alarming increase in violence against them. The fact is, we cannot truly heal individually until we heal collectively. We cannot ever heal as long as our actions cause harm to others.

3. EXCLUDING OTHER VOICES/EXPERIENCES

Sometimes a community or a nation believes it has put systems in place that will alleviate the suffering of the collective when in fact it has only taken into account the experiences of those in the dominant culture. What can feel like healing to one group can exacerbate the pain of another. The trauma that comes out of the current climate crisis is a good example. Indigenous people often feel shut out of climate discussions, even though their ability to live on and care for the land has been severely compromised. Even more than that, they feel the solutions put into place by those in power are counterintuitive to the values, wisdom, and deep understanding they have had for many generations.[5]

Another good example is what happened during the AIDS crisis in the 1980s and 1990s. AIDS was characterized as a white gay male disease, according to Black gay activist Phill Wilson, but the "epidemic I was experiencing didn't look anything like that," he said. The Black HIV community was excluded from HIV research studies. So Wilson cofounded the Black AIDS Institute, a self-described think-and-do-tank "to end HIV in Black communities by engaging and mobilizing Black institutions and individuals to confront the epidemic."

4. LACK OF VALIDATION BY THOSE IN POWER

Of course it's vital to acknowledge collectively that you have been victims of a grave injustice or a destructive natural disaster. Being part of that shared experience is the first step toward collective healing. However, unless the collective trauma is validated and recognized by an outside group—preferably with power to repair the damage—the collective cannot fully heal. Eva and Emilio, whom we mentioned earlier, came from a close-knit community in Spain, yet discovered that it was unable, or unwilling, to give them the support and validation they needed to heal their family wounds. When they moved to Miami, they found a new community that opened their arms to them and gave them the assurance they needed that they were not alone.

That's not a universal story, though; often, when immigrants or refugees come into a new country, they encounter a lack of recognition of what is happening in their country of origin. In other words, their new community does not recognize the trauma they are going through, which makes it much more difficult to heal from it.

5. INTERRUPTIONS FROM OUTSIDE FORCES

We see multiple examples of communities naturally and organically coming together to grieve and to heal—only to be interrupted when they are forced to focus on legal, financial, or political issues. A prime example of this is found in the Surfside building collapse in Miami. The process of healing got interrupted by the demands of lawyers, judges, and "experts" offering their opinions and forcing the families to focus on legal issues. This created tension and opposition between the families of the victims and the survivors; between apartment owners and those who were renting; between community members who had money and those who did not; between locals and outsiders, and finally, those who wanted to create a memorial and those who refused to support them. The safety of their collective was breached, and the sanctity of their connection was severed.

Recovering Collective Connections

When fear sets in, trust erodes, and connections are severed between families and neighbors, it becomes imperative to repair and rebuild those connections before recovery and healing can begin. Jack Saul and neuropsychiatrist Judith Landau propose certain themes that typically allow communities to build collective resilience and recovery after psychosocial trauma.*

---

* For more information, see *Collective Trauma, Collective Healing: Promoting Community Resilience in the Aftermath of Disaster*, by Jack Saul (New York: Routledge, 2014).

I. BUILDING COMMUNITY AND ENHANCING SOCIAL CONNECTEDNESS

Dr. Landau calls this the "matrix of healing," where we mend or reinforce the connections we had before and forge new ones.

2. COLLECTIVELY TELLING THE STORY OF THE COMMUNITY'S EXPERIENCE AND RESPONSE

The stories we tell of the experiences we've had keep the collective experience alive. Touching on other people's traumas within the collective experience allows for collective healing. When one person shares their experience, other people feel safe to share theirs, and then healing can happen, not in isolation, but in community. This storytelling must include and amplify those whose voices have been silenced. By bringing them into the collective, we can break the divisiveness among groups and individuals, the loneliness and fragmentation that trauma fosters. This is how we recognize the interdependence between the individual and the collective, acknowledge our collective suffering, and move toward collective healing.

3. REESTABLISHING THE RHYTHMS AND ROUTINES OF LIFE AND ENGAGING IN COLLECTIVE RITUALS

Although there is rarely a return to "normal," engaging in routines and rituals can provide a community with some sense of normalcy and stability. These can be new practices or routines that the community comes up with together or things they've done in the past that have sustained or soothed them. In the case of the Surfside building collapse, for example, the community almost immediately organized itself to create opportunities in which people could gather. Organically they began to come together twice a day every day, in the same place, to listen to one another, to share their experiences, and to exchange ideas about the immediate situation and next steps. Coming together in that way created a routine and a ritual for healing.

4. ARRIVING AT A POSITIVE VISION OF THE FUTURE WITH RENEWED HOPE

Part of collective resilience involves reimagining a more positive future. Figuring out how to move forward through creative outlets such as art, music, theater, and dance can help with the healing process.

From Collective Healing Comes Collective Growth

The five-stage model of PTG works for collective, systemic, and cultural traumas as well as individual suffering. Think of the stages as a collective journey, from which we emerge from isolation and paralysis, no longer dissociated from ourselves and others, and together unlock our collective wisdom, bringing consciousness and transformation to all.

STAGE 1: RADICAL ACCEPTANCE

As the Buddhists teach us, before we can heal, we first must accept that we are suffering, acknowledge there's a cause of suffering, and recognize there is an end to it and a path to get us there, if we choose to take it. But the thing is, we can't bypass the pain; in fact, ironically, the more we resist and deny our reality, the greater our suffering becomes.

This is why the first stage of PTG is Radical Acceptance.

Radically accepting our suffering is the first step on the path to healing. This shared acceptance happens within the collective, the community experiencing the effects of a traumatic event. What does this mean on a collective level? It means that we must recognize and name the emotions, feelings, reactions, and circumstances we are going through *as a community*. It means we can no longer avoid or deny what is happening. Consider the pandemic and how it is affecting a particular community of people right now: What is their shared experience? Individuals in crisis can sit with their feelings, name them, and identify where those feelings live in their bodies. But the collective must identify the emotions that are most prevalent within the community—is it fear, confusion, anger, isolation? A sense of dread, longing, frustration? Through talking together, members of the collective can recognize and accept their experience, which is the first step toward healing and growing as a community.

There's beauty in bringing together a diversity of voices who share a common traumatic event, often with very different, even opposing narratives. This can include a ruling government and the opposition party; straight people and LGBTQ+; those from a dominant culture and those who feel oppressed or marginalized; union workers and their employers. To be able to acknowledge the pain and suffering both sides feel and recognize the responsibility that each one carries is a radical act of deep listening and compassionate action.

STAGE 2: SAFETY AND PROTECTION

To go beyond radical acceptance, we must create a safe container that will allow further healing to happen. This is the stage in which we give ourselves permission to explore and express our feelings within a group setting because we are ready to counteract the isolation, fragmentation, paralysis, and dissociation that trauma brings. It's an *internal* sense of safety within the group experience in which we feel protected and valued enough to begin to process our grief, to be witnessed and to bear witness to others.

Often that means the group feels safer when they limit outside interference. During the first month after the Surfside building collapsed, Jews and Latinos, residents and vacationers, rich and poor, Black and white, gay and straight, young and old, all came together, sharing in the collective grief. What helped them in the moment was the container that they created. I was one of the psychologists providing support, there to bear witness, but I was also part of the community, along with first responders, chaplains, and religious and community leaders. The outpouring of love and support from different communities and organizations from all over the world strengthened their sense of safety and protection. At the same time, the families of the victims created their own container of safety with each other, able to have their own resources to come together. *We don't need someone from the outside coming in to tell us what to do or how to feel. We are the only ones who know what we're going through. Our experience is not their experience.* It's not that there was no knowledge from the outside, but there was something about the strength of their shared experience.

One thing I've noticed in my own work with refugees from Central and South America is that in order to create safety and protection, I need to be mindful to keep their cultural perspective and their language, careful not to impose any foreign solutions. I speak to them in Spanish, asking them questions about what they eat, how they heal, what their rituals are, what resources they have within their own communities.

On a more systemic or cultural level, creating safe spaces allows us to have the difficult conversations we need to have as a society, instead of repressing, denying, or dissociating. After Hurricane Katrina devastated New Orleans, for example, community organizers brought together representatives from diverse populations within the city and outlying areas to offer a safe space in which to hear their stories, understand their needs, and witness their suffering.

STAGE 3: A NEW NARRATIVE

Often in this stage a community realizes that what has worked in the past isn't working anymore. This is when they consider a new way of being and the need to create a new paradigm and a new group identity.

This is a natural extension of the previous stage: people felt safe enough to tell their stories on an individual and communal level, but now they're expanding those narratives and, together, seeing what's possible. They know what hasn't worked, what has caused them pain; now it's time to imagine something new. Jack Saul calls this a "dialogical process," in which the group can "open up by letting the stories breathe," by moving from static to dynamic stories of the difficulties their people have had. Communities do this in dialogue with one another as a "way to get out of the constrained narrative" of their collective past and move toward a freer future. In this regenerative stage, everything is on the table—how they tell their collective story, how they define themselves, what kind of narratives they use to describe who they are, how they envision their future. They begin to realize they can shift the discourse and the narrative of their traumas they've been carrying on a familial, cultural, national, and global level. And from that realization they can come together to reimagine, re-create, and reframe their narrative and their future with more freedom.

The Cambodian refugees who fled the Pol Pot regime and the genocide inflicted upon their people by the Khmer Rouge and settled in the Bronx in New York City and in Los Angeles offer a beautiful example of reimagining and redefining who they are. After coming to the United States, the Cambodians slowly began to create a sustainable community in their adopted home. They had to navigate their new cities, a new language, and for many, new ways of making a living. They began to figure out how to survive, adjust, and even thrive. They realized they could bring the strength, resources, and resilience that allowed them to survive the wars to their new situation and build a new life.

STAGE 4: INTEGRATION

This is the stage of the "both/and," a collective reset fueled by collective trauma. The collective acknowledges their traumatic past, how it affected their lives and the lives of their ancestors and children. They don't acknowledge it as a reality in the present moment that determines their decisions, but as a part of the collective identity, the history of their people; it becomes something to remember and to learn from. But now they are ready to integrate it into a new and authentic way of being.

The Cambodians found ways to integrate so much of what they had left behind—the culture and their rituals, including their traumatic past—into their new home. They were proud of their heritage and wanted to share it in a way that Americans could taste, feel, and experience it. They created festivals, played music, displayed their art, opened small neighborhood restaurants featuring their native foods. They integrated the old ways—generations of wisdom and knowledge—with the new, helping the younger generations become leaders in their own right. They had found a new identity that combined their Cambodian ways of being with the newfound American culture.

Only by integrating the past—all the pain and suffering endured as a collective—will we be able to be fully available in our present lives. Consciously integrating the wounds of our ancestors allows us to reframe them, extract the wisdom from within those wounds, and break the cycle of intergenerational trauma for our children and grandchildren.

STAGE 5: WISDOM AND GROWTH

Moving from integration into wisdom and growth isn't easy, nor is it a necessarily natural progression for individuals or communities. But the fact is that collective trauma—be it 9/11, a pandemic, or a family tragedy—can serve as a connector to make us stronger, more empathic, and more compassionate. We can come out of the experience with a greater sense of purpose and new priorities. It is the reconnection with another person, or with other people, the reaching out for help or the providing of it, that gives us that opportunity to grow as a community. It sheds light into the invisible wounds so many marginalized members of our society are suffering from and also into the actions of those who have caused the suffering.

Committing to wisdom and growth requires a higher level of consciousness, a commitment to deep listening, and an understanding as a collective. In this stage, the community is invited to call in the wisdom of their lineage, their ancestors, and past cultures. How have they been informed by the past? What are the gifts inherent in the wounds of that past the collective can bring forth into the light? How can they recognize the traumas of the past, so they don't continue in a cycle of repetition?

It's important to realize this stage requires a shift—a leap, really—into a more connected, spiritual understanding of what it means to be in community and in the world. It commands the collective to reevaluate its sense of purpose and the work it does in the world. What is its purpose? How is the collective as a whole meant to be of service? It's often said that our purpose is born from our suffering. That out of the wisdom that emerges from our suffering comes an intuitive understanding that we are interconnected with each other and interdependent; that the pain we experience is part of the human condition, which informs our mission in life. The healing within our communities is what can begin to heal the world.

As a result of going through collective posttraumatic growth, groups, societies, and cultures will gain a better understanding of themselves, become more conscious about where they've come from and their shared history. When we are part of a community we have more tolerance for one another and more meaningful relationships, and we collectively develop a deeper sense of purpose. By accepting our trauma, we gain clarity and a new level of self-acceptance; we shift our narrative from blame and guilt to growth and wisdom. With a common vision and a set of goals, which usually entails helping others in the community, the collective can repair and heal from within.

In Part II, we dive deeper into the stages of posttraumatic growth, looking at how each stage develops, what happens inside, and how we can put it into practice. You'll be able to get clarity on how to apply the stages to situations in your own life, individually and collectively. The invitation is to start where you are and return as often as you need to.

||

Moving Through
the Stages

Chapter 7

The Stage of Awareness:
Radical Acceptance

Your vision will become clear only when you look into
your heart. Who looks outside, dreams. Who looks inside,
awakens.

—CARL GUSTAV JUNG

THE STAGE OF AWARENESS:
KEY THEMES

Vulnerability—The weak self in a malevolent,
shattered world; defenseless, helpless, weak

Isolation—The abandoned self in an indifferent
world; isolated, worthless, hopeless

Paralysis—The bewildered self in a chaotic,
meaningless, and unresponsive world; paralyzed,
disorganized, and disordered

This first stage, Radical Acceptance, begins with the after-
effects of a traumatic event, when we realize that something

terrible has happened and we are *in the trauma*. We can no longer pretend everything is fine. Everything feels out of control; we don't know who we are, how things work, or how to relate to others. We might be hypervigilant or dissociated, plagued by nightmares, or have the trauma on continual replay in our mind.

The trauma could stem from any type of experience—from a miscarriage, a breakup, or a job loss; physical or emotional abuse or a terrible accident. The story of Alejandro, the young man who survived the school shooting, is certainly more extreme. His whole world shattered and his view of himself along with it. In this stage, the traumatized person literally experiences *a shattering of the system*.

When we experience something traumatic—whether it's a catastrophic event, a heartache too painful to bear, or a dismissal from a job we love—we may consciously or even unconsciously develop coping mechanisms that allow us to keep going. These adaptive behaviors can make us dissociate, deny, or detach from the pain—keep us functioning in ways in which we can continue to live our life without feeling the pain, or loss, or suffering. Sometimes these mechanisms are very sophisticated, other times they're quite simple. They may work for a while, even years, and then . . . they don't. Instead of helping you, they're now hurting you. But here's the thing: if this happens to you, you may not necessarily *notice* they've stopped working. It's a bit like grabbing a garden hose to put out a fire in your living room. It worked perfectly. The fire is out. But you keep the hose turned on full force anyway, not noticing that the water continues to rise and rise and rise. You are now drowning in the very thing that was supposed to save you. The strategy you created to save your house has actually made things worse.

My fellow psychologist and dear friend from Venezuela, Carolina Arbelaez, has a wonderful way of expressing this paradoxical behavior. This is what she shared with me:

> The psychological defenses or coping mechanisms in trauma are like provisional bridges that we construct in disaster areas so as not to leave people or towns disconnected and unable to communicate. But then, these bridges stay there forever, and we never tend to deeper, more profound solutions that would allow for a more stable and authentic healing. (In much the same way, we postpone a deeper, more authentic resolution to the trauma that would take us to a healthier, more stable and authentic life.)
>
> We repair only halfway in order to continue our daily functioning, which gives us a false sense of "normalcy." But the situation on the inside is another story; the darkness and the humidity of the pain favors the growth of an existential mold. It eats up the will to live. It has no access to the sun's rays.
>
> Having certain awareness allows us to "see" the damage. The way out requires energy; how many messages of *Don't live, You are no good, You are not worth it,* have we accumulated in our cells? How very wounded we are, walking day to day dressed up as "normal" without attending to our wounds, made-up, undervalued, "forgotten," in the eternal chaos of our closets.

As Carolina points out, coping mechanisms (temporary bridges) are really no more than short-term fixes designed to keep us functioning day to day. But when the bridge collapses, when our defense mechanisms stop working, when the suffering we are experiencing in the moment becomes worse than the pain we've so skillfully avoided, it's time to surrender. As they say in Alcoholics Anonymous, we've hit rock bottom. Everything is messed up, we've become unbearable to be around, and we realize something needs to shift. It's time to "attend" to the wounds buried within the deep recesses of our being. It's time to radically accept that these wounds, which may have originated from something that happened yesterday, last week, or many years ago, are very much alive in the present. We have entered the Stage of Awareness: Radical Acceptance.

As we talked about in Chapter 6, Radical Acceptance also applies to acknowledging collective trauma, the obvious and the invisible wounds and moral injuries people and communities carry with them. Families, communities, marginalized peoples, and war-torn countries often erect barriers, much like individuals do, which keep them from acknowledging the cultural and systemic suffering. As Judith Herman says, "Denial, repression, and dissociation operate on a social, as well as an individual level." To begin to heal, they must be able to "see the damage" first and then radically accept that the suffering of the individual exists within the suffering of the collective. Thomas Hübl in his book *Healing Collective Trauma* describes what he calls the "trauma signature" of a group of people:

It's as if a massive elephant sits in the human living room; few may see or acknowledge it, but we are all impacted by its presence. Everything about our societies—from geopolitics to business, climate, technology, healthcare, entertainment and celebrity, and much more—is dominated by the existence of this elephant, by the residue of our collective trauma. **And as long as we fail to acknowledge or adequately care for it, the elephant will grow larger** [emphasis mine].

Becoming Aware of the Pain

Although you may have experienced previously unexplained physical or emotional symptoms of nervous system dysregulation, in Radical Acceptance chances are you've become more conscious of your feelings and your behaviors. You may even be able to distinguish between a "normal" emotional response and a dysregulated trauma response. This is the Stage of Awareness, in which someone remembers and acknowledges.

Paula, my patient I first mentioned in Chapter 5, is a perfect example. She told me one day she turned to see her five-year-old daughter standing in front of her—and she froze. She could barely breathe as she suddenly realized, *Oh my God, I was sexually abused when I was her age. I am a survivor of sexual abuse.* In that moment, she knew she not only had to accept that she was victimized, but that she had to name her experience, recognize it as trauma, and take steps to heal it, not just for her sake, but for her daughter's, too.

Another patient of mine, a young guy I'll call Oren, loved to party hard, drinking, doing cocaine, staying out all night. He told me he never really thought he had a problem—he was just having fun—until his best friend staged an intervention. Immediately after that, he says, he went into a spiral of denial, blaming his friend for overreacting and abandoning him. Then one day he got into his car after an all-night bender, and ran off the road, ending up with multiple injuries. Lying in the hospital, completely incapacitated, he got it. *I am a drug addict and if I keep going the way I'm going, I'm going to die.*

As Paula and Oren, and countless others like them, realized: to accept something is happening that causes you pain is a radical act, even if you can't quite articulate it (like Paula did) or give it a name (like Oren did). It takes courage to be vulnerable, to sit with feelings we'd rather not feel, see patterns of behavior we'd rather not see, remember experiences we'd prefer to keep buried. It's a confusing state to be in and it can leave anyone shattered, bewildered, and scared. This is where you finally say *I can't live like this anymore. I don't want to pretend everything is fine. I can no longer keep this addiction going or stay in denial.* When that happens to us, it's not uncommon to feel cut off from family, isolated from community, abandoned by the world, and disconnected from our own body and emotions. Nothing quite makes sense; the world is chaotic and unresponsive. No one else can help us; it's something we must accept within ourselves.

The thing is that lasting change can *only* come from within; it never comes from the outside. It doesn't matter what kind of change. It can be a change in your body, in your mind, in your religion. It has to come from the inside, from a realization that *something* is happening. As Dr. van der Kolk explains, trauma is the residue living inside of you, the wounds that won't heal. You are experiencing a past traumatic event as though it were happening in the present moment. This is a trauma response. Only by going within, seeing, feeling, and acknowledging your wounds will you be able to radically accept that you are suffering. Trauma lives in *your* body and only *you* have the key and the power to unlock its hold on you. That's what makes the Radical Acceptance stage so challenging for some—and liberating for others.

The singer and actor Lady Gaga explains this very well in an interview she did with Oprah Winfrey in 2020 (and again, as part of Oprah and Prince Harry's TV series, *The Me You Can't See*). I watched as she shared how she came to embrace Radical Acceptance after many years of unrelenting pain. She talked about how she had been repeatedly raped at nineteen by an unnamed music producer, locked away in a studio for months until he dumped her near her parents' house, pregnant and vomiting. She didn't have a therapist or any way of dealing with what happened, she said. Her life was moving at warp speed. She became a star right away, thrust onto the stage, traveling and making music—so she pushed the whole thing out of her mind. Until, as she recounts, she developed intense pain all over her body, which felt just like the pain she had experienced after she was raped. Pain alternating with numbness; both of these were trauma responses. On top of that, she started to cut herself; on occasion, she'd throw herself against the wall—anything to get some relief, however short-lived, from the other pain she was feeling. As she told Oprah, all of this was her way of *showing* people she was in pain because she didn't know how to tell them.

She finally got a diagnosis of PTSD in 2016—eleven years after she was raped—and another diagnosis of fibromyalgia, a chronic disease that presents as intense pain, which research has demonstrated can sometimes be caused by physical abuse and PTSD. In fact, one Israeli study that evaluated war veterans bears this out. According to its lead investigator, Howard

Amital, MD, the fibromyalgia-PTSD link was much stronger than that for PTSD and major depression, despite the fact that the severity of the two psychiatric conditions was similar.[1]

She admitted in the interview that she ended up having a psychotic break and was briefly hospitalized. There were days, weeks afterward, in which she could barely get off the couch. Doctors were trying to decide how they could get her to move. One of her doctors finally said to her, "You have to radically accept that you're going to be in pain every single day." She told Oprah that although she thought his advice sounded ridiculous, she agreed, and slowly, slowly, slowly, her pain began to lessen to the point where she could move and, ultimately, start performing again. Lady Gaga admitted that radically accepting her pain as a trauma response, and conceding that she needed help, was difficult, but not nearly as difficult as living a life of pain and suffering with seemingly no end in sight.

Radical Acceptance Is Not Easy

When you've been traumatized it's as though you've lost a vital part of yourself. You've become disconnected from the part of you that still believes in life, still believes you're worthy of love. Burdened by a sense of hopelessness and helplessness, the idea of radically accepting where you are can feel impossible. As a result, you may not be ready to make that leap. And that's okay. You may not have the resources or the motivation to move out of your despair just yet. I've had many patients over the years who tell me it took years of accumulating pain and unpredictable behaviors before something jarred them into a realization that they wanted to live, that they wanted—and deserved—a happier life.

What's Happening Inside

When we're in trauma and we have unprocessed emotions stored in our body, our nervous system goes into survival mode, affecting us physically, mentally, and psychologically. We become emotionally dysregulated, in states of hyperarousal and hypervigilance, dissociation and numbness, avoidance, agitation, and fear, in an attempt to cope with the pain. When that happens, the body may experience any of the following survival responses:

Fight. When our nervous system is on hyperalert, we can become agitated, distracted, and defensive, believing everyone is against us. The world is a dangerous place; everything is a threat. When this happens to us, we may find ourselves picking fights with our partner, family members, friends, or coworkers. Our temper could explode without warning, becoming violent, loud, and in-your-face aggressive. In other words, people may find us really difficult to be around.

Flight. Alternatively, a trauma response can sometimes make it impossible for us to be around other people. The world is chaotic and disorganized; everything feels like it's too much. We may not be able to sit still; we have excess nervous energy that we don't know what to do with that can sometimes devolve into a full-on panic attack. When people are in a flight response, they become masters at avoidance and distraction. When faced with a situation that feels the slightest bit uncomfortable or confrontational, we can dissociate or check out—and sometimes even physically leave the room. In this state, addictive behaviors—e.g., using drugs and alcohol—are also common ways of disconnection and denial. We'd rather keep busy, throw ourselves into work, than sit with our emotions or discuss anything personal.

Freeze. It's not uncommon to feel stuck and numb when we're in pain without knowing what is causing such paralysis. In the freeze response, everything seems impossible. The world is indifferent, we can often feel cut off, isolated from friends and family, worthless and depressed. It can be almost impossible to engage our mind to make decisions—or access our imagination and creativity—making it difficult to find our way out of this state. In fact, we may have days when we just can't seem to get out of bed or off the couch. Lady Gaga's experience is a prime example of the freeze state.

Fawn. This is the state in which we react with emotional codependency and lack of boundaries, a state in which we are so fragile and unsure of ourselves that we give up any sense of agency. Our sense of self is shattered, and the world has become a confusing place to navigate. When this is our experience, we may be so afraid of rejection (or of violence or harm or confrontation) that we consciously or unconsciously avoid any behaviors that might upset someone. We respond from fear, from a lack of confidence, and allow others to make decisions for us, to tell us how to be, what to believe, and how to act. We are incapable of being assertive and we're at the mercy of others.

How to Work with Radical Acceptance

It's important first to understand that deep emotions are not, in and of themselves, traumatic. We can welcome our emotions for what they are: responses to life, a reaction to something that has touched us in some way. We can realize, for example, that we're really sad right now. We can put our sadness into context—what's it connected to? Where does our sadness live? Being emotionally connected gives us a way to understand that our sadness is attached to a certain experience or even an old memory. My patient Bella lived for a long time with a deep, pervasive sadness, which she fought against, avoided, denied, and ultimately blamed for much of her mental health struggles. Bella had been adopted as a baby by an older couple, who were first-generation Holocaust survivors. She always felt out of place growing up. Not because she didn't believe her parents loved her. They did. But as Polish Holocaust survivors they carried a burden from their past she could never fully understand. Even as she got older, she couldn't shake the feeling that she didn't belong; that she had no voice of her own.

This went on for many years and then, one day, something shifted. She told me later that she had walked into her apartment after work, looked around, and stopped. "I really understood in that moment that I was completely alone. And I felt the pain of that. I didn't want to keep blaming my parents or looking outside of myself for a solution. I was ready to own the fact that I was hurting, I was sad, and I didn't want to feel the way I felt anymore. I didn't want to keep going like this." In that moment of Radical Acceptance, Bella made a decision to seek help.

Bella managed to separate her feelings from the story she had been telling herself all these years about the why, the when, and the where, and simply feel what was coming up. When we're able to do that, when we can find that feeling in our body, we may be able to notice it, and let it move through us. Having a strong emotional connection with ourselves can help us figure out when to act on our feelings and when to simply acknowledge them and then let them go. And that may help us to recognize our trauma and name it.

For some of us, just being able to radically accept how our traumas have affected our past and current behaviors is enough. In fact, it can be quite liberating to discover, name, and completely accept the cause of our suffering. But no matter how liberating it feels, it may be quite difficult to go through this process. Here are ways to identify that you are ready for radical acceptance.

YOU'RE READY FOR RADICAL ACCEPTANCE WHEN . . .

- Your coping mechanisms have stopped working.
- Your defense mechanisms (and behaviors) bring you more pain and suffering than joy.
- You are paralyzed and stuck in life.
- Your emotions easily overwhelm you.
- You can no longer stand the intensity of your anxiety.
- You are experiencing unexplained physical pain and emotional distress.
- You are fed up with being fed up.
- You admit that your relationships are a disaster.
- You are tired of all the drama.
- You don't want to live in fear or loneliness anymore.
- You have no name for what you are experiencing.
- You feel hopeless and helpless and cut off from others.
- You realize you have a childhood story of trauma.

Vocabulary of Emotions

Now that you are beginning to identify and name your emotions, here's a list that can help you expand your vocabulary.

Exhausted	Confused	Ecstatic	Guilty
Angry	Satisfied	Frustrated	Sad
Embarrassed	Happy	Mischievous	Disgusted
Enraged	Ashamed	Cautious	Calm
Overwhelmed	Hopeful	Lonely	Loving
Bored	Surprised	Anxious	Shocked
Thrilled	Joyful	Excited	Cheerful
Grateful	Balanced	Rejected	Uncomfortable
Worried	Broken	Nervous	Concerned
Worthless	Paralyzed	Powerless	Disappointed
Suspicious	Confident	Afraid	Depressed
Jealous	Shy	Despair	Melancholic
Troubled	Uptight	Hurt	Inspired

AFFIRMATIONS

Sometimes it helps to remind ourselves that we are indeed worthy of happiness and connection. We can do that by creating positive statements we repeat as often as we need or want to.

- I have everything I need to begin to heal.
- I give myself permission to be human.

- I don't need to fix anything; I can simply observe.
- I am kind to myself and tender with my feelings.
- My feelings make sense and are legitimate.
- I accept all parts of me, even if I don't always understand them.
- I am worthy of love.
- I can radically accept how I'm feeling right now.

RADICAL ACCEPTANCE PRACTICE

Here's one awareness practice that may help you begin to get in touch with your emotions.

1. Sit or lie down, making yourself as comfortable as possible. You can lay your head on a pillow, wrap yourself in a blanket, lean your back against a wall. Whatever will allow you to stay for a while.

2. Take a few moments to notice your breath. Softening your gaze (or closing your eyes), gently inhale and exhale through the nose, making a sound. With every exhale, remind yourself that you are whole, you are human, and you are okay.

3. Allow the breath to be circular; that is, don't try to stop it. Let the exhale naturally follow the inhale, which will bring about the exhale.

4. As you continue this breathing pattern, thoughts and feelings will naturally surface. Allow them to arise, linger, and dissolve. Don't try to fix anything; don't analyze. Simply witness.

5. As thoughts and feelings arise, can you name them? You may want to write them down and then journal about what came up during this practice.

6. What did you discover? Can you radically accept it? *I radically accept that I am . . .*

Chapter 8

The Stage of Awakening: Safety and Protection

Everything can be taken from a man but one thing: the last of the human freedoms—to choose one's attitude in any given set of circumstances, to choose one's own way.

—VIKTOR FRANKL

THE STAGE OF AWAKENING: KEY THEMES

Protection—Self feels protected, unburdened

Caring—World is caring, trustworthy; self doesn't feel so all alone

Responsiveness—Self feels freed up; others feel the person's pain; world is less chaotic

At this point we have radically accepted that we're in pain, that we feel helpless, hopeless, and stuck. The loneliness and isolation we're experiencing is making our life miserable. By realizing that this is what we're going through—and acknowledging that we can't do it alone—we begin to consider the *possibility* of connecting with someone else for support. Just this subtle mindset shift can move us ever so slightly into the realm of safety and protection, which is the second stage of posttraumatic growth.

If you're like many people who have experienced a traumatic event, however, the thought of actually venturing outside of your comfort zone can be daunting, even paralyzing. Nonetheless, when you recognize, in Radical Acceptance, that your suffering has become burdensome, is weighing heavily on your heart, you may decide that it's time to change. That you're ready to change. And yet, to do that, you need to make a move—physically, emotionally, and energetically.

Safety and Protection is the stage in which we begin to wake up. In which we become conscious of ourselves, others, and the world. In which we experience the beginning of an awakening. This stage is all about moving and removing—that is, moving toward what makes us feel safe and removing ourselves from people and places that trigger us.

This Stage of Awakening is where you slowly and carefully seek out safety and protection. This can mean reaching out to someone you trust and beginning to share what you've been through. That someone could be your therapist, a close friend, family member, yoga teacher, a mentor, or even a group of people—anyone whose presence gives you strength to tell your story and will respond with *We believe you. It did happen. We still love you and appreciate you.*

Or it might be an actual place you go to feel safe and protected. I encourage my patients to look for somewhere that holds a special meaning for them and stirs within them a sense of calm and safety. The place could be anywhere that brings with it a sense of peace and positive associations. Maybe for you it's at the ocean or in the mountains; it could be a special room in your home or even an imaginary place you can go to in your mind. The important thing is that you find a safe container that will allow you to consider that there might be another way of understanding the world and understanding yourself.

Even when someone feels safe, that doesn't always mean they feel comfortable expressing their feelings. When my patient Liana came to see me initially, she felt lost, confused, and very depressed. She seemed to feel safe in my office, and yet she didn't seem to want to talk at all. It was only when I handed her some paper and crayons that she began to express herself. She would write down parts of her story that she wanted to share with me. She wrote that she had been cutting herself and acting out in other ways that felt self-destructive. Over the course of our sessions together, she began to see how her behavior allowed her to cut through her numbness in order for her to at least feel something; a cry for help and a way of showing others she was in pain because she couldn't tell them. Slowly she realized she was able to stop self-harming when she felt safe enough to release her feelings. She could share parts of her story without shutting down. When we're in trauma response, it's so difficult—and yet so necessary—to accept the compassionate listening of others. As Liana's story demonstrates, there is nothing more powerful than being seen, being held, and being heard.

Finding Support

When we're able to connect with someone else who really listens to what we have to say—even if it's just a casual friend or a chance encounter—the world looks and feels a bit kinder, more manageable and less chaotic. Being in a relationship with another person we can trust helps us feel heard without being judged. In this moment we are safe and protected.

This stage brings to mind an experience I had many years ago working at the Bellevue Program for Survivors of Torture Clinic in New York City. I was seeing refugees and asylum seekers who came to New York from all over the world. I remember one case in particular. A young man came into our center, confused and frightened. He spoke no English. As soon as he heard me speak Spanish, I could see his body begin to relax; once I told him that the center was a safe place, a sanctuary within the hospital, and that he would not be deported, he was so grateful he wept—and then he began to tell me his story. He slowly trusted me enough to be vulnerable and honest. I saw how important providing a safe place was for the healing process. This is where I learned never to underestimate the power of being present, even if you don't know what to say or how to fix it.

There are many ways to receive the kindness and compassion of others, to be safe and protected. It doesn't always involve sitting in a therapist's office. One of my patients, who had gone through a difficult divorce, went with a friend to a 5Rhythms movement class, a mixture of improv, dance, and meditation. She arrived there feeling awkward, out of place, and convinced that everyone would notice she didn't belong. But, as she told me, the teacher had "created such a nurturing space that I couldn't help but join in. I remember going around the circle, moving and crying and shedding all the shame I felt inside. I never expected to be so safely held by people I had never met before. It really was beautiful."

Going on a yoga or meditation retreat or attending a weekend relax-and-renew workshop is another way to cultivate this sense of safety. Some people may even find solace in leaving town and going somewhere they've never been before. They find it easier somehow to accept the kindness of strangers and share aspects of themselves knowing they may never see those people again.

The kindness and compassion of others is the very foundation of this stage, and in some respects, goes against what society dictates: *Buck up, be strong. If you fall down, get up and keep going. Don't show emotion—that just means you're weak. If life hurts, deal with it, but certainly don't talk about it.* Instead, this Stage of Awakening provides the space we need to pause, contemplate, and allow our feelings to arise. We feel safe enough to take things slow, go at our own pace. It's not always an easy path to step onto, however, even when we know it's the right thing to do. It takes courage to sit with our pain, examine and experience it in real time, and even more courage to share all that with another human being. It doesn't always come out in tidy, predictable ways. And that's okay! Sometimes it expresses itself in bursts of anger, fits of rage, and torrents of tears.

My patient Rita was like that. She called me one morning early in the pandemic, after she had been quarantining with her family for a couple of months. She was sobbing. "I need help, Doctor, I'm dying, I don't know what I'm going to do. This is the worst thing that's ever happened in my life, I'm desperate, I need to talk to you, I'm about to go crazy."

By the time she got to my office she had calmed down enough that I could understand what she was saying. She started telling me she'd been married for twenty-five years, and she and her husband and their four girls were all at home now because of the pandemic, which was unusual. One morning she heard her husband's phone go off several times, so she picked it up and . . . by then she was crying so hard, she couldn't speak. Finally, she said, she saw proof he was having an affair—with the neighbor! And it was not just a one-night stand. It'd been going on for a few years. She was devastated. She burst into tears again, until finally she looked at me and said, "I don't know what to do. I'm giving up, I'm surrendering to this, I'm in your hands. Please, just tell me what to do because I can't even think straight." I didn't tell her what to do; that's not my job. I listened compassionately and simply held space for her to express her emotions in whatever way she needed to.

Rita's story is not unusual. I've had other patients come to my office in a fit of fury. *I'm so angry because my mother rejected me. I'm angry that I let it happen. I'm angry at her, but I can't rage at her, so I'm going to scream at my therapist.* Their emotions were raw, they were raw, and yet they had no way to express themselves. Not because I've made them angry, but because they finally feel safe enough to express real feelings that, until now, have been bottled up inside them. It's a way of rinsing the body of the toxic pain, anger, and sadness they feel.

I've had other patients come in barely able to function, and barely feeling anything at all. Bill, the firefighter I mentioned in Chapter 3, is a good example. As a first responder during

9/11, he witnessed the horrific deaths of hundreds of people, including many of his friends and colleagues who died in the rubble. He suffered deeply, but he didn't know how to talk about it. He cut himself off from his family and coworkers; he began to drink heavily and refused to talk to anyone. Finally, after a suicide attempt, he realized he needed help. When he came to see me, he was agitated and yet, at the same time, numb and dissociated from his feelings. He didn't want to talk much, which was fine, and he didn't think he could really explain why he felt so miserable. My role was to honor the process, to create a space where he felt safe enough to share his story and feelings, and to listen compassionately to him talk.

During our time together, I acknowledged and validated his suffering by repeatedly saying, "It's okay; you're safe here. I recognize how difficult this is; how painful this must be." I reassured him that he was safe to express himself in any way he chose—he could talk, yell, sing, cry, or dance his pain, or simply do nothing. I had no agenda for him. Knowing I believed him, and that I really was listening to him without judging him in any way, put him at ease. He slowly started to trust me enough that he could begin to open up. Obviously, it didn't all happen in one session—and not all sessions were the same. Sometimes he had a lot to share, other times he closed down. All of this is a normal response to trauma, and a normal way for someone to work through this stage.

What's Happening Inside

As we explored in Radical Acceptance, trauma can be a bit of a paradox. When we're suffering, we might just want to be left alone; we don't want to be out in the world, because the world is a threatening and confusing place. No one could possibly understand what we're going through, and, anyway, it's too much work to try and explain it. At the same time, we've accepted that isolation is making our trauma response worse, that the only way to heal is to move out of our isolation and look for people we feel comfortable with and can trust. Isolation breeds loneliness and loneliness dysregulates our nervous system—which is designed for connection—and that makes it harder to have relationships built on trust. It can feel like a vicious cycle. But if this is your experience, know that it's a normal, physiological reaction.

Even after we have stepped out of our comfort zone and reached out to someone for help, our nervous system may still be in reactive mode. It may not be that easy to feel safe right away. It's not unusual to go in and out of a fight-flight-freeze-fawn response, especially at the beginning. *I may have managed to get here* [to this therapist's office, yoga studio, support group], *but what if it was a mistake? It's all too overwhelming. No, I don't want to sit down. Well, maybe I can stay, but don't look at me. I can't handle that. I shouldn't have come but it feels kind of good, I should give it a shot.* Don't be surprised if your emotions are all over the place and your mind is struggling to settle. That's because trauma messes with the mind's ability to be present without invoking the past. In some ways I think of it as a dance between two parts of the brain: the amygdala, home of implicit (emotional or unconscious) memory, and the hippocampus, home of explicit memory (that is, what's actually happening in the moment).

Implicit memory is a response connected to something that happened in the past that we may not even be consciously aware of. For example, if you learned to ride a bike when you were little, that memory is stored away and surfaces whenever you decide to get on a bike. You don't have to relearn. When implicit memories have strong emotional content associated with them, the amygdala, which is part of our emotional brain, gets triggered. When we're fearful, for example, the amygdala's neurons feed on that fear, and our stress and anxiety strengthen those neural connections. In turn, the fear we're feeling makes us more anxious and depressed. The problem is that the amygdala responds not only to real fear, but also to the *memory of fear*, which can cause us to view the world from a trauma perspective, from the lens of past unprocessed emotions. For example, if you were bitten by a dog when you little, every time you come into contact with a dog, you feel scared.

Explicit memory is often defined as "declarative memory," in which we consciously recall the facts of an experience or even remember dates, times, or formulas when studying for an exam. Every time we're able to do that, we strengthen and increase the neurons in the hippocampus, and we get better at distinguishing between what is factual and what isn't.

When we've experienced something traumatic in our past, it becomes almost impossible to create new present-day memories—if what's happening now reminds us of what we went through before—without the old, often unconscious memories intruding. In scientific terms, our fear-on-repeat causes the amygdala to grow larger and the hippocampus to grow smaller.[1] In other words, the amygdala hijacks the hippocampus and keeps it from creating new memories that aren't entangled with unconscious memories from our past.

Remember the example of Leon in Chapter 5? He's the father who wouldn't allow his kids to go swimming, ride bikes, or play sports. He had grown up with a mother whose own mother almost drowned and convinced her children that water was dangerous. Leon's fear was fed, compounded, and reinforced by an implicit memory not only from his past, but from his mother's past and his grandmother's. He wasn't able to create brand-new experiences with his kids that weren't filled with fear.

The vagus nerve: our social connector. When we connect with another person in a way that feels good or have a sweet experience in a workshop or class, our nervous system responds accordingly, bringing us into what neuroscientist Stephen Porges calls our social engagement state. Our sympathetic fight-flight-freeze-fawn response decreases and our parasympathetic tend-and-befriend response increases. This happens through the action of the ventral (or front) vagus nerve, what Porges calls the "love nerve" or the "caretaking nerve" in the body. When we are in a "ventral vagal state," we feel at home inside our body, grounded, safe, and present. The vagus nerve has a psycho-spiritual role, from a safety and protection perspective: it helps us receive and make sense of our experiences and connects us to our "gut brain" or wisdom mind. It is part of our mammalian brain, the center of emotion and learning, known as the limbic system. According to Dacher Keltner's research at the Social Interaction Lab at the University of California, Berkeley, this means we have evolved "with remarkable tendencies toward kindness, generosity and reverence." We are not only hardwired to be kind and compassionate but are predisposed to *receive* the kindness and compassion of others.[2]

A story I once read about American cultural anthropologist Margaret Mead validates what Keltner's research demonstrates. It goes like this:

A student once asked anthropologist Margaret Mead, "What is the earliest sign of civilization?" The student expected her to say a clay pot, a grinding stone, or maybe a weapon. Margaret Mead said she knew that an ancient people had reached the point of becoming a true society whenever she found a healed femur, the longest bone in the body, which links the hip to the knee.

It takes about six weeks of rest for a fractured femur to heal. A healed femur shows that someone cared for the injured person, did their hunting and gathering, stayed with them, and offered physical protection and companionship until the injury could mend.

Mead explained that where the law of the jungle—the survival of the fittest—rules, no healed femurs are found. The first sign of civilization is an act of compassion, seen in a healed femur.

Although some say this story is apocryphal, I love the beauty of its message: it has long been inherent in our humanity to show kindness and compassion to those who are most vulnerable.

How to Work with Safety and Protection

Sometimes it's hard to accept an act of compassion from others when we're hurting. It takes courage to ask for help. And yet, it is in the asking that we begin to crack open the armor that shields our heart and let in the kindness of others. It is in the act of surrendering to the care and support of others—even for a short time—that healing can begin.

Three elements need to be present in this stage. I call them collectively the VAR technique: validation, acknowledgment, and recognition. This technique, which I adapted from psychologist and professor Kenneth V. Hardy, an important mentor to me and whose work continues to inspire me, is essential for safety and protection to happen.

THE VAR TECHNIQUE

Validation is synonymous with compassionate listening. It is when you feel the person you're sharing with is truly listening to your story from the heart, and they can hear what you're saying, without judging you, telling you what you did wrong, or dictating how you should feel.

Acknowledgment means someone (or a group of people) can see things from your perspective, can bear witness to how your experience has affected you in such a way that you feel seen—even if they don't share that same perspective.

Recognition means someone else accepts that the pain you're going through is real, it's hard, and it's affected you emotionally and physically. It's not necessary that they agree with you or think the same way you do. It matters that they see, listen, and support you no matter what you're going through and no matter what you say or do.

Validation, acknowledgment, and recognition can be expressed in different ways. Here are a few that can be used in Safety and Protection.

Attunement. There's nothing quite as soothing as hearing someone say, "I believe you. I am here for you no matter what." To know they understand and meet you where you are physically and emotionally—in the present moment—is huge. In other words, having someone who is attuned to how you're feeling. Therapists often do this through "emotional mirroring," by repeating back to you what they notice in a way that compassionately and empathically acknowledges, validates, and recognizes how you're feeling and what you're going through.

Attunement happens in all healthy relationships and, for those who are lucky, it began in infancy, with their primary caregiver. The only way a baby knows how to signal that she is in distress is by crying. When her caregiver responds to her cries by picking her up, holding her close, and soothing her, the baby feels safe and protected. When a small child delights in something she's discovered, having her mother respond with equal delight shows her that she's being seen, that she exists, and someone loves and understands her. Even if that never happened to you as an infant or in early childhood, it's still possible to reenact that experience in safe relationships as an adult.

Like the good-enough parent who soothes *and* gives space for feelings to arise and self-awareness to grow, a good-enough therapist, mentor, friend, family, or a group of people can do the same for you. They can acknowledge what you're going through, validate your feelings, and recognize the effects the experience has had on you. Such compassionate listening leaves space for you to express whatever you need to express—scream, cry, rage, shake—and examine it when you're ready. Mark Epstein, a psychiatrist, Buddhist practitioner, and author of *The Trauma of Everyday Life,* says that such an understanding can then "point toward the good pattern that has long been forgotten." In other words, bringing your shadow (your shame, blame, rage, et cetera) into your conscious awareness helps you also remember your gifts. Admitting that you do have needs is the first step to being able to ask for what you need.

Co-regulation. When we're in trauma, it can be really hard to get control over our emotions, which makes it difficult to engage with anyone or anything outside of ourselves. Our nervous system is dysregulated, and we need someone who can model what it feels like to be grounded; someone whose steady and reassuring presence can help us follow their lead. We can do that through a process called "co-regulation," in which one person's nervous system can sensitively interact with another person's in a way that facilitates greater emotional balance and physical health.

It's no secret that other people's words and behaviors can have a damaging effect on our nervous system and our emotional well-being; co-regulation allows us to experience the reverse as well. When someone is calm and present, our nervous system can align with theirs, which will, in turn, help us feel more grounded and present. This happens not only within human interactions but also with animals, whether they are therapy dogs or family pets.

There are many ways to experience co-regulation. Communing with nature, receiving energy from the trees in a forest, or being by the ocean can have a calming effect on the whole body. Certain practices, such as trauma-informed yoga or guided visualizations, can give us a taste of what a few moments of peace feel like. In a therapy session, your therapist may pause and take a few grounding breaths and invite you to follow along or encourage you to dance or even jump around. Having a cup of tea with a friend who is committed to compassionate listening, or taking a walk with that person, can be just the thing you need to feel a little less anxious.

To be in the presence of others who have gone through similar experiences and have come out the other side can offer us a powerful way to regulate our emotions. When someone models possibility and growth, we can begin to see that for ourselves. Empathizing with others can often help us learn to regulate our own emotions. In an article for *Yoga International,* cancer survivors admitted that practicing yoga together "offered a respite from the emotional chaos and the physical challenges they face." Jeannine, whose own journey with a brain tumor sometimes threw her into a state of agitation and fear, believes that being in a yoga class with other women going through cancer helped her manage her emotions and connect with her body in a more loving way. She says she "took comfort in the group experience and saw it as an invitation for everyone to move as a collective," which was in itself profoundly healing.[3]

To have someone recognize that what we went through was difficult and painful—and that our anger, shame, fear, or dissociation is a normal response—authenticates our experience and allows us to validate, acknowledge, and recognize our own trauma as well, and soften our self-recrimination at the same time.

Listening to the body. Allowing others to bear witness to our suffering without apology can help us recognize the broken parts within us so that we can begin to heal our relationship with our body, our mind, and our heart. We can begin to validate and recognize what we've experienced and explore the wounds the trauma has left behind in our own body. In the first stage, we already radically accepted that we are suffering. Now that we feel safe, protected, and loved by others, we can slowly do the same to ourselves.

Sometimes we need the validation and recognition of others to begin to see the light within ourselves. Connecting with others, listening to their stories, and engaging with them socially can have a powerful effect on our ability to love ourselves, to see our own worth through the eyes of another. Because trauma lives in the body, as Dr. van der Kolk says, it is through the body that we begin to acknowledge and heal our wounds. We can learn to listen deeply to what our body is asking for, honoring whatever is surfacing, in a tender and friendly way, much as we would do for someone else.

When we feel safe in our own body, we can enter into a relationship with our thoughts, feelings, and sensations and come back into the present moment. We do this by using conscious breathing techniques, yoga, guided meditation, and any number of body-awareness practices.

Vulnerability. Our experience can't truly be acknowledged, validated, and recognized unless we can be completely honest with ourselves and with others, willing to admit our failures and share our pain. Not an easy thing to do, even within a safe container. It requires trust, and vulnerability. So many cultures view vulnerability as synonymous with weakness;

they see it as shameful. But it's really the opposite. Vulnerability takes courage.

Popular speaker, researcher, and *New York Times* bestselling author Brené Brown writes about shame and vulnerability. She calls vulnerability "an excruciating act" of allowing ourselves to be seen. The thing about vulnerability is that we don't really know how others will react to what we've just told them or what we're about to share. And yet, we do it anyway. Because, as Brown says, vulnerability is the path we must take to find our way back to each other, and to ourselves. It's a commitment to "radical honesty," which is really the only way we can connect. And true connection, Brown reminds us, is the essence of human experience and, as I've been saying throughout these pages, the key ingredient to healing our pain.[4]

We can't heal what we don't recognize, and chances are we've spent a long time (maybe even a lifetime) hiding our pain, keeping our feelings locked away inside. Isolation, fear, shame, secrecy, and distrust are some of the emotional armor we wrap around ourselves. As we begin to see the world as less threatening and more accepting, the armor becomes too heavy to bear. Feeling brave enough to be vulnerable means that we begin to loosen the ties that hold our defenses in place. That often includes doing a little emotional housecleaning, taking inventory about what is getting in the way of connecting and healing.

My patient Kellie was so shut down and afraid to be open or expose herself around anyone or in any circumstance that she armored herself by sending what she called a "representative" to interact with others. She would show up, but never as her true, vulnerable self. As a consequence, she missed out on having real experiences and being present in her life.

In this stage, you can tune in to your gut feelings and honor them. When you think about a particular person or an experience, have you ever had an immediate negative reaction that you could feel in your body? If so, that may mean you need to let them go. We've all held on to things way past their prime: the relationships that have turned toxic or are triggering, the ways we punish ourselves, such as cutting, addictions, demeaning jobs—anything that reminds us of our traumatic past or diminishes our self-worth.

How We Armor Ourselves

Hiding behind a false persona. When it feels too scary to be yourself around other people, you create a false persona, often acting in ways you think they'll approve of.

Pushing emotions away. It's not easy feeling what you feel. When it becomes too much to bear, you either ignore, push away, deny, or repress your emotions.

Transferring blame. It's common to see other people or situations as the reason you act or feel the way you do. *I was just fine until . . .*

How We De-Armor Ourselves

In order to release any physical and emotional armor, it's important to first check in with what you're feeling and where you're feeling it. And then begin to release the tension in your body, using touch and breath.

Stop and notice. When you're in a situation that feels uncomfortable or triggering, take a pause. What does your armor feel like physically? Where does it feel particularly thick or heavy? Do you feel it most in your shoulders, jaw, neck, or chest? Try moving your body a little bit—move your shoulders up toward your ears and release them; shake everything out.

The power of touch. If you have more time, give yourself a massage, starting with your feet and ankles and moving up your legs; and then focus on your arms, shoulders, neck, and head, and then gently massage around your eyes, your forehead, cheeks, and mouth.

Practicing mindful breathing. As you are massaging your body, consciously direct your breath to the places you are focusing on. Gently inhale and fully exhale, softening and releasing any tension you feel.

Reach out. Connect with someone you trust so that you can talk things out, describe what's going on, and get the support you need to calm your nervous system.

This stage is not an easy one to navigate. It asks us to continue removing the barriers we've erected, to shed the armor that has shielded our heart, and be willing to stand naked and raw. There's nothing left that binds us. Nowhere else to hide. We have removed ourselves from the paralysis that imprisoned us—that feeling of being stuck following trauma—and we have moved toward the arms reaching out to hold us. When we've chosen vulnerability and connection over fear and isolation, we're ready to embrace our creativity, imagine new possibilities, and open ourselves up to a more understanding and loving world.

ARE YOU READY FOR SAFETY AND PROTECTION?

Sometimes you're not quite ready to be raw and vulnerable in front of other people but you are ready to feel held or to venture out into the world. If that's the case, you may want to consider:

- Taking a walk in your neighborhood, going to the local farmers market, or spending time in nature or on the beach

- Sitting in a café working or writing in your journal

- Singing, humming, chanting—anything that will bring sound and vibration into your body

- Exploring relaxation techniques, like guided meditation or deep, slow deliberate breathing

- Taking cold showers, splashing your face with cold water, or putting your hands into a bowl of ice

Whatever you choose, stay away from situations that are triggering or that activate your trauma response. For example, if closing your eyes during meditation makes you anxious, keep your eyes open.

GET MOVING

Physical movement is an excellent way to get out of your head and move the energy, especially if you feel stuck with your shame, insecurities, and fears on repeat. Here are some suggestions:

1. Choose any kind of physical practice that will remind your body that it's capable, perhaps even stronger than you thought it was. Walk, swim, do an active yoga class, take a bike ride.

2. If the idea of movement feels overwhelming, start with something simple like a walking meditation, in which you bring your attention into your feet and mindfully take one step at a time. This can give you a little confidence and keeps your mind focused solely in the present moment.

3. Sing, dance, laugh, play silly games. Take a moment to pause and focus on what you're experiencing in your body right now. Do not interpret it. Just feel whatever arises.

4. Sometimes too much silence and not enough activity can spiral you back into rumination. Instead of doing restorative yoga or guided meditation, begin with something more energetic to get out of your head and into your body.

Therapy Modalities

Here is a list—by no means exhaustive or complete—of different treatments, therapies, and practices that could be helpful in treating trauma. Regardless of the modality you choose, one condition should be in place: you should feel safe and protected and have a sense of trust in the person who is offering the help in order to do this work. Listen to your body, and pay attention to any alarms or triggers that arise when you are seeking help.

Functional life coaching

Internal Family Systems (IFS)

Sensorimotor psychotherapy

Accelerated Resolution Therapy

Somatic Experiencing

Emotionally focused therapy

Neurofeedback

Emotional freedom technique

Psychedelic-assisted psychotherapy

Eye movement desensitization and reprocessing (EMDR)

Play therapy

Reality therapy

Trauma-informed yoga

Trauma-informed meditation

Rapid Resolution Therapy (RRT)

ACT therapy

Accelerated Experiential Dynamic Psychotherapy (AEDP)

Cognitive Behavioral Therapy (CBT)

Dialectic Behavioral Therapy (DBT)

Hypnotherapy

PSYCH-K

Acupuncture

Vagus nerve technique

Mindfulness-Based Stress Reduction (MBSR)

Energy healing therapy

Group therapy

Prolonged exposure therapy

Narrative exposure therapy

Chapter 9

The Stage of Becoming: A New Narrative

Our job is not to deny the story, but to defy the ending—to rise strong, recognize our story and rumble with the truth until we get to a place where we think, yes. This is what happened, and I will choose how the story ends.

—BRENÉ BROWN

THE STAGE OF BECOMING: KEY THEMES

Support—The self feels strengthened and empowered in a world that makes sense, is "there"

Validation—The self feels valued in an accepting world; worthy, encouraged, hopeful

Perspective—The self is participating, exploring in a world that feels intelligible; creative, curious

Radical Acceptance and Safety and Protection are critical steps in the journey toward posttraumatic growth. Navigating these stages has allowed us to become acutely aware of how our suffering has kept us isolated and miserable, and has helped us recognize that we no longer want to be in pain. Once we felt safe enough to reach out to others, we were able to tell our story and begin to heal our wounds. Being in relationship with others has helped us become more conscious of how our past experiences have defined us and have either limited or prevented us from living our life fully.

We've made great strides, and now we're ready to move forward, to commit to transformation and growth. In order to do that, however, it's critical to go through this Stage of Becoming. Because this is where we get to figure out how we want to grow, what we want to nurture within ourselves. This is where we can push for the true change. This is when we get to reimagine and rebuild our life.

When people leave the stage of Safety and Protection, the old paradigm is broken; the story they've told about themselves and the world a thousand times doesn't work anymore. There's little left of the old life. It's gone. Shattered. There's no going back; there's only moving forward. They've been shedding layers of trauma experiences, processing and dissolving each of their defenses. Now they have an opportunity to see things as though for the very first time, and that can feel raw and new. It's as if the veil has been taken off and they're no longer seeing the world from a survival mode. The good news is, as they gather new information, maybe even remembering what was important *before* the trauma, they can begin to reconstruct their belief system and shape it into a new reality, into a new identity.

This is the Stage of *Becoming*: a transitional, exploratory one where we get a chance to start over. This is a crucial step in which we can consider new perspectives, try out new sets of beliefs to replace the old, rewrite our story, and imagine (and ultimately create) a whole new identity. As with all the stages, this doesn't happen in isolation; it happens with the help of our therapist and others in our life whom we can trust. What's important to remember here is that this paradigm shift is still theoretical and has not yet been internalized or put into practice. We can think of it instead as the gateway to rebuilding our life and the world in ways that make sense, in order to find peace. Consider this stage as a dress rehearsal for a new life.

Not for Everyone

Some people are able to achieve Radical Acceptance and Safety and Protection and then stop the journey there. This may be because the suffering they've experienced has not shaken them to the core; therefore there's no need to become anything radically different from how they are now. Getting the validation, acknowledgment, and recognition they seek from their therapist, family, and friends, they've been able to put the trauma behind them and bounce back to their previous lives. They can see their traumatic events not as something that has shattered their lives, but as temporary setbacks that allowed them to become more resilient.

You may remember Miranda, the doctor in Chapter 4 where we talked about resilience. She's a good example of what I'm describing here. Someone whose life was not shattered in the face of adversity. Even though she continues to be deeply affected by her mother's death, she hasn't allowed herself to fall apart; she knows how to get back on track. She is a tough, solution-driven, and capable woman who takes care of her family and her patients. Her traumatic experience did not destroy her core beliefs about herself and the world, so her coping skills continue to work.

Rebuild and Reimagine

I've long thought of trauma recovery as a hero's journey, with plenty of rocky roads and dead ends as well as moments of great beauty and illumination. The pain and suffering people go through give them insight into who they are. The people they meet along the way—therapists, mentors, friends, spiritual teachers—help them to see that wisdom and growth can emerge from their wounds, even though the path can be difficult.

In Safety and Protection, you found a more accepting world within a nurturing circle of trust, and that felt good. Now this stage invites you to get a taste of what transformation feels like. Going into this stage you're already more connected to people and less triggered. You're calmer and your nervous system is less reactive. You may find that your mind is expanding, and that you're ready and eager to accept the invitation to continue the process of growth and change.

I think of this stage as a new beginning, one in which we are empowered to get out into the world and see what's possible. After the work we've done so far, our view of the world may be more nuanced. It's no longer either/or; it's both/and. It's not all good nor is it inherently evil. People can be kind, and they can also be cruel. This new perspective embraces the complexities in life.

But first, we have to be willing to completely let go of what *used to be* in order to begin to imagine what *can be*. Unfortunately, when we're in a trauma response, we are unable to access our imagination. Trauma disables the capacity to envision new possibilities and find creative solutions to problems. Like I discussed in the last chapter, we have to be ready to drop the shield that has protected us and shed the armor that has bound us to our trauma and surrender to the mystery of becoming. It's a delicate and vulnerable time, which can be both stimulating and terrifying. We are entering a period of seemingly infinite possibilities, and although we may feel a sense of urgency, we need to slow down. We need to be patient with ourselves, and allow space for new possibilities and new ways of thinking to arise. That way we can determine what feels right and good to keep and what needs to be discarded.

The good news is you never have to move into this stage alone. You explore what's possible within a container of support with people you trust. Your support system is still here— not only to listen, but also to encourage you to try out new things; to applaud you when things look promising and pick you up when you falter. Use such support as scaffolding, as a temporary structure that holds the experience and the knowledge you need in order to rebuild. A patient once told me that she thinks of me as a doula, someone who can guide her through the birth canal when she's ready to be reborn. And healing from trauma really is a rebuild and rebirth. After all, everything you've believed until now, all the assumptions you've had about yourself, others, and the world are gone. Everything has collapsed around you and now you need to figure out what's next. You need to reach out to people who are doing things that are creatively interesting, so you can begin to try some of those things out for yourself.

A good example comes from a Cambodian refugee I worked with, who goes by her initials, S. P. She endured unbelievable suffering in her own country during the genocide of the Pol Pot regime. She lost her family and many members of her community before she was finally able to escape to the United States, where she settled in the Bronx, in a community of other Cambodian refugees. She found support in therapy and through her American social worker. She told me that she looked to her social worker for ways of reinventing herself. She figured out what to eat, how to dress, where to go, and even how to talk to other Americans by copying her social worker's behavior—and asking her advice—until she felt comfortable carving out an identity for herself. This is the way she explained it to me:

> The closest person I have in my life is my social worker. We talk a lot. She gave me support and encouraged me to go on with my English lessons and my job. She's given me a role model to follow. She helped me a lot with everything. Anything that I have problems with she always gives me advice. She is the one who encourages me to do things; she pushes me to do things I never did in my life. I usually never give credit to myself about what I do, so she always reminds me of the good things I do and helps me not to put myself down and get over it.

My patient Alexa is yet another example of someone who has embraced this Stage of Becoming in a beautiful way. By the time she came to see me, she was thirty-five years old, completely closed off, rigid, and deeply depressed. She rarely left her house except to go to work and on occasion to visit her one friend from childhood. It took a lot for her to even call me for an appointment, and even more to come to my office. But slowly she began to trust me enough to tell her story. Over time, I learned that her mother, who had been emotionally abused by her own father, had spiraled into drug addiction and, as a result, was emotionally unavailable. Alexa also felt distant from her father, who was emotionally absent and whom she suspected was cheating on her mother. As a teenager, Alexa had a series of relationships that were not healthy and even one that bordered on abusive. She told me she refused to repeat the traumas she had inherited. With no role models to guide her toward a healthy relationship, she stopped dating completely. For eighteen years.

She was surprised at how much she revealed in our sessions together. Not even her best friend, and certainly not her coworkers, knew this much about her past. She told people very little about herself. But, the more space I gave her, the more she trusted me. The more she trusted me, the easier it became for her to trust others, she said. I gave her homework to do—encouraging her to reach out to a friend and tell part of her story and report back. So she did. And they listened and they understood. She felt like the world was beginning to open up to her. That she could keep exploring. She was inspired to try something new, so she joined a soccer team. She discovered she was really good at soccer! She said to me, "I'm trying on what it feels like to be more flexible and not so rigid about how I plan my day or go about things." She's trying new stuff every day, little by little, and seeing how it fits. She really can't believe what's happening.

Alexa's experience points to an important distinction in this stage. Rebuilding is not the same as repairing. In other words, in this stage, we're not repairing old relationships; in fact, we're weeding out the ones that have been unhealthy or made us miserable. Instead, we're relating to those we've *chosen* to reconnect with differently. We're rebuilding connections in ways that make sense to our new narrative, our new sense of self. Alexa's friends had no idea about her inner life, past or present, and even less about how she felt. She didn't dwell on explaining herself or apologize for not being more available; she simply shared her truth by showing up fully and being more authentic with her feelings. As she began enjoying the intimacy of old and new friends, she felt her rigid boundaries relax.

What's Happening Inside

When we begin to explore the world, connect with other people, and reimagine what's possible in our lives, the myriad options can be overwhelming. And they can leave us feeling vulnerable and exposed. Getting to know the signals of the body, opening up the mind, and listening to the desires of the heart can help us discern what feels true and nurturing and what we're able to tolerate or not.

The body. In this stage you'll continue to work on becoming more at home within your physical container. You may alternate between periods of calm abiding and periods of acute distress when you first start down this path, which is not unusual. After all, your body may not have always been a safe or predictable place to be. But you're learning that the more comfortable you feel in your own skin, the more easily and naturally you can connect with others, which is essential to healing trauma.

This can manifest in different ways to different people. Because trauma can disconnect us from our body, we must learn how to listen more carefully to what it needs and learn to respond to its cues. For you, that might mean eating more consciously, exercising, or laughing more; you may need to prioritize rest, add in moments of reflection, or make sure you include opportunities to hang out with friends or family. Ask yourself periodically, *How am I doing and what do I need?*

As it gets easier to inhabit your body, you may find that it starts to communicate more effectively with you: you may notice when something doesn't feel right sooner than you used to. That's because tuning in to the body keeps us focused on what is happening *as it's happening*. Often a physical cue, such as a tightness in our chest or jaw, signals feelings of fear, agitation, or being overwhelmed, which can mean we're uncomfortable in a new situation. When that happens at this Stage of Becoming, you can reach out to someone in your support network whose reassuring presence can, in turn, help you regulate your nervous system and better understand what's going on. Once you get more confident with the new life you're creating, you'll be able to turn to certain self-care practices yourself, such as breathing techniques, guided meditations, or any other inward techniques, to self-regulate instead of relying on co-regulation.

These practices aren't only designed to make us feel better; they are also a key part of the process of self-discovery. They can help you get to know the different parts of your internal landscape, and notice where you need to put your attention. This is an important step toward growing post-trauma. When we don't pay attention to our emotions, express them, and then allow them to move through us, they stay repressed within the body, which can make us chronically ill, both physically and psychologically. As psychiatrist and Buddhist practitioner Mark Epstein reminds us, "That creates a blockage that doesn't allow for growth."

As we get to know ourselves in a kinder, gentler way, our nervous system responds by dampening down the body's fight-flight-freeze-fawn response and heightening our vagal tone, part of what humanistic psychologist Scott Barry Kaufman calls our "calm-and-connect system." This makes it easier for us to enter into new situations, including new relationships. But not just *any* relationships. In his book *Transcend,* Kaufman writes that we need to have *high-quality* connections that "get us in tune with another human being—whether it's confiding a vulnerability to someone, gossiping about a common enemy, or sharing simple moments of laughter and joy." He goes on to say that the calm-and-connect system involves a whole suite of biological responses that work together "to intensify a deep connection with another human being."

The mind. The Stage of Becoming offers an array of opportunities to get curious, ask questions, learn new things, and expand our understanding of the world. But in order to do that, as I've said before, we have to let go of everything we're still holding on to from the past and be okay with not knowing. We have to empty out in order to refill.

All this reminds me of a popular Zen story. A young scholar came to visit a Zen master known all over Japan for teaching others how to become enlightened. He asked the master to teach him the ways of Zen. But each time the master began to speak, the scholar interrupted him, telling him all about *his* experiences and what *he* thought instead of listening to the teachings. Finally, the master offered to pour him a cup of tea. Once he filled his guest's cup, however, he kept pouring until the tea spilled out of the cup, onto the table, onto the floor, and ultimately all over the young man's clothes. The young man jumped up and yelled, "What are you doing? Can't you see the cup is full already?" The master quietly replied, "Precisely. You are like the cup. So full of your own ideas that nothing more can fit in. Come back to me when your cup is empty."

Like the young scholar, when we are overly invested in our own ways of thinking and being—whether they work or not—we leave no room for becoming anything else or entertaining anything new. And yet we have a desire to prove ourselves, a constant need for validation. We become stuck in the "fixed mindset," where there's no desire to be curious or think creatively, no willingness to imagine or wonder. Trauma can do that to the mind; it can cause the mind to contract around limiting beliefs, further shutting out the world and tricking us into believing we can't trust anyone, including ourselves. But now that you are free to approach the world from a safe base, grounded in trust, you can begin to empty the mind of old paradigms and move into a growth mindset. A growth mindset allows you to stretch beyond what you think you're capable of and expand your capacity to cultivate nurturing, loving relationships. A bonus of a clearer mind: you get to experiment with what it's like to be kinder to yourself. What it's like to let go of self-bullying or self-hatred and instead embrace self-care, self-compassion, and self-love. You can become your own ally.

As we gain more confidence and clarity, it becomes easier to imagine opportunities that can enable us to make sense of our experience and relate to it differently. When her mother died of a brain tumor, ten-year-old Stella's grief was compounded by her inability to grasp why it happened and what her life would be like from that moment on. She began to realize that what she had with her mother and father no longer existed, that her understanding of the world had been shattered, and there wasn't anything she could do to get her old life back.

In this stage, she became preoccupied with death, particularly fearful that she would die or that her father would die and leave her all alone. She wanted to make sense of what was happening, so she asked me to help her map out what was going on in her brain. We sat on the floor and drew a big picture of what her brain looked like, creating several compartments, including one marked "dying from illness." She took little toys and objects, which represented thoughts, feelings, and experiences she had, and put them in specific places. She saw how her brain had changed and how her experience had made her feel different. She collected crystals she felt could help her feel better, give her more strength, and be more compassionate. As she continued to feel braver and safer, she took a risk by telling her new friends at her new school that her mother had died. And she felt okay about it. By the time she was twelve, she had mapped out a new identity for herself— she enrolled in a dance studio where she took dance classes three times a week and made new friends. In addition, she got involved with social justice issues at her school and became passionate about defending animal rights and creating awareness about the environment.

Achieving Coherence

Making choices from a more open, intuitive place brings the heart and mind together to create more self-awareness and more confidence; this helps us imagine a new paradigm for ourselves. You may find you're more conscious of how your old trauma-born fears, judgments, and other reactions have been limiting your ability to be kinder and more present. Many of my patients tell me when they realized that for themselves, it felt like their heart had been cracked open to reveal more compassion and more understanding than they thought they were capable of.

When we begin to take action and make decisions based on how we honestly feel, our body, mind, and heart are no longer at odds with one another; they have entered into a state of unity, what psychologists call coherence. If you think back to Chapter 3, where we introduced trauma, the images shared are those of disconnection and shattering. In this stage, we are able to move away from that discord and experience the benefits of coherence, which might include:

- The world and our place in it make more sense. We experience more days of calm and connection and expand our ability to self-regulate our emotions.

- We can tell the difference between relationships that foster connection and those that breed separation and suffering, and we can work toward creating more of the former and releasing more of the latter.

- We can separate the present (new experiences, healthier relationships, new memories) from the past (old fears and other emotions that came out of our traumas).
- Our emotions are identifiable, and we are able to name them; we are more attuned to where they live in our body. Equally important, we no longer identify with our emotions; we can now take some distance from them.
- We begin to take charge of our mental habits and can redirect our focus of attention in more helpful, successful directions.

Let's remember that coherence is not a permanent state. Early in this stage you may get only glimpses of clarity and sometimes a fleeting sense of unity, but those grow as you begin to feel more at home in your body, have more agency over your thought processes, and develop a more trusting connection with your intuition.

Constructive thinking. In moving from awareness to awakening to becoming, your relationship with your traumatic past has begun to shift. It's not as though you've forgotten what caused your pain or kept you from participating fully in your life. It's just that you've started to put some distance between what happened then and the new life you're envisioning now. Most of us are familiar with obsessive thinking, in which we kept our past on repeat as a constant reminder that anything can happen, and nothing is predictable or safe. All of this is accompanied by high levels of anxiety.

However, there is a more useful way of thinking, as I mentioned in Chapter 4, that can actually lead to self-awareness. Constructive thinking is often called "*deliberate* rumination" and it's the body-mind-heart's attempt to make meaning from what we've been through. It's a way of contextualizing your trauma—placing it in a time and a place—so that you remember it, but it doesn't get in the way of your willingness to rebuild your life or reimagine your future.

Making meaning out of our traumatic experiences often involves a healthy dose of what philosopher Viktor Frankl called "tragic optimism." Tragic optimism allows us to *accept* what has happened in the past. To acknowledge that our feelings are legitimate, they are part of who we are, they are valid, and it's actually possible to be okay with whatever arises—fear, anxiety, even joy or relief. Tragic optimism is *not* what psychologists call "toxic positivity," a very unhelpful and unhealthy habit of glossing over painful emotions and declaring: *Everything's good, it all happened for a reason. Just forget about it, you'll be fine!*

Take the example of Rita and her husband, Ryan, who were struggling with infidelity issues. His affair shattered their marriage and forced them to look seriously at their relationship and at themselves. They didn't want to continue to pretend everything was fine. They refused to shove everything under the rug and didn't want to give up on the possibility of reconciling. They worked hard to get to the point where they were able to look at what happened and say, *Okay, we can't change what happened, but let's see if we can accept that it did happen and if it's possible to process it and move forward.* They decided to reinvent their relationship. Their original marriage contract had been broken and was now obsolete. It was time for them to rewrite their contract and recommit to their relationship so they could move forward.

Creating new habits. Habits are hard to break. Even when we know our old ways of doing things don't work, it's not easy to just let things go. Indeed, old habits die hard, as the saying goes, because they are wired into our brains in such a way that they happen automatically, but that doesn't make them impossible to change. Three neuroscientists at MIT discovered that although our habits may be deeply ingrained, "the brain's planning centers can shut them off," allowing us to form new ones. The researchers identified an area of the brain that can switch between old habits and new, which means that the old ways don't necessarily go away permanently; instead, we can learn from them and we can choose to prioritize new, healthier ones.[1] One way we can choose new habits over the old ones is through daily affirmations. According to Joe Dispenza, a chiropractor, researcher, and author of *Breaking the Habit of Being Yourself,* "The affirmations we repeat to ourselves on a daily basis are the programs we live by and they can either aid us or inhibit us from creating, growing, and experiencing new things in our lives."

So what makes it so difficult to build new, healthier habits, even when you're ready to emerge from your old self and reclaim a new way of being? Fear. The fear of not being loved, accepted, and recognized. It's scary and destabilizing to completely let go of something that you've identified with for so long. When you find yourself struggling with this, remember that it's normal to feel fear, but that on a deep level, you already know it's possible to let go of these habits, actions, and patterns that are no longer serving you. After all, you've been in discomfort before and have been able to tolerate the not-knowing and even welcome it.

Picture yourself swinging on a flying trapeze, preparing to let go of the bar and fly through the air. Visualize the moment you have to let go, when your feet are no longer on the ground, and your hands are holding nothing but the open air, waiting to make contact with the other trapeze. You are suspended in space, with nothing to hold on to and no guarantee you'll land safely. This is what it's like to take a leap of faith. It is in that moment where transformation happens. Here are a few things that may help your process:

- Be intentional about your desire to change. Your whole being needs to be invested in your transformation.

- Know that it takes deliberate action and plenty of willpower to stay the course. Keep reminding yourself the old no longer works and you've chosen the new on purpose.

- The more you listen to your inner dialogue, the quicker you'll be able to notice your thoughts and emotions as they arise—and your reactions to them.

- Consider some of the ways in which your thinking becomes rigid or narrow. What would it feel like to imagine a new possibility as an opportunity instead of an obstacle? Instead of automatically thinking, *I could never do that, there's no way,* flip the script and say to yourself, *I bet I could do that. I'm willing to explore that possibility.* And then give your mind permission to wander, visualizing this new opportunity. Remember, this is the time to try on new things, to entertain fresh ways of seeing yourself in the world; you don't need to commit to anything. This is the time to reimagine what you're capable of without letting anything get in your way.

- Imagine the "you" you want to become. What are the gifts you have to offer others? See your future self doing what you would love to do, being the friend you'd like to have.

The Possibilities Are Endless

There's often a pause between letting go of old behaviors, trying on new ones, and then claiming them as your own. This can look like a transitional moment, a time of being in limbo, not having complete certainty, being suspended in time (much like the trapeze example). This gap is a potent time of self-reflection and self-awareness. An opportunity to release any stuck energy that may still be blocking your growth and move forward with a sense of anticipation. With no obstacles standing between your body, mind, and heart, you begin to have more clarity; everything is alive with possibility.

After Alejandro survived the school shooting and had slowly begun to heal he would often talk to me about how he looked at life in a new way. His dream of being a professional soccer player had been shattered and he had to reimagine who he was without that. He started to see himself as someone who could be strong for his family and his friends. He believed that his God had a higher purpose for him, and that it would evolve over time. He just needed to be patient and open to whatever the future held. This reminds me of the famous Viktor Frankl quote, which says:

Between stimulus and response there is a space.
In that space is our power to choose our response.
In our response lies our growth and our freedom.

Like Alejandro, many of us have an idea of where we're headed but aren't quite sure how to get there or what awaits us when we do. We're in the process of redefining who we are, renegotiating relationships, and recalibrating our place in the world. The operative words for this stage are **movement, imagination,** and **creativity.** We can begin to move the energy through our body; reimagine our place in the world; re-create our narrative without shame, blame, or guilt. And we can begin to replace the life we left behind with the life we are imagining and rebuilding for ourselves. You may notice a wellspring of questions rising to the surface, questions like, *Who am I in relation to others? What are the stories I wish to tell? In what ways can I express my true self? What belief systems are out there that make sense?* By deepening your relationship to yourself, you can assume more agency over your own self-care.

As we free the mind from the shackles of trauma contraction, we become more flexible and creative. Changes have started to happen—in context, in conversations with others—and now with more self-awareness. When we have a more conscious relationship with ourselves, we can begin to rebuild our relationships with others.

QUESTIONS TO CONSIDER

Here are some questions to ask yourself as you begin to consider new ways of being in the world, new identities to try on.

1. What are some of the beliefs that you grew up with? What kind of messages do you remember hearing from your parents, your grandparents, or other family members as you were growing up? These can include spoken (explicit) and unspoken (implicit) messages. For example: all men are cheaters; children should be seen and not heard; women are weak.

2. What beliefs have you decided to let go of because they don't really work for you anymore? What have you replaced them with?

3. What else defines you besides your gender, your work, your religion, your sexual orientation, or your ethnicity?

4. If you could be anything else—or do anything different—what would that be?

5. Keep a gratitude journal and add to it every evening before you go to bed. What were you grateful for at the end of the day? Be specific. What did you do today that made you smile? What did you do today that contributed to someone else's happiness? Whom are you most grateful for?

Again, be specific. What is it about that person that brought them to mind?

6. Do you have a creative outlet (e.g., painting, drawing, dancing)? If not, what do you find yourself gravitating toward? Is there a way you can allow yourself the space and time to explore a creative hobby that might interest you?

7. Who are the people who inspire you? People in your life or people you've read about. Maybe they've overcome obstacles and have reinvented themselves or have gone on to do something they never thought possible.

8. Some people find it easier to tell their story if they can imagine writing it to someone they love, such as a family member or an old friend. Picture this—and choose your person. What do you remember? What do you want them to know about you?

9. What do you do to feel calmer when you're anxious or afraid? What sorts of self-soothing practices work for you? What practices would you like to try that you've never done before?

10. In reframing your narrative, what have you discovered about yourself that was most surprising?

11. As you've become more comfortable in your body and are able to self-regulate more easily, what are the "I am" statements you can make now?

Building New Belief Systems

By this stage in your journey, you've opened up to new paradigms. Eager to see the world from a different perspective and understand life and yourself in a deeper way, you've started exploring new belief systems, ones that are quite different from what you've known before. I'm not just talking about religious traditions or spiritual beliefs, though some people gravitate to an organized religion or a set of spiritual practices during this stage. A new belief system could be anything that you're passionate about and identify with. It could be anything that resonates with you, anything that brings a sense of order to the new paradigm you're building and helps you feel connected to others and more engaged in the world. Some people adopt a vegan lifestyle or join a yogic community or go on regular retreats. Others become fascinated by a scientist or motivational speaker, a musician, a poet, or an artist whose work speaks to them, or even have a desire to explore psychedelics in a healing, therapeutic context. Still others embrace new cultural traditions or try out new professions. It's really different for everyone.

As you become more self-confident and self-aware, you may naturally gravitate toward what feels most supportive for your healing—and equally important, most authentic. You can begin to listen more internally and no longer have to rely so heavily on the guidance and experiences of others.

Writing a New Narrative

As we slowly assume more control, or agency, over our life, we see that we have the power to reframe our narrative in any way that more closely aligns with who we want to be. Our traumatic memories become events that happened in our past so they can no longer intrude on our ability to create new experiences in the present.

Writing our narrative or telling our story is the way we make sense of our life—how we interpret our experiences, either as they happen or as we're able to reflect upon them afterward. Instead of "I am divorced and I'm so ashamed, so lost, so fractured," a woman who has been through a contentious divorce might be able to say: "Yes, I got a divorce, I'm finding that life as a single person can be rewarding. Who knew? I'm learning so much about myself." The narrative separates us from what we consider our problem or weakness. What happened to you does not define you. You are not your trauma.

Reframing our narrative can be really hard to do. It may require help from a therapist or mentor, or from a supportive group of people going through similar experiences. Alcoholics who join AA, for example, or women who are part of a support group for rape survivors, may benefit from giving support to and receiving support from others.

The work we've done thus far has helped us move the trauma energy out of the body and transform it. We are taking away the trauma's power and beginning to explore it in a different, healthier way. Gloria, the young woman we met in Chapter 3 who ended up in Rikers Island, is one of the most powerful examples of this. By the time she was released into a psychiatric ward, she was severely traumatized. After she was discharged, she worked with a mentor who encouraged her to embark on a healing journey. Along the way, she began to express herself through her art. With a supportive community and plenty of therapeutic guidance, she gained a deeper understanding of what had happened to her, and she channeled the pain of her deep trauma into her paintings. She allowed her sadness and depression to be expressed through the colors and the shapes she painted as she poured her pain and suffering onto her canvas. She let her trauma live in her art.

Perhaps the most remarkable thing about her process is that she created an alter ego as a painter. She was no longer Gloria, who had been raped and tortured. She was Kiki, an accomplished artist in her own right. She had rewritten and retold the story of her life in art in order to heal the pain of her past and begin to create a more empowered future.

Creating an alter ego was Gloria's way of reimagining her life and rewriting her narrative without her traumatic past invading her new beginning. She didn't deny what happened, but she put it into context. As Nigerian poet and high priestess Ehime Ora once wrote, "You gotta resurrect the deep pain that lives within you and give it a place to live that's not within your body." That's precisely what Gloria did. And that's exactly what this Stage of Becoming is inviting all of us to do.

The next stage, the Stage of Being: Integration, summons us to revisit the trauma and move into relationship with it. We've created a new paradigm in the Stage of Becoming. In the Stage of Being we will integrate this new self with the old.

ESSENTIAL TOOLS FOR THE STAGE OF BECOMING

Focus on positive thoughts. Do spend some time each day deliberately thinking about any challenges that came up, the solutions that occurred to you, and what new things you may want to try.

Lean on others for support. This is key because we are social beings, and it is by interacting with others, receiving and giving support, and knowing we're connected to one another that we keep moving forward.

Express yourself creatively. Paint, draw, dance, make music, write poetry, do anything that helps you express feelings that may not feel accessible through words.

Stay connected to your purpose. Knowing there is something much greater than yourself helps, especially in times of doubt or confusion. Create structure around your goals.

Stay open to new experiences. Be flexible, avoid self-criticism as much as possible. Be open to new ideas and embrace challenges that come your way.

Fake it until you make it. When you begin to feel trapped in fear, negativity, or doubt, try putting a smile on your face and cultivate the opposite emotion. You may be surprised at how well that works!

Words to Remember

Here is a list of words and phrases you can refer to as you step onto the path of Becoming. As you read each word, consider how you can apply it to your relationship to yourself, to others, and to the world.

BEGIN IN A WORLD OF POSSIBILITIES

Reconnect

Rebuild

Reimagine

Reinvent

Regenerate

Reprocess

Reactivate

Relate differently

Release the old

Reorganize priorities

Re-create new memories

Reshape habits

Resource self

New narratives

New possibilities

New perspectives

New paradigms

New growth mindset

More flexibility

More openness

More creativity

More willingness

TRANSFORM TO A WORLD THAT MAKES SENSE

Self-resilience

Self-regulation

Self-coherence

Self-care

Self-confidence

Self-love

Self-trust

Self-renewal

Self-reliance

Self-reflection

New beginning

New belief systems

New identity

New relationships

Chapter 10

The Stage of Being: Integration

In a deeper sense, a great deal of human suffering exists because of the denial of the past and the inability to acknowledge and integrate it. But when the decision is made to finally look at and feel the past, everything shifts.

—THOMAS HÜBL

THE STAGE OF BEING: KEY THEMES

Resilience—The self feels sturdy, capable, and able to cope in a world that is benevolent enough

Belonging—The self feels worthwhile, valuable, and self-assured in a world that offers a sense of community and a place within it

Reconciliation—The self is reconstructed in a framework that integrates the new posttraumatic narrative and intertwines it into the whole; you are reclaiming the self

At this point in the journey toward posttraumatic growth, you may feel that you're finally on firmer ground, more self-assured, and that the world makes more sense. That the work you've done to create a new identity has given you more self-confidence, maybe even set you on a new path that has taken you from *I think I can* to *I know I can.*

At this stage, my patients often tell me that they don't doubt themselves so much anymore. That they feel stronger and more self-assured. By exploring new possibilities and trying on new perspectives, they've been able to discard what used to be in order to imagine what could be. It's not that they deny their trauma, it's that they realize what they went through is in the past; it's not part of their present experience. Through trial and error, starts and stops, they have emerged with a new story to tell and have replaced their old identity with a new one (*I am no longer becoming. This is who I am*), one that focuses on the present and looks to the future.

As people move from the Stage of Becoming into the Stage of Being they often become more comfortable living in the present moment, generating new memories, creating new habits and letting the old ones fall away. So much healing has taken place in this liminal stage, what psychologist and best-selling author Dr. Joan Borysenko calls "the time between no longer and not yet."[1] You've embodied those changes; you own your new identity. You've stopped feeding your trauma and can see what's possible without being controlled by it. If you're already seeing a shift in yourself—even a small one— the power of inner transformation is beginning. All the new changes you've gone through, and all the times you pushed yourself out of your comfort zone, have reshaped you in some way; they have become part of who you are. You can now say, *I did that! I took a risk. I made the decision to do something different and I did it! This is who I am now.*

For many people, that's enough. They feel capable of being in the world in a healthier, more connected way. Their relationships are more meaningful, they're much more resilient and more present. They're ready and eager to embrace their new identity without really needing to think too much about their past, including their traumatic experiences. They've put their past behind them and have grown in spite of what happened to them. They can say, *I'm good now, I don't have to think about the past any longer. I have a new identity and I am resilient.*

The Old World Meets the New

For true transformation to occur, however, it's not enough to create and embody only the *new* identity. We must also incorporate the past to create a whole. We must integrate all parts of ourselves: the changes we've made, the work we've done up until now, and the traumas that have lived within us and caused us pain. There's wisdom within all of it—and there's no leaving any of it behind. That's what the Stage of Being: Integration is all about. It is the stage of both/and. We may still remember our past trauma experience; we may even be able to talk about it to other people, but—and here's the main, crucial point—*we are no longer experiencing it as though it were happening in the present moment.* We are not reliving the abuse or the war or the divorce or the loss of a child. We can remember it and engage with it without experiencing a trauma response; it is a memory relegated to the past that now informs the present in a healthier way. As Dr. van der

Kolk says, when you are able "to integrate the old trauma with the new, you no longer see the trauma as if it's happening in the present moment; you can actually talk about the trauma in the past."

True transformation honors the wisdom within the wounds as well as the new, empowered self. The mantra becomes: *I am who I am because of my trauma, not in spite of it.* This stage invites us to rework our new narrative further, and write a new chapter, one that integrates our new self with our old trauma and celebrates our wholeness. We can acknowledge that we are strong, because we survived. The more unified we become, the more we are able to hold all our contradictions with kindness—our vulnerability and our resiliency, our aloneness and our sense of belonging, our rage and our compassion.

Gloria reported she could lay her alter ego to rest and admit *she* was the artist—and she was also someone who spent time in prison, who was a victim of rape, beaten down by violent abuse, and a refugee. She could own that identity at the same time as she could unabashedly declare she was also a woman who had people who love her, who was capable of developing and keeping more intimate and meaningful relationships and was proud of who she had become.

The refugees I've worked with over the years offer important lessons for us about what it means to integrate our past traumas into our present lives. They come into a new country with a story to tell, the story of their past, eager to begin anew. They often face a lot of adversity and trauma before they are able to adjust and create a new identity for themselves. Some end up assimilating into the culture, which means they deny their own story, their own cultural ways, and embrace only their new life. Others are able to acculturate, which means they integrate their cultural and spiritual beliefs, their ancestral wisdom, and their customs into their host culture, the old ways into the new. The Venezuelan refugees I've known and worked with in the United States, are a good example of this. Much like the Cambodians who settled in the Bronx, the Venezuelan families brought their culture—their food, music, dance, and even their language—with them and introduced it into the neighborhoods in which they live. They talk about their past, not in a traumatized way, but proudly. It feels good to share their stories, and equally important, to be creating new ones at the same time.

What's Happening Inside

Telling our whole story even to ourselves—without being triggered—can help us reclaim our identity. We may find, when we no longer have a relationship with our past that is mired in shame and regret, that it's a lot easier to own the trauma and accept it as part of who we are.

All of this has a balancing effect on our physiology. In Integration, the nervous system is no longer in survival mode. Even if we begin to feel worried or anxious or a bit overwhelmed, we have tools available that can help us come back into balance more quickly. Practicing any kind of mindful self-care, such as yoga or meditation, Reiki or massage, a walk in nature or a midafternoon nap, elevates the parasympathetic nervous system so that we feel more grounded and connected and enjoy more moments of serenity and ease with fewer triggers to react to.

It's important to remember that integrating our trauma into our narrative is not the same as dissociating from it or becoming numb to it. Dr. van der Kolk warns against what he calls "desensitization," in which traumatized individuals learn *not* to feel or react to their emotions; that way they can separate themselves from their experiences and from the emotions those experiences trigger. Integration, on the other hand, invites us to bring our emotions to the surface and get to know what they feel like in our body by noticing them as they are happening. Then we can use the tools of self-awareness to increase our capacity to respond and regulate instead of reacting or burying them. Noticing what's happening, naming what we're feeling, keeps the mind anchored in the present moment, which can make it easier to release any attachments to the past and focus on making peace with it.

RECLAIMING YOUR PAST

In order to reclaim the parts of you that may have been hidden away or buried, it's important to bring them forth so that you interact with them. In this journaling exercise, name your trauma and the emotions that arise—grief, anger, shame, whatever is connected to your past experience. What does your trauma have to say to you? What do you want to say in response? Write for at least ten minutes without thinking or editing or worrying about grammar. Write whatever comes into your mind. When you're finished, close your journal and simply sit quietly for several minutes and feel whatever arises. From there, you can burn the pages, throw them away, or simply store them in a closet somewhere.

REWRITING YOUR NARRATIVE

During the Stage of Becoming, you were invited to write a new story, a story in which you reimagined your life not limited because of the effects of your past traumas. In this stage of Integration, you have another opportunity to rewrite your narrative, this time integrating your old life and your new, empowered one.

1. Now that you've integrated your past into your new narrative, what is the story you are telling now? How has your story changed? How has this new narrative changed the way you feel about yourself?

2. Can you come up with a few "I" statements that describe who you are now? Examples might be something like, *I am a survivor of child abuse, and I'm also a strong, capable woman who is in a healthy, loving relationship.* Or, *I have accepted my past trauma as part of who I am now.*

3. Are you okay with letting go of old relationships that don't work any longer and embracing new ones?

4. Can you talk about your past without shame?

5. Can you see your past trauma as part of who you are now, something that no longer prevents you from living a full life?

From Fragmentation to Wholeness

This stage of the posttraumatic growth model is more of an internal investigation, a way of reconnecting with the self. It asks us to investigate how we self-identify and what we've left behind. This is important because true transformation requires that we integrate all of ourselves—the good, the bad, and the ugly. We can't just take the parts we've chosen to bring to the light and express outwardly—the stuff we appreciate about ourselves and our new identity. We have to include the parts we don't like so much or maybe have hidden away, our shadow self, and the parts that have been hurt by others.

It's helpful to remember that each and every part of you has a voice and a story to tell. When you are willing and ready to listen to each one, you can receive its messages and respond with compassion. Healing requires loving yourself, accepting the whole of you, and learning how to trust your intuition. When you can be tender with yourself, soften around the sharp edges of suffering, you can move from fragmentation to wholeness and emerge authentically and unapologetically yourself.

My friend Ana demonstrates this in a beautiful and most unusual way. Ana had been sexually abused by her father for many years and had worked hard to heal her trauma. As part of her healing process, she wanted to create a visible representation of what it meant to stop hiding her trauma and begin integrating it into her life. She asked a makeup artist to paint two halves of her face and then photograph her. One half represented who she was when she was abused; the other half, who she is now. The images were so startling and powerful that she and her makeup artist decided that this could be a moving and healing experience for others who have suffered abuse. So they've teamed up with an organization that works with teenagers who have been abused, to paint their faces and photograph them as part of their healing process.

Collecting All the Broken Pieces

The early part of this stage is all about collecting the lost, forgotten, or broken pieces we need to fold into our new narrative. I have a piece of pottery in my office, a ceramic bowl created using the ancient Japanese art of kintsugi, which we touched on in Chapter 3. I keep it there because it beautifully depicts how it's possible to put our broken parts back together again. It also reminds me and my patients that the goal is not to "fix" what's broken or toss it aside, but to integrate it into our being in a way that honors the beauty of our imperfections and celebrates our uniqueness. Kintsugi's philosophy of transformation reminds us not only that everything is impermanent, but that there's reason to illuminate the changes, to celebrate and embrace them for the depth of awareness they bring to our lives. Our wounds become the precious fabric, the golden thread that weaves together our life stories and gives them meaning.

We can see this philosophy of transformation happening throughout the stages of posttraumatic growth. In Radical Acceptance, the pottery is broken, and the pieces lie scattered all over the floor. We come to recognize there's no way we can fix it by ourselves or clean up the mess. In Safety and

Protection, we reach out to others who agree to help us gather the pieces back together. In A New Narrative, we have an opportunity to reimagine the vase, rearrange the pieces in a different way, decide how much gold dust or lacquer we need to attach the broken pieces, and determine what else we can add to create something even more beautiful than the original. Now, in Integration, the Stage of Being, we put it all together. The broken pieces represent the wounds from our past, maybe even how we used to see ourselves. The gold and lacquer we've chosen to keep the pieces together represent all we've become—the value of connection, our compassionate nature, and the contributions we are capable of making in the world. Now we can look at the piece of pottery and think, *Wow, everything is really fitting together*. There's a place for everything, and it all makes more sense. Our trauma, our old self, is an integral part of who we are now. We can see it in a new way. We are whole. We are complete.

This metaphor of kintsugi reminds me of my patients Eva and Emilio, the couple with three children I talked about previously, who immigrated to the United States from Spain. The whole family was traumatized by their realization that the children's grandfather had been sexually abusing children, including possibly their own. Instead of supporting them, the extended family and much of their community turned against them, accusing them of attempting to extort money from the grandfather, who was a very wealthy and influential man in Spain. Their whole lives were shattered, and their young children were traumatized. They had to radically accept their situation was never going to get any better unless they left their home and their country. They came to the United States, where they slowly found safety within a community that believed their story and could help them pick up the pieces. Once they felt safe, they could begin rebuilding their lives. I encouraged them to create a sacred space—the gold and lacquer—that would hold the family together and strengthen the bonds between the siblings, between Eva and Emilio, and within the whole family. They did this by forming conscious connections within the community that were authentic and intimate, friendships in which they could show up fully and truthfully.

Recovering the Gifts of Our Soul

So far, much of the transformation that's occurred has been focused internally, with changes taking place inside of us. All of this may seem counterintuitive because healing happens through connection, and relationships are key to making progress. But it makes sense if you think about it: As you're healing your relationship to yourself, you are slowly moving back into the world and touching the lives of others in more authentic ways. We have brought all of ourselves—our past and future as well as the present—to the surface. We have made peace with our shadow—the shame, blame, guilt, and all the behaviors we aren't proud of—and can see the wisdom within it. We are retrieving the lost parts of us that have been pushed aside or repressed and are now calling them home to our true nature, to our soul. We do this in order to reconnect with all that is beautiful and noble about being human, to be able to say, *I am the shadow as well as the light.*

During my studies of shamanic medicine with a mentor in Miami and then in the mountains of Peru, I learned a powerful way to recover and reclaim essential aspects of ourselves we have lost as a result of pain, trauma, and stress. It requires that we dive into the depth of our being, to what the shamans call "the four chambers of the soul" and bring the lost pieces home. Although I've modified it over the years for myself and my patients, this soul retrieval journey begins by visualizing yourself descending a stairway into a four-chambered soul.[2]

1. In the first chamber, the chamber of wounds, we face the source of our wound, what has caused our soul to flee.

2. In the second chamber, the chamber of contracts, we meet the limited beliefs we had and promises we made at the time of our loss. We get to renegotiate those now.

3. In the third one, the chamber of grace, we see beyond the anguish of our wounds into the beauty and the wisdom that lie within them, and we are able to recover the grace, passion, and trust that will make us whole again.

4. In the fourth chamber, the chamber of treasures, we excavate the most precious gifts of our soul, which we are responsible for sharing with the world.

As we gently, reverently, gather up all the lost pieces and fold them into who we have become, something completely new emerges. That, the shamans say, becomes our medicine, the gift we have to offer the world. All the work we have done leading up to now has been in service to a purpose much larger than ourselves, the purpose we are here to fulfill.

As we explore in Wisdom and Growth, the Stage of Transforming, by learning to trust our wisdom, by embracing our true nature, we see that our transformation is intimately connected with our purpose and our intention to make the world a better place.

INTEGRATING NEW HABITS

In an article for the *New York Times*, Tara Parker-Pope offered five steps to creating and *keeping* new, healthier habits. Using her framework, I've suggested ways in which we can be successful in incorporating new habits into our daily lives.

Stack your habits. Fold a new habit into things you already do so that the new habit seems like an extension, not a replacement. A friend of mine wanted to start her day by reading something inspirational, but she could never seem to make it happen consistently. She finally figured out that she could use her morning coffee time as a time to read as well. After a month of doing that, she says she can't imagine starting her day any other way.

Start small. Don't let your enthusiasm cause you to sign up for more than you can realistically accomplish. In other words, instead of promising yourself that you'll do a sixty-minute workout every day, see what it feels like to do a few stretches or strengthening movements while your tea or coffee is brewing or before you get into the shower. Or lie down and put your feet up the wall for five minutes at the end of your workday.

Be persistent and consistent. Tara Parker-Pope points to a study that showed how long it takes to make a routine stick. The research says that can take anywhere from 18 to 254 days—the median being 66 days! So pick something you feel you can do every day or at the same time each week. Maybe it's a twenty-minute walk after lunch or a commitment you make to volunteer every week.

Make it easy for yourself. Creating an intention or having a clear purpose for what you're doing helps keep it top of mind. It can help keep your motivation strong.

Reward yourself. Don't wait until you've exercised or meditated for a week, a month, or sixty-six days to reward yourself for your efforts. Build in immediate rewards. What would make your activity more pleasurable, something to look forward to? A word of caution, though: don't multitask your new habit.

Have an accountability partner. I added an extra one: reaching out to a friend you trust can help you stay the course. Sometimes that friend is also the habit-making partner, with whom you share your morning or evening walk; sometimes that friend is the person you check in with three times a week to name your progress or your challenges or to get encouragement to keep going.

Chapter 11

The Stage of Transforming: Wisdom and Growth

Where you stumble . . . there lies your treasure. The very cave you were afraid to enter turns out to be the source of what you were looking for.

—JOSEPH CAMPBELL

THE STAGE OF TRANSFORMING: KEY THEMES

Consciousness—The self is appreciative, has a greater sense of personal strength, and is more grateful in a world that is more benevolent and alive; the self is more aware and awake

Connection—The self is intuitive and trusting in a world that feels more compassionate and meaningful

Transcendence—The self has initiative, a goal, and a mission in a world that feels manageable and organized; the self engages in acts of service, activism, and advocacy for self and others

After all the work we've done to heal our wounds, this is the stage in which we are more aware, more conscious, and more awake. We are heroes in our own journey, everyday heroes who have had the courage to dive deep within our being, naming, healing, and integrating our traumatic past experiences into our lives. We reemerge with a profound understanding of the interconnectedness of all life and the desire to share what we've learned on the path.

We've all heard amazing stories of the more well-known heroes who have overcome traumatic experiences and have gone on to do incredible things; to change the world, even. Many modern heroes have origin stories that are steeped in trauma. Oprah's story of repeated sexual abuse beginning at the age of nine; Malala, the young Pakistani girl, who survived being shot in the head by the Taliban for championing a woman's right to education, and who went on to establish the Malala Fund, "a charity dedicated to giving every girl an opportunity to achieve a future she chooses." And Lady Gaga, whose story I recounted in Chapter 7. Her horrific experience of being sexually abused by a music producer—and her experience of being bullied as a child—allowed her to see the wisdom within the wounds of her trauma and dedicate her career as a "rebellion against all the things in the world that I see to be unkind." She didn't do what she does for fame; she did it for impact.

Of all the stages of posttraumatic growth, this is my favorite stage, and is at the core of my work. It's the stage I want everyone to get to, because this is where true transformation happens. I often tell my patients that once they've worked so hard to change their lives, there'll be something else to look forward to, something more beautiful to experience. The journey's rarely easy; it can be painful and difficult. But if you do a lot of hard work on yourself and you're willing to walk through the fire, you will have transcended the trauma and grown because of it.

I sometimes liken this stage to the aftermath of a heavy summer rainstorm. The wind and rain have washed away the dirt, leaving fallen twigs and small branches in their wake, and the heaviness of the summer heat has vanished. The sun is out, the sky is blue, and everything is saturated with color, looking brighter and more beautiful than ever. All our senses have awakened, and we are connected to our surroundings— fully present. We are grateful for the storm that has cleansed the earth and brought such clarity and beauty, even as we are relieved that it has passed. We know storms will come again, some without warning, some more destructive than others, but in this moment we realize we've been transformed, that our view of the world—and our place in it—has changed. We are grateful to be alive, and we know that anything is possible.

The thing is, once we have experienced such profound transformation, there's no going back. We've awakened to our true nature. We've seen what's possible, and now we can't un-see it, we can't unknow something we've already discovered. After her struggle to break free, a butterfly can't return to being a caterpillar, although she embodies its essence. Just like the butterfly, you have emerged fully formed and changed. You have not only healed your trauma, but your trauma— your inner storm—has been the catalyst for wisdom and growth. For your beautiful reawakening. Of course there'll be fluctuations, and some days you will feel stronger and more self-assured than others, but this change is permanent.

You can now see yourself and the world through a different, sharper lens.

Your job is to remember who you are now—integrated and whole—and to own it. Remember what this feels like. You will return to it over and over again, throughout your life.

What Happens in Wisdom and Growth?

We bring a keen sense of identity and belonging to this stage; we feel more confident, compassionate, and present in the world. Our priorities have shifted. We've become more conscious of who we are as individuals and as part of the collective; we have a clearer understanding of what's important in our lives and have a deeper desire to share what we've discovered with others.

The road leading to posttraumatic growth, however, is rarely an easy one. It is often a rocky and difficult journey. We must become completely undone in order to piece ourselves back together. Our core beliefs were shattered, and our hearts were cracked open countless times. Yet we have slowly and consciously transformed; we have rebuilt, rewritten, and recommitted to a new set of beliefs, and we have found that our heart is indeed big enough to hold all our complexities with love and understanding. We can connect with others in a more meaningful way and show up fully in a world that makes more sense, is more manageable and more meaningful. Much like the caterpillar who had to shed everything she was in order to become a beautiful butterfly, we have transcended the old to be born anew.

Remember Emilio, whose world was destroyed when he found out that his own father was a sexual predator and was manipulating so many people in his favor? Emilio was transformed by separating himself from his home country and creating something brand-new: a family with different values and a fresh way of understanding life. Through hard work, therapy, and support from his new community, he not only created a new identity for himself, but was inspired to found an organization that offers a sense of community for recent immigrants.

A Phenomenon Grounded in Science

For many people, the whole idea that you can heal from your trauma and grow because of it sounds naive at best and even a little absurd. So I think it's important, before we dive deeper into what this stage of posttraumatic growth offers us, to remember the phenomenon has been studied in various disciplines. Since 2012, the number of studies has grown extensively in fields such as neurobiology, clinical psychology, epigenetics, sociology, and psychiatric epidemiology. In fact, we've cited the work of many of the leading researchers in Chapter 2. And the consensus is that PTG is not just a theory, but it is what people can actually experience, and it has changed the lives of countless people who have suffered from trauma.

There are many different avenues that take us along this journey to posttraumatic growth. Some people get to this stage by working with a clinical psychologist who specializes in trauma and believes that posttraumatic growth is possible. Others have had help from their family or friends, a mentor, or a group of people (such as those in Alcoholics Anonymous) who are going through similar experiences—"Expert companions" as Richard Tedeschi calls them. Still others benefit by more unconventional means, such as working with shamanic healers or using psychedelics as medicine, which in the last few years has been hailed by researchers as an "emerging paradigm" in transforming trauma into growth.

Some people who work in trauma-related fields believe that posttraumatic growth can happen naturally, unprompted or even spontaneously. That may happen in a small number of cases, but the wisdom and growth I'm describing here is more than an "aha" moment or a spontaneous awakening. It requires a commitment to the process and a facilitator to guide it. I have been blessed to witness many moments of clarity and expansion in my own patients. Those moments feel like the light of a revelation is bursting forth out of the darkness of despair, reminding us all, as Rumi writes, "The wound is the place where the light enters you." Such epiphanies give people hope that healing and growth are possible and keep them moving forward.

Wisdom and Growth requires us to commit to a complete transformation—psychological, physiological, and emotional. It requires us to think not just of our life, but also of those who came before us: of intergenerational trauma and our role in the cycle of inherited pain. As we will discuss in this chapter, this Stage of Transforming resides in a spiritual dimension, and it has the power to forever change us.

The Five Pillars

This fifth stage of posttraumatic growth touches every aspect of our lives. We come to it deeply changed from where we were at the start of our journey. We are connected to others and our community in countless ways. We appreciate life and are full of gratitude for what we have. We feel strong and capable, as well as vulnerable and open. Our relationships are more meaningful, and we understand that there's something much bigger than ourselves that connects us to the universe and to one another. We know we're here to serve others through a mission born from our wounds.

When people go through posttraumatic growth, according to Richard Tedeschi and Lawrence Calhoun's research, they develop measurable capacities that either weren't there before or had been obscured because of their trauma. They show up as five specific domains.

In the clinical work I've done with my patients, in my research, and in my personal experience, I have also observed unexpected gifts of growth and transformation and the characteristics that keep showing up in people who get to this stage of Wisdom and Growth. Based on Tedeschi's domains, I've also grouped these areas into five pillars: **appreciation of life, personal strength, meaningful relationships, a deeper spiritual connection,** and **purpose and meaning.**

APPRECIATION OF LIFE

After all you've been through, you now feel like you have a fresh outlook on life. You don't want to miss a single thing or waste a moment. You made it through, and you have a greater appreciation for what it means to be alive. Your senses have reawakened and you're aware of your surroundings in ways you probably haven't been in a long time. You're enjoying these moments, savoring them, without being distracted by your previously chaotic mind. I had a patient in Florida tell me he was so surprised to discover he could hear the ocean from his apartment balcony—and he had lived there for ten years. Another patient told me she was getting so much joy in walking in the woods by her house because she could really appreciate what surrounds her.

Tal Ben-Shahar, my dear colleague, is the founder of the Happiness Studies Academy; his course on positive psychology is the most popular course in the history of Harvard University. He says whatever you appreciate, increases. It increases because "to appreciate" *means* to increase. When we invest in something, we're delighted when it appreciates in value or worth. The same thing happens when we invest in our surroundings—they become more valuable. They appreciate.

You feel more at peace now and you're grateful. Grateful for everything, even all the experiences you had to go through to get here, even for the things you lost (which can include losing people you love, missed opportunities, discarded core beliefs that failed you, or relationships that have ended). You may still be mourning these losses, even as you are paradoxically grateful for what they have brought you.

Having said that, sometimes I feel like we use the term "gratitude" a little too loosely. It can be a way of minimizing what we've been through, or a way of avoiding it or putting it out of our minds. Well-meaning friends or colleagues often tell us to look on the bright side, to just be grateful, and to remember that everything happens for a reason. That's not gratitude. It's what is called "toxic positivity," and it can actually make us feel worse about ourselves and our situation, not better.

When I talk about Wisdom and Growth, I'm talking about "tragic optimism," which allows us to find the meaning within the pain before we're able to be grateful for what we've experienced. Tragic optimism isn't something that happens while we're in a trauma response; it is what comes out of all the work we've done to heal and grow from our past experiences. And the gratitude that emerges goes beyond being happy for what we have and encompasses a deeper appreciation for and connection to all of life—even (and sometimes especially) the painful parts.

Posttraumatic growth is full of paradoxes. Making friends with death in order to appreciate life is a big one, because out of our loss comes growth. Beth, a woman I work with who has stage 4 breast cancer, admitted knowing with relative certainty that she's going to die soon gave her a new appreciation for living. The prospect of death has brought a greater sense of immediacy to her life and, paradoxically, more joy. She is making the most of the time she has—she's hanging out with family and good friends; she's laughing more, and crying, too. She wants her life to have meaning and her work in the world to help others—and she does that by creating cancer support groups specifically for women with stage 4 cancers. She's incredibly grateful for the beauty she has had in her life. She personifies what poet Rainer Maria Rilke says: "Death is our friend precisely because it brings us into absolute and passionate presence with all that is here, that is natural, that is love."

Appreciation of life—and the ability to embrace the reality of death—often brings contentment. Material stuff becomes unimportant. Your priorities shift; you feel less urgency to be more successful, to have more things, to make more money. The longing, *I'd be happier if only . . .* falls away. You become acutely aware of what you've lost, of course, but also of what you still have. You may find you appreciate your family and friends more, or your ability to breathe, move, go outside, play with your children or grandchildren. Gratitude brings with it the realization you have everything you need to be happy, to be whole, and to embrace life fully.

PERSONAL STRENGTH

Almost without exception, people who have gone through horrific experiences and have come to the stage of Wisdom and Growth say they feel stronger and more capable for having done so. Many are even surprised they found the skills to do what they did.

We don't know how strong we are sometimes until being strong is the only option we have. Gloria personifies this. She found incredible strength in her transformation, strength she didn't even know she had after having been beaten down physically and psychologically. It came out of an intense desire not only to survive, but to make her suffering mean something, to transcend the pain and give birth to something new. She resolved to fight against injustice by joining an organization working to shut down the Rikers Island prison, and to help women who have immigrated to the United States navigate all the complexities and challenges that come with their decision. In his book *Transformed by Trauma,* Tedeschi explains:

> When something has been ripped away, people who experience posttraumatic growth recognize that what has been hidden from them can be seen again. The sleeping giant

lying dormant inside can be awakened and a new perspective and approach to life can unfold. Incredible strength and resolve can come to light and the person changes the life course.

Personal strength in this stage illuminates yet another paradox: in strength lies our vulnerability, and acknowledging and accepting our vulnerability gives us strength. For some people, the "sleeping giant" that has awakened within may be newly discovered self-confidence or courage. For others it could be advocating for themselves; still others find more self-reliance. We now have the confidence to ask for what we need, the strength to face whatever comes our way, and the wisdom to think before we act.

Paradoxically, we are unafraid—and strong enough—to show our vulnerability, to name our weaknesses and own our limitations. We can ask for help, admit we may be out of our league and that we can't do it alone. Here's a story that so powerfully demonstrates this paradox, how a man's incredible strength almost prevented him from healing his trauma and moving into growth. I've already talked about Stella in Chapter 9, the young girl whose mother died of a brain tumor. This is the story of her father, Diego.

When his wife was first diagnosed, Diego did everything he could to find a treatment that would save her. Despite his efforts, she died within the year. He and Stella were devastated. In their own grief, his wife's family blamed him and tried to take Stella away from him. He fought hard to keep her, and he won. Although he was deeply grieving, he focused all his strength and attention on Stella, making sure she was okay. They began therapy together and created a routine of rituals to soothe each other. They built an altar for her mother, which they filled with some of her favorite things; several photos of her and also of them as a family, Stella's stuffed animals and special crystals. They created a dedicated corner in the house where they would sit together and tell stories about their lives before the tragedy, laughing about things they remembered, admitting how much they missed her. They would cry a lot together. In the beginning, our sessions were heart-wrenching.

In time, Diego felt that they would benefit from moving to a new, bigger community where Stella could make more friends and they wouldn't feel so isolated. The community embraced them both and Stella felt welcomed at her new school. Diego was so proud of the progress Stella was making and the way that she was working through her grief and trauma. He seemed to be doing okay, too. He even remarried.

Not long after they moved into their new family's home, however, Diego fell apart. He had been focused on everyone else and hadn't allowed himself to work through his own grief. There were plenty of times he would express his sadness, but then he'd push his feelings aside and keep going. He had to be strong for his daughter, his parents, and the rest of his family. He had a new life now, in a wonderful community, with a loving family. Stella was happier than he had seen her in years and yet . . . he was, as he told me, "broken in ways [he] hadn't even been aware of until now." He finally accepted that he needed help. During our time together, he's been working on embracing his vulnerability, asking for what he needs, and being patient and gentle with himself. In admitting his vulnerability, he has found his new personal strength. He's choosing to use this new superpower to help other families grappling with chronic illnesses navigate the often complicated health-care system, something he's well equipped to do thanks to his personal experience and his professional background.

MEANINGFUL RELATIONSHIPS

In this stage, relationships become more nurturing and mean-ingful; we deepen them by being more present, kinder, and more compassionate in our interactions with others. We pri-oritize more meaningful connections and more emotionally intimate conversations. We see synergies—things that bring us together—rather than focusing on our differences or what keeps us apart. We relish relationships that are co-creative and loving, in which there's a shared bond of trust and comfort. This can often help us love without expecting so much in return.

Turns out that relationships are indeed the key to our growth and our happiness. As my friend Esther Perel, psy-chotherapist and author of *Mating in Captivity*, says, "The quality of our relationships determines the quality of our life." It's not how many books you have in your library, how many awards you receive for the work you do, where you live or how smart you are. It's the attention you pay to the relationships you have. Not just with your families, studies suggest, but the long-lasting friendships you nurture. People who have authentic, loving relationships have a higher prob-ability of living longer and being happier.

A longitudinal study conducted through Harvard Univer-sity bore this out. Beginning in 1938, researchers gathered tens of thousands of pages on the more than seven hundred men they tracked in their study. The results confirmed that "good relationships make us happier and healthier," according to Robert Waldinger, a psychiatry professor at Harvard Medical School and the lead researcher of the study. He emphasized the fact it's the quality and the closeness of those relationships, not just that we have them. It turns out, as he says, that "people who are more socially connected to family, to friends, to community are happier, they're physically healthier and they live longer than people who are less well connected."

By this point you have let go of relationships that no longer work. They may have stopped working because you're different now, barely recognizable as your old self. As author Joan Didion would say, "I have already lost touch with a couple of people I used to be." Maybe they don't work because they've run their course and there's nothing more to say; maybe you've let them go because they remind you of your past in a way that doesn't honor your growth and transformation. Regardless of the reason, you know that life is too short and precious to waste time on superficial relationships with people who don't value connection. You feel the difference between past friendships that caused you harm—and launched your nervous system into a fight-flight-freeze-fawn response—and the new ones that have a calming effect on your whole body. Instead of fighting now, you are kinder and more patient. Instead of fleeing, you stay put, listen, and respond. Instead of freezing, you communicate openly and honestly. Instead of fawning, you enter into the relationship without the need to placate or please the other person, and you set healthy boundaries.

At this stage, we only want relationships that provide a sense of belonging—a family, a group, or a tribe—in a way that we feel heard, supported, and held. That might mean we connect with others who've had similar experiences they are willing to share, and we can support them with our understanding and presence. When we know the role each person—and the group as a whole—plays in our lives, we can meet them fully, as equals, without falling into old patterns of reactivity. We are no longer afraid of losing ourselves in these relationships—nor are we willing to do that. We know who we are, we value ourselves, and we can stay connected with our true essence in the process. In fact, I find patients in this stage can be more authentically themselves without apology and are better at setting boundaries while leaving room for flexibility.

I remember talking with a group of women who had endured horrific losses when the Surfside building in Miami collapsed. They told me that before their experiences, when someone's spouse or parent died, they would say all the things they were taught to say: *It must be so hard. I'm so sorry for your loss. Call me if there's anything I can do.* Now that they have gone through such heartache, they're not interested in empty clichés. They want relationships that allow them to speak authentically, speak the truth from the heart. They know what loss feels like and what they needed when they were in such pain. The wisdom that came out of their experience has shown them the way to respond more compassionately and empathically.

We are building stronger and more intimate relationships in part because we know what it feels like to be lost and alone. We want to connect; we no longer feel we have anything to hide. We are connecting in ways that will allow us to be ourselves without being judged or dismissed and to show up for others in the same way. We want honest discussions with people who are interested in speaking the truth with kindness and compassion. When that happens, we know we can listen with more empathy because we are no longer hearing what they have to say through the lens of our trauma. We clear our minds, set aside our own thoughts, feelings, and reactions, and commit our full attention to the person in front of us.

Rita and Ryan, whom we first met in Chapter 8, understand how a relationship can get lost and how a whole new relationship, one that is stronger and more intimate, can emerge by committing fully and lovingly to the process. After Rita learned that Ryan had been having an ongoing affair, they started couples therapy and realized after several sessions that the way they were functioning as a couple was not working. They needed to learn who they were separately and who they were together. They were willing to do the work.

Today they don't deny what they have gone through, but they also acknowledge how much they have grown as a couple *because* of it. They understand each other's fears and past trauma. They're able to be there for each other, communicate their needs, and be more present during conflicts. Today they have made a fresh start, created a new covenant between them, which has opened up space for them to truly listen to each other and to spend time together, not because they have to, but because they want to.

A DEEPER SPIRITUAL CONNECTION

We have embraced the gift of connection while moving through the stages of posttraumatic growth. We have awakened to the realization that we are interconnected to the web of life. You matter and you are not alone. You are a part of everything, and everything lives within you. You have experienced the power of unconditional love—both by giving it freely and by receiving it gracefully. And you have found wisdom within your suffering that you feel called to share with others.

To be clear, this has nothing to do with institutional religion; in fact, spirituality and religion are very distinct concepts. Spirituality is not a scripted set of beliefs that comes from an outside source. It's an overwhelming sense of union with everything, a feeling that we belong to something much bigger than ourselves. And in embracing such deep interconnection, we begin to act in ways that unite instead of divide. I love what Buddhist monk and revered teacher Thich Nhat Hanh said:

> If you can see the nature of interbeing between you and the other person, you can see that his suffering is your own suffering, and your happiness is his own happiness. With this way of seeing, you speak and act differently. This in itself can relieve so much suffering.

Lisa Miller is a clinical psychologist and the author of *The Awakened Brain* who has researched extensively on the genetic connection between the brain and spirituality. Her understanding of spiritual connection aligns with mine. She defines spirituality as a "moment of deep connection with another being or in nature. A feeling of awe or transcendence. An experience of startling synchronicity. Feeling held or inspired by something greater than yourself."

To be spiritually awakened means to enter into a state of being where we are connected with ourselves, with others, and with the world in a very conscious way. This connection envelops us, and we feel it within us and all around us. We may understand higher consciousness as spirit, universal consciousness, nature, or a unified force field. We may feel this connection in our everyday lives as we embrace a deeper sense of purpose in the world, and vow to lift others up with our presence, our actions, and our love. We may feel it through intergenerational ties, as we receive the wisdom of our ancestors, and work to transcend their struggles and pass on their gifts. Its presence is our future, as we pass on the wisdom we've gained from our own experiences to our descendants, those who will come after us, and work to stop the trauma cycle from repeating. And finally, it is all around us, as we are lovingly interconnected to our family, friends, and community, those who care for us as well as those who challenge us.

Finding meaning in suffering. Spirituality is an integral part of posttraumatic transformation, and without it we are more likely to fall back into pain. I wasn't always sure about that. Years ago, when I started doing this work, I thought it was enough for my patients to accept their trauma and begin to repair their lives, reconstructing a core set of beliefs that would help them put the pieces of their lives back together and move on. But I saw that the change wasn't solid or long lasting. Something was missing. What if they could find the *meaning* within their suffering, the wisdom in the wound? What if they could see what their experience had to teach them?

I was pleasantly surprised when many of my patients were willing to explore such philosophical and existential questions about themselves and about life. I asked them things like "How do you understand what's happened to you on an existential level?" "What keeps you going?" "What do you believe in?" Some told me that they never really thought about what they believed in or what really mattered or what they felt most connected to, especially when it came to spirituality. And no one ever really asked them those questions before. It was oddly freeing, they said, to get underneath the pain and understand their trauma in a different way. It was hard, but they were able to articulate those feelings and see the spiritual connection and association. They had spent so long feeling isolated and alone in that experience that the realization they were part of something bigger than themselves was incredibly liberating.

We experience transcendence, or spirituality, in many aspects of our lives. Some people find a sense of peace and unity through meditation, prayer, being in nature, or reading poetry or spiritual texts. Others feel unmitigated joy at being alive, spontaneously choosing activities that delight their senses. And still others lose themselves in art, music, or sports. We all become one with the experience, absorbed in the moment.

Frida Kahlo, the fierce and passionate Mexican artist, is someone whose life and work have always inspired me. When she was young, she wanted to study medicine, but a horrific accident in a streetcar shattered her spine and crushed other parts of her body, and school was out of the question. Unable to move for months after undergoing multiple operations, she admitted that she had always wanted to be an artist. She had a contraption built above her bed so that she could paint lying down and began to produce powerful works of art that depicted both her broken body (the trauma) and her likeness as a whole, strong, and beautiful woman (her transformation). She absorbed herself completely in her art. She once said, "I paint my own reality. The only thing I know is that I paint because I need to, and I paint whatever passes through my head without any other consideration."

Synchronicity. When we're deeply connected and awakened to what's happening within us and around us, we see synchronicities everywhere. These are not so much coincidences, but rather seemingly uncanny things that happen as the result of being open, sensitive, and attentive to the wider associations you are manifesting. For example, by the time Stella was fourteen, and had been moving through the stages of posttraumatic growth, she told her father she wanted him to remarry. Not just to anyone, however. She told me she visualized him marrying a kind woman who also had daughters and dogs because she wanted older sisters and she loved nothing more than taking care of animals. The odds were hardly in her favor and yet . . . that's exactly what ended up happening. By seeing our lives as more than a series of single, isolated events, we see things through a wider lens, and we see continuity instead of fragmentation.

The science of spirituality. I know that talking about being spiritual and experiencing a sense of interconnection can seem mystical and esoteric. But, in fact, the connection between spirituality and mental health has been extensively studied and tested through multiple approaches. Indeed, there's evidence to suggest that spirituality actually develops as a *result* of struggle.

Dr. Miller describes an interesting finding from her ongoing research with fourteen- to twenty-six-year-olds. She and her team discovered that those who had strong personal spirituality by the time they reached twenty-six were two and a half times more likely to have been depressed in the past. In other words, Dr. Miller writes, "spiritual formation doesn't seem to be an *alternative* to depression so much as a way of being that emerges alongside or through struggle." Even more striking, she notes, "those who had strong spirituality by age twenty-six were 75 percent protected against a recurrence of major depression for the next ten years." In other words, spirituality develops as a result of major trauma. Furthermore, once the brain is awakened, spirituality is also awakened and becomes a protective factor in future depression and traumatic symptoms, making us 80 percent less likely to suffer depression.

Dr. Miller goes on to describe how we are actually neurologically programmed to "awaken, expand, and transform through trauma." She says it shows up in three distinct areas of the brain: the ventral attention network, where we see that the world is alive and talking to us; the frontotemporal network, where we feel the warm, loving embrace of others and of life itself; and the parietal lobe, where we know that we matter, belong, and are never alone.

What I know to be true from my own experiences and those of my patients—and what Dr. Miller's neurological research confirms—is that we all have within us the capacity for spiritual connection; that we are hardwired to listen to and receive what the universe is telling us, to be able to give and receive love, and to belong to something bigger than ourselves. And all of that has the power to transform our lives and to heal our traumatic past. Spiritual awareness is something that lives within us always. It's our job to remember—

and to know that it is a powerful protective factor that will help us stay connected to what is true and meaningful in our journey through posttraumatic growth.

In working with Alejandro, the young man who survived a school shooting, and his family, something truly remarkable happened. Alejandro's father, whose own trauma in the aftermath of the shooting was immense, had a profound spiritual awakening. He told me that it pains him to see how much his son is still suffering, and yet he feels so much compassion for the young man who shot him. Out of his own pain came the realization that the young man must have also been suffering horribly to have murdered so many people. He faced the shooter at the trial, wanting to understand what would drive a fifteen-year-old kid to do something so terrible. Alejandro's father continues to be on a mission to connect with parents of teenagers in hopes of preventing that from ever happening again.

LOVING KINDNESS MEDITATION

When we realize we are all interconnected, we understand we have a responsibility not only to heal our own suffering, but also to ease the pain of others. We can do so by offering this loving kindness meditation as part of our daily practice. According to the Buddhist tradition, we offer kindness and compassion not only for ourselves and those we love, but also for those we struggle with. Here is a typical loving kindness meditation; feel free to add any other statements that resonate with you.

To begin, sit in a comfortable position and set an intention to practice with a full heart and without judgment. Spend a few minutes simply breathing naturally, visualizing a time when you felt really happy and at ease. And now silently say the following statements:

> May I be filled with loving kindness
>
> May I feel peaceful
>
> May I feel safe and protected from harm
>
> May I be healthy and happy

Repeat this prayer over and over again for several minutes, feeling as though you were held in loving kindness.

Next repeat the prayer three more times, first for someone you love with all your heart; second for someone your feel neutral about; and third someone you really struggle with or dislike intensely. In each case, substitute the word "you" for "I." As you bring each person to mind, see if you can hold them in your heart with tenderness, as you offer them this prayer. It may not always be easy—especially for the person you struggle with—but that's okay. It may, in time, grow easier. Keep at it.

PURPOSE AND MEANING

This pillar of posttraumatic growth is the culmination of all the struggles we've been through, all the work we've done, all the wisdom we have received. Everything we have experienced has brought us to this moment of true connection to ourselves, to others, and to the world. We see life with more clarity, we relish meaningful relationships, and we know we're connected to a higher power. We are more at peace with who we are. We are more conscious of our role in the world, and we have a responsibility to create more conscious connection, to use our gifts for the benefit of others, and to make the world a more compassionate, more inclusive place. We can no longer stay small. We have a higher purpose: our mission in the world becomes clearer.

Our pain, the very thing we have healed from, fuels our purpose. As I often tell my patients, it becomes our "superpower." For example, if someone was bullied as a kid because they were a weak and vulnerable target, they may make it their mission to ensure that no one else is *ever* bullied again. They may advocate for those who are vulnerable, they might even create services or opportunities for bullies to get help with their traumas. In other words, we are invited to ask ourselves this question: How do the struggles from our trauma inspire us to make a difference in our own world?

My cousin Debbie's personal journey through grief demonstrates how someone's superpower can lead to a life committed to selfless service. Here's her story in her own words:

My father, a strong man, hardworking, visionary and entrepreneur as well as an inveterate dreamer, romantic poet, and lover of life, died on Yom Kippur, the holiest day on the Jewish calendar. I don't know how I would have felt if he left any other day of the year, but for some strange reason, knowing that it was that particular day and not another, leads me to think he was not only an extraordinary and special being for me, but the universe also recognized him as such.

Exactly one year later, I lost my mother to a long and terrible illness. My mother, a woman who gave everything for her family, a being of light, with a pure heart and an advanced soul; a woman of few words, but the right words. My best friend, my adviser, my conscience. The one that taught me to believe in humanity, not to lose hope, and that good always triumphs.

The physical loss of my bastions, the beings I have loved the most, left, as expected, a great emptiness. This emptiness, impossible to describe, gave me the strength to create ShirAnit, a nonprofit organization that helps people after the loss of a loved one, during the first seven days of mourning. Being there for others has given me a new purpose. Honoring my parents has become my life mission. Seeing them, through my actions, through the lessons they instilled in me, is my way of keeping them alive. The emptiness is still there, but the pure and eternal Love that unites us is the engine that drives me to move on, to be a better person and to continue with a legacy.

The depth of Debbie's grief moved her to figure out a way to ease the pain of others who had lost people they loved. So she founded ShirAnit, which supports families who are going through the mourning process, known in the Jewish tradition as shiva. She and her volunteers prepare people's homes for the weeklong ritual, including setting up the space, organizing everything according to tradition, sometimes preparing and bringing the food, and, on occasion, even sitting with the mourners. Debbie says it's been a powerful way to stay spiritually connected to her parents and, at the same time, give back to her community. And truly, she's a testament to what happens when we make our work in the world an integral part of our spiritual practice.

It is not unusual for my patients who have endured great suffering to tell me they are grateful for what they went through. In fact, they often say they wouldn't change a thing, that they wouldn't be who they are today without the traumatic experiences they were once convinced would destroy them. Even as they mourn their losses, they can hold the realization that their pain has allowed them to be reborn into something new. Their pain has given them the purpose and meaning they've been searching for.

A few years ago, a tragedy in a neighborhood close to mine became the catalyst that allowed a family and an entire community to heal. Two teenagers were out riding their bikes near their house when a car came around the corner, striking the younger one. He was rushed to the hospital, where he lingered for a couple of days before he died from his injuries.

Hundreds of kids held a vigil outside of his window. They lit candles and took turns stepping up to the window holding signs they had made to express their hope and their love. They sang songs to him, prayed together, and held one another. And then he died. The whole town was devastated. He loved music more than anything, so the school created a music festival in his honor. Several of the kids came to see me and shared their grief, and also told me how much they loved him and how much they learned from him. They said things like, "We appreciate life so much more. We've organized ourselves in different ways; we've become better friends with one another; we're now helping other children, tutoring them in school and teaching them to play new instruments and organizing musical events."

His mother has turned her pain into her purpose by supporting other women who have gone through similar experiences. At the same time, she continues to grieve the loss of her son. Some days, she says she can barely get out of bed; other days she's going out into the community, speaking to other parents, sharing her own wisdom as well as her grief.

Tedeschi says that our suffering becomes tolerable because there's now a point to it, a raison d'être for all we've been through. It doesn't mean that our pain goes away or that we minimize the impact of our past experiences. It just means if we can find our purpose within the pain, we didn't suffer in vain. The most profound way to make meaning out of our suffering is to take the wisdom we gained and use it to serve others. In this pillar of purpose and meaning, we are taking the work we've done within ourselves and moving it out into the world in a more conscious and compassionate way. We are more aligned with who we are and what we want. This alignment may reveal itself in all sorts of different ways. But the bottom line is that the work of healing ourselves and our relationships is what changes the world; it's what fuels our desire to help others. We know how it feels to suffer and we want to do whatever we can to make sure no one else has to go through such pain. Out of our particular brokenness comes the medicine of compassion we can offer others.

Early on in the book, I introduced María, from the Dominican Republic, whose father sold her to a *brujo*, an old sorcerer, when she was nine years old. The old man took her away, drugged her, and then violently raped her. The physical torture she endured was so grave that it severely damaged her internally. The emotional toll on her was even more devastating, as she describes in her memoir, *I Say No More* (*Yo Digo No Más*). Although it took her many years of therapy, María vowed that her experience would not be in vain, that she would use it as a vehicle to help other women. What gave her the strength and determination to make meaning from such suffering? The birth of her son, who she felt could become "an accidental victim" of her trauma. Here's how she describes it:

> From the moment I became a mother, I made the decision to overcome the toxic residue of my childhood experience. I would stop regretting the past and worrying about the future so I could enjoy the present. I decided to change my role from victim to protagonist and to become the heroine of my own story. I chose to release criticism and opt for recognition; to shun excuses and focus on my purpose, not my problems; and to find the gift or lesson in each situation to make every moment a worthwhile memory. I wanted to take control of my life and rewrite my painful story as one of triumph and realization.
>
> The journey did not happen overnight, and certainly not on a direct or well-paved path. I have encountered storms and reefs as well as moments of smooth sailing. The only constant was that I never stopped moving forward. I continued growing and always aspired to reach

further. My original goal was to overcome my trauma and nourish my personal growth. It was a personal challenge for me, with the specific purpose of healing myself in order to properly raise and educate my children.

Out of that original purpose—to stop the cycle of abuse from being passed on to her children—came an even broader mission to ensure that no other woman would have to endure such abuse alone, that there would always be services for those who needed them. As part of that promise, she co-created the Formé Medical Center in New York, which provides services primarily to the vulnerable Hispanic community, especially those who are undocumented immigrants living in the United States. And more recently, she created the #YoDigoNoMás movement, which includes an online platform to provide a safe space for women and men to break their silence and tell their stories of abuse.[1]

We all know many people like María, who have not only advocated for themselves but become vocal champions for others. The list is endless. Black mothers, in particular, have turned their immense pain into action many times over. Sybrina Fulton is one of them. Not long after her son, Trayvon Martin, a seventeen-year-old high school student, was gunned down while walking in his father's Miami neighborhood, Sybrina became an activist, determined to change minds, hearts, and laws so that no other mother would have to bear such unbearable pain. She knew she couldn't stay quiet in her grief. She said, "It took my son being shot down to make me stand up."

Initially Trayvon was Sybrina's sole focus, but she soon discovered that her mission was "so much bigger than Trayvon." She founded the Trayvon Martin Foundation, which focuses on issues around gun violence, African American youth empowerment, and family support. She also hosts an annual Circle of Mothers weekend in Florida, in which a hundred or more mothers from across the country who have lost children or family members to gun violence come together to heal "mind, body and soul . . . We laugh together, we cry together, we hug together . . . You don't have to know each other to do that; we have compassion. I'm not saying that guys don't, but it's easier for us to heal as a group."

Going Forward

Posttraumatic growth is certainly not an easy road to navigate and it's anything but linear. I see the entire five-stage process as a spiral, inviting us to move up and down the helix as life presents us with challenges and opportunities to heal and transform. You may, for example, have gotten to this stage after years of working through your childhood trauma, only to have something else cause you to fall apart and make you feel like you're back to square one. That's okay. The presence of growth does not mean the absence of pain. But it does mean we feel capable enough to face our suffering. We know we can do this because we've done it before, because now we feel more connected to a support system. We have the relationships; we have a sense of belonging with ourselves and others. Once we've experienced wisdom and growth, we have more tools at our disposal to meet our trauma and transcend it.

There's a saying in the Buddhist tradition, often attributed

FINDING YOUR LIFE PURPOSE

Ikigai is an ancient Japanese framework for helping you integrate your passion and talents with your purpose in a sustainable and meaningful way. Ikigai has no literal translation, but according to Yukari Mitsuhashi, it is essentially "the reason you get up in the morning," it's what brings you happiness in life.[2] Everyone has their own ikigai, as Tim Tamashiro explains in *How to Ikigai*. But it does require time, effort, and a commitment to self-reflection and self-discovery to find it for yourself. Here are some questions to consider as you embark on this journey:

What do you like to do the most in life?

What brings you the most pleasure or satisfaction?

What is the capacity you have that comes easy to you or that you are very good at it?

What is your special talent that people notice all the time?

What is the world in need of right now?

What do you think you could do that you could be of service and make money doing?

to the Buddha himself: *Pain is inevitable, but suffering is optional.* We can choose how to respond. In the final chapter, we'll take a look at several factors that can protect us from falling back into old trauma responses and ways of implementing them.

HOW YOU CAN TELL YOU HAVE PTG

1. Do you feel you have grown because of your trauma experience?

2. Are you able to enjoy the small things in life?

3. Do you have a clearer sense of what your priorities are?

4. Do you feel that your relationships are becoming more intimate and meaningful?

5. Have you begun to take any risks to explore other possibilities in your life?

6. Have you rewritten the story of your life?

7. Are you finding yourself to be more spiritually connected or aware?

8. Do you find more meaning in your life or have you found your life purpose?

9. Have you scored a 47 or above on the Posttraumatic Changes Questionnaire (see page 285)?

Chapter 12

Staying Elevated

When you come out of the storm, you won't be the same person who walked in; that's what this storm is all about.
—HARUKI MURAKAMI

The work we have done to transform our lives and transcend the pain of our past has irrevocably changed us. We have emerged stronger in the broken places, like an exquisite piece of kintsugi pottery; we have become more beautiful because of our wounds, more conscious, awake, and connected to everything around us. Our work now is to continue to commit fully to the process, to find ways to stay curious and open and to keep moving and growing—in other words, to stay elevated.

Just because we've gone through this amazing journey of growth and awareness doesn't mean we'll never experience trauma again. The road map that has led us into the Promised Land of posttraumatic growth is not linear, nor is it sequential. It is deeply personal and unique to each of us. Sometimes we lose our way and instead of moving forward, our path circles around and we find ourselves heading back to where we started. We may have successfully dealt with and healed our trauma from a heart-wrenching divorce, for example, but never worked on the resentment we felt after being fired from our job.

Posttraumatic growth doesn't mean that we won't face *new* obstacles and challenges either, or that, in facing them, we won't feel frightened or sad or challenged in some way. Suffering is part of the human experience, and nothing can shield us from future heartbreak. We can heal and grow from our experiences in a war-torn country, for example, but fall completely apart when a car crash claims the life of someone we love.

How can posttraumatic growth make us stronger and more resilient and yet leave us so vulnerable to pain? First of all, we can hold both of these truths simultaneously: that we are forever transformed, *and* that life is messy and unpredictable, which makes healing from trauma a process we must continually tend to. There's one more very important truth: Having gone through the stages of posttraumatic growth, we know beyond a doubt that growth after trauma is possible—and that we have what we need to make it happen. We also know that the process has its own timetable, that we can't rush it—if we try to move too quickly, we risk being re-traumatized.

The tools we've already accumulated on our transformative journey have become our permanent internal allies; protective factors that help us maintain the growth that has awakened our innate power of transformation. The key to such transformation is *conscious connection* in every aspect of our lives. Every single one of these protective factors plays a part in this connection. We feel connected to ourselves—to personality traits we've developed and nurtured, which allow us to be more open, flexible, and curious; connected to others—our families (biological or chosen), our friends and communities, our culture and our ancestors; and connected to something greater than ourselves—nature or a higher consciousness perhaps—that allows us to see the interconnectedness of all beings.

Sustaining Factors

These characteristics are the same ones I see repeatedly in my patients who have gone through PTG, although there are certainly others. They continue to sustain and protect a growth state and help us in staying elevated: deliberate rumination; emotional intelligence; openness, flexibility, and adaptability; newfound resilience; maintaining spiritual awareness; maintaining community and a sense of belonging; and being of service, giving back to the community.

DELIBERATE RUMINATION

Even when you have gone through posttraumatic growth and come out stronger and more conscious, you can still get triggered by an old trauma response. You might hear a song that takes you back to an incident that happened a long time ago; you may have a chance encounter with someone who recently broke your heart; or you may smell a particular scent that reminds you of something you would rather forget. The good news is you now know how to meet those triggers and extract the wisdom and the lessons they are here to teach you. You can do this through deliberate or constructive rumination, a skill you've developed along the road to healing. A skill that allows you to work on an issue with the intention of finding meaning in the experience.

Several studies suggest that constructive rumination does indeed play an important role in staying in posttraumatic growth. Why? Because it can help you move through the problem and find solutions instead of getting stuck in repetitive or obsessive thought. Setting aside a specific time during your day allows you to think creatively about a particular problem or challenge with intention and purpose. In a 2006 study by Stephen Joseph and P. Alex Linley, they found that the more deliberate form of meaning-making gave people a way to look for the significance of what happened and its implications in their own lives.[1] Other studies suggest that the timing of this process is important because deliberate rumination doesn't really work too soon after the event. It does, however, lead to healing and growth when it happens later on as a means of self-reflection.

The role of gratitude. The most interesting studies showed that deliberate rumination has an even more powerful effect when it's combined with gratitude. Gratitude strengthens and reinforces the effects of deliberate rumination, and vice versa: deliberate rumination increases a sense of gratitude.

These studies seem to support the idea that people are often grateful for their experience no matter how awful it was, even years after it happened. They can understand and appreciate the benefits they've gained but still feel the pain. It goes beyond happiness to encompass a whole state of well-being. People who use rumination constructively, combined with gratitude after a traumatic experience, are much more likely to accept that such painful experiences are part of what it means to be human.

EMOTIONAL INTELLIGENCE

One of the ways we've been able to identify, meet, and heal our trauma is by developing a higher emotional intelligence, which is a way of contextualizing and making sense of our past experiences and learning from them. Emotional intelligence is a measure of how well we recognize, understand, and manage our emotions when we're stressed and overwhelmed; how we recognize and understand what other people are saying and feeling; and how we realize the impact our own emotions have on other people.

Studies confirm that our emotional intelligence is heightened as we move through growth, and our ability to manage our emotions helps us stay elevated. To stay elevated, we know how important it is to express our emotions as they're happening and not keep them stuck in our bodies. Through emotional intelligence we have a vocabulary to do that. Linley's study in 2011 showed that those who scored highest in emotional intelligence *and* expressed their emotions had the highest levels of growth.

Going forward, your high emotional intelligence can serve you well in a number of ways. First of all, greater emotional intelligence brings greater self-awareness, and a greater ability to assess a situation, which makes it easier to respond appropriately and not get triggered. Second, it gives you a tool to manage your inner dialogue. It can help you, for example, when you are going down the rabbit hole of negative self-talk and invite you to notice what you're feeling and make a decision to pause and recalibrate. It can also provide you with better problem-solving skills, according to a 2004 study led by Moshe Zeidner, psychology professor emeritus from the University of Haifa, without denying the existence of the problem itself or being carried away by the negative emotions it brings up. Finally, positive emotions or optimism, coupled with good supportive relationships, enhances your ability to thrive.

Our emotional intelligence helps us read other people's emotions, and recognize and understand what they're telling us, without projecting our own insecurities, judgments, or reactions onto them. We know how to pause, listen to what's being said, and notice the feelings behind the words (even when they're not so obvious), and then respond without reverting to old, pre-growth habits of blame and shame. Responding with more kindness and less judgment strengthens our connection to others and helps us meet them where they are.

OPENNESS, FLEXIBILITY, AND ADAPTABILITY

Some of the core beliefs we had about ourselves and the world before embarking on the journey toward growth have fallen away. We have consciously and deliberately broken free of what no longer works for us and have taken on a new identity. We've developed new ways of being in the world and we have no intention of going back to what we were before. Feeling comfortable in our own skin, knowing who we are— and, equally important, who we are not—has given us a sense of freedom to explore within a widening lens of curiosity and flexibility. When we embrace what Zen master Suzuki Roshi called a "beginner's mind," we are connected and awake to everything life has to offer, and open to the possibilities it has in store for us. People who have never thought of themselves as risk-takers, for example, may now try things they've never tried before. Those who have always felt awkward and shy have come out of their shell and connected with people in ways they never thought possible. Others have found their creative outlet and take great joy in painting, sewing, sculpting, dancing, writing—anything that awakens their imagination. These positive personality changes appear to be permanent. Not only that, but according to one study, they seem to make a difference in how people dealt with *future* challenges, including being less depressed and better able to gain mastery over the situation.

Being open, flexible, and adaptable continues to fuel your curiosity and your ability to go with the flow and be able to change gears when you need to. And it gives you a more positive and optimistic attitude about where you are now and what lies ahead. One study in 2014 measured positive personality changes in 256 college students. It showed that being optimistic, seeing the world and their place in it in a positive light, and having a strong sense of social connection all contribute to posttraumatic growth. In another study, researchers discovered that such personality changes are, in fact, enduring. They produce long-lasting changes in what and how we think, how we feel, and how we behave.

Everything you've discovered about yourself keeps you growing and your mind and heart expanding. You are more present and more adaptable to the changes and challenges of life. This "growth mindset" can profoundly awaken your intellect, your creativity, and your ability to give and accept friendship and love. When you believe in your ability to keep growing and learning, you can reach ever-higher levels of achievement in whatever you choose to do. Growing beyond your trauma has taught you that you have the power to transform, that you are capable of anything you set your mind and heart on, and that you have the strength, focus, and resilience to face whatever future challenges come your way.

NEWFOUND RESILIENCE

Resilience developed from posttraumatic growth is an important trait we've acquired as a result of all we've gone through. It's resilience *after* wisdom and growth, and it can help us stay elevated long after we've healed and grown from our traumas. It differs from the resilience we talked about earlier in the book, the kind of resilience people use to quickly adjust to adversity and to bounce back.

The road to posttraumatic growth doesn't start with resilience; instead, this form of resilience is something we develop; it emerges through our struggle as an outcome of the work we've done. It can be part of our personal strength: it gives us the sense that if we could survive this, we can survive anything. Richard Tedeschi defines posttraumatic growth resilience like this:

> One important relationship between resilience and posttraumatic growth comes after a person has been in the posttraumatic growth process for a while. When core beliefs are rebuilt in a better form, they are better able to withstand future traumas. Therefore, people who have a stronger set of core beliefs are becoming more resilient. We can, therefore, say that posttraumatic growth provides a pathway to resilience.

MAINTAINING SPIRITUAL AWARENESS

When we've experienced the fullness of our shared humanity, we see that there is no separation between ourselves and others. We feel their joys as well as their suffering, and it becomes impossible to turn away. We are all One. To believe otherwise, as Albert Einstein once said, is an "optical delusion of consciousness."

This heightened sense of spirituality, which we experience in posttraumatic growth, infuses every aspect of our lives and influences every action we take—from the way we care for ourselves and the generosity and tenderness we show toward the people in our lives, to the commitment we've made to fulfill our mission in life. As we discussed in the last chapter, maintaining a spiritual connection is one of the most powerful ways we can stay elevated, according to the research Dr. Lisa Miller headed up in the late 1990s. One study in particular showed that those who were highly spiritual and had gone through major depression in the past were *90 percent protected* against a recurrence of depression. They had, as Dr. Miller explains in her book, "cultivated a spiritual response."

What I found most interesting in the research were the specific *expressions* of spirituality that Dr. Miller and her team discovered could best protect us from present and future trauma: relational spirituality—practicing altruism and love of one's neighbor—and intergenerational transmissions of spirituality—the passing of the "the spiritual torch" specifically from mother or grandmother to daughter.

Relational Spirituality. Dr. Miller's studies suggest that when we connect with others, through acts of kindness and selfless service (altruism) or by loving our neighbor as ourselves (the proverbial Golden Rule), it produces thickness in the cortical brain (cerebral cortex), the part of the brain that processes emotional stimuli and is in charge of reasoning, planning, and mood. In fact, Dr. Miller believes that a spiritual brain is a healthy brain and that relational spirituality in particular may even be curative for depression. This resonates with the work I do because *all* trauma is relational and so is our healing journey through posttraumatic growth. I've certainly seen its effects on my patients' lives, especially those who were stuck in the paralyzing effects of their past. When I encouraged them to go do something helpful for someone in need, they were surprised at how even a simple act of altruism could shift their attention away from their own pain. As Leo Tolstoy famously said, "Kindness enriches our life; with kindness mysterious things become clear, difficult things become easy, and dull things become cheerful."

Intergenerational Transmission of Spirituality. The idea that the protective effects of spirituality can be passed down through the generations is especially fascinating. It begins with the understanding that humans are genetically inclined toward spirituality—and that it can protect us from depression and other trauma responses. In his book *The God Gene: How Faith Is Hardwired into Our Genes,* molecular biologist Dean Hamer explains that human spirituality has an innate genetic component to it, which "refers to the fact that humans inherit a predisposition to be spiritual."[2] Knowing that spirituality is innate allows us to cultivate the capacity to intentionally become more spiritual in our daily lives, connecting nature and nurture, biology and behavior.

Dr. Lisa Miller's own study showed that a child is 80 percent protected against depression when her spiritual life is shared with her mother.[3] In *The Awakened Brain,* she goes on to say that even with all other variables present for depression—the mother's depression, poverty, bad home environment, and a disorganized parenting style—intergenerational spirituality still held an 80 percent protective benefit. Intergenerational spirituality is a way that we stay connected on a deep level to the wisdom of our ancestors. In nurturing our spiritual practice, we are able to pass along that wisdom to our children and grandchildren, helping them to stay in posttraumatic growth as well.

MAINTAINING COMMUNITY AND A SENSE OF BELONGING

By now we know that we heal, grow, and transform in relationship. We know that trauma expands in isolation and shrinks in connection with others. We know we are relational beings, social beings who need human touch—not just physical, but emotional and intellectual as well—in order to thrive and grow. We are also spiritual beings, who understand that we are part of the larger web of life, and that we have a vital role to play in the world. We can celebrate and embrace our differences as well as our similarities and hold each other sacred.

This inner sense of oneness is a protective factor that makes you feel as though you're never alone. You can be in solitude and experience a deep connection to everything around you, to all of life and to everything that came before you. In fact, your alone times have taken on a greater significance—they give you opportunities to listen to your inner dialogue and, at the same time, experience what the outer world has to offer. A study led by Laura Marie Edinger-Schons, a researcher at the

University of Manheim, showed that people with a "higher sense of oneness" felt a greater sense of life satisfaction, which stayed with them long after the study was over. She wrote that these oneness beliefs "are much better predictors of life satisfaction than religious beliefs," and you can experience them in multiple ways—through being in nature, surfing, doing yoga, making music, being "in a state of flow."[4]

We often feel most supported when we're with family—either biological or chosen. We feel accepted and recognized; we can be ourselves in ways we can't with anyone else. Also, when we hang out with people with whom we resonate—those in our workplace, those in our tribe or community, and even those we occasionally cross paths with—we can feel supported, needed, and alive. Connection nourishes our growth. We see interconnections like this in nature all the time. For example, a lot has been written about the ways trees communicate and take care of one another. They are part of a social network in which they share information with each other that is important to the health of the whole forest. According to Suzanne Simard, professor of ecology at the University of British Columbia, they've also been known "to share nutrients at critical times to keep each other healthy," even across species.[5] Mother or "hub" trees take care of other trees through an interconnected network facilitated by the mycelium or fungi that live within the trees' root system. The mycelium, the threadlike vegetative portion of fungi, is a good example of a social colony. Its network is like a superhighway of vital information within the natural world, transferring the right nutrients to the right plants at the right time. These are beautiful examples of interconnectedness.

In our own lives, we also see a protective and nurturing

connection within communities. Town centers, farmers markets, cafés, music venues, and other public places offer opportunities to be part of a larger community and provide a sense of belonging that protects us from sliding backward into isolation.

There are many ways of consciously creating community or being an integral part of one. You may have a group of friends you only see on occasion and yet when you're with them you can be yourself in ways you can't with anyone else. You may belong to a community whose members share your cultural identity; another whose mission aligns with yours; or a spiritual or intentional community that meets to practice together and explore philosophical or existential questions. Often, when we're aligned with our purpose, we naturally gravitate toward others who have the same desire or intention—or they somehow find us and call us in. This gives us a sense of belonging that says, *I'm not alone in this* and *Together we can make a difference.*

There have been several studies that show the importance of family, social support, and connection for continuing posttraumatic growth. Some confirm the need to belong as a "fundamental human motivation"; others show that a decreased sense of belonging is associated with an increase in depression. Still others say that being socially connected increases longevity, decreases anxiety, and makes people more trusting and empathic.

It's important to keep in mind you don't have to be an extrovert, someone who has a full social calendar, to experience a sense of belonging. You can be shy or introverted by nature and still be connected to others, because connection is a felt sense, a bodily sensation, and sometimes a heart connection.

In an article in *Psychology Today,* Emma Seppälä, PhD, author of *The Happiness Track,* explains how that works:

> Researchers agree that the benefits of connection are actually linked to your subjective sense of connection. In other words, if you feel connected to others on the inside, you reap the benefits thereof!

Usually the sense of belonging isn't a one-way street. When we feel supported, heard, and loved within a community, we embrace the opportunity to support others in return.

BEING OF SERVICE, GIVING BACK

We stay in growth by being of service. It's nearly impossible to go through posttraumatic growth and not emerge with a longing to share with others what we've learned along the way. When we understand that there is no separation between ourselves and all other beings, we feel a responsibility to do what we can to alleviate the suffering of others. We resolve that no one else should experience the pain we've gone through, and our pain becomes our purpose. In turn, by helping others, we may feel more valued, more confident, and more optimistic about the world in which we live.

Transforming hearts and minds heals the world—and there are many ways to be in service to that goal. Depending on your mission—and your way of showing up in the world—you can choose to make your activism far-reaching and public by doing such things as creating nonprofits, organizing demonstrations, working with marginalized people, and speaking out publicly on an issue. There are so many inspiring examples of people within the pages of this book who have transformed their trauma into service. No matter how you get involved, your actions can also help you stay in a growth state.

While many people move into service in big, public ways, others turn their pain into purpose in more intimate, but no less impactful, ways. And when they do, their acts of kindness can spread well beyond their initial intention. These are the everyday heroes who show up for others when others can't show up for themselves. One young woman I know, a personal chef whose own turbulent childhood often left her wondering if there'd be enough money to buy food, is one of those helpers. She seems to intuit when someone's having a hard time or needs a little extra. You're not feeling well? She'll prepare and drop off your next three meals. You need to go somewhere? She'll drive you. She listens to what's underneath your words. Her generous spirit is both compassionate and action oriented.

When we notice the suffering in the world, we can consciously choose to put our intentions where we think we can do the most good. When we can do that—as mentors, teachers, therapists, friends, or family—the effect of our efforts is felt far beyond our circle of influence. We are changing the world.

We see examples of the ripple effect everywhere. Every time a young immigrant is welcomed into his new country by another family who had immigrated and is made to feel held and supported, both emotionally and financially. Every time a mentor or counselor helps a child find common ground with the other kids he's bullying. Every time a woman has successfully fled an abusive marriage and decides to provide services and support for other women who are still struggling.

Those whose lives they have changed pay it forward as their desire to help others grows stronger. So much of the focus on trauma has been the pain and suffering it inflicts, the collateral damage it leaves behind. All of this shows us, as one of my patients so wisely put it, that trauma also brings collateral beauty. The process of healing brings with it wisdom and growth and transformation, a deeper connection with ourselves, with others, and with the world.

This commitment to serving the greater good doesn't come from a sense of guilt or shame or because we have something to prove. It comes from a place of compassion and connection, a desire to make sense of our experiences. The key to staying elevated and continuing to grow after trauma is the commitment we make to be true to ourselves and to share our wisdom. Being authentic aligns us with our mission, which in turn may alleviate the suffering of others. And how do we do that? As Buddhist meditation teacher Ralph De La Rosa says, "Follow your heartbreak. Whatever has torn you down in this life, go offer your heart and hard work to people still caught there." That's when you know you are leading from the heart, practicing truly compassionate service.

In an era of emotional and social isolation, one exacerbated by the trauma of all sorts of pandemics, going through the stages of posttraumatic growth will allow each of us to be more intimately connected, to have a greater sense of belonging, to be more active in our community, to have a sense of purpose, and to give our relationships a higher priority. A new, more closely intertwined and conscious world is about to be born.

Posttraumatic Growth Inventory

Richard Tedeschi and Lawrence Calhoun developed the Posttraumatic Growth Inventory (PTGI) to assess the posttraumatic growth and self-improvement a person undergoes. A twenty-one-item scale built on the five-factor model of Tedeschi, this inventory is one of the most valid and reliable resources for evaluating personal growth following a stressful encounter.

The statements included in the inventory are related to the following five factors:

Factor I—**Relating to Others**
Factor II—**New Possibilities**
Factor III—**Personal Strength**
Factor IV—**Spiritual Enhancement**
Factor V—**Appreciation**

Each of the twenty-one items falls under one of the five factors and is scored accordingly. A summation of the scores indicates the level of posttraumatic growth.

The advantage of this scale is that the categorization of scores according to the five factors is suggestive of which area of self-development is predominant and which area might be a little behind.

For example, a high total score implies that the person has undergone a positive transformation. But a closer look at the scores of each section would provide a more in-depth insight into what has changed significantly and what aspects of the self may still need some improvement.

The PTGI was initially developed to measure favorable outcomes following a stressful life event. But with time, it became popular as a test that provides direction to the participants about their future actions and suggests a scope for self-improvement.

Where Can I Find the Scale?

As mentioned earlier, the PTGI consists of twenty-one statements, each coming under one of the five categories mentioned by Tedeschi and Calhoun in their initial proposition.

Participants indicate their scores on a six-point scale where:

- 0 implies—I did not experience this as a result of my crisis.
- 1 implies—I experienced this change to a very small degree as a result of my crisis.
- 2 implies—I experienced this change to a small degree as a result of my crisis.
- 3 implies—I experienced this change to a moderate degree as a result of my crisis.
- 4 implies—I experienced this change to a great degree as a result of my crisis.
- 5 implies—I experienced this change to a very great degree as a result of my crisis.

Here is an overview of the test items along with the categorization of the five factors.

Factor	Item Numbers
1—**Relating to Others**	6, 8, 9, 15, 16, 20, 21
2—**New Possibilities**	3, 7, 11, 14, 17, 18
3—**Personal Strength**	4, 10, 12, 19
4—**Spiritual Enhancement**	5
5—**Appreciation**	1, 2, 13

The Posttraumatic Growth Inventory

PTGI is widely available online. Below is an illustration of the form:

SCORING

0   1   2   3   4   5

1. I changed my priorities about what is important in life.
2. I have a greater appreciation for the value of my own life.
3. I have developed new interests.
4. I have a greater feeling of self-reliance.
5. I have a better understanding of spiritual matters.

6. I more clearly see that I can count on people in times of trouble.
7. I established a new path for my life.
8. I have a greater sense of closeness with others.
9. I am more willing to express my emotions.
10. I know that I can handle difficulties.
11. I can do better things with my life.
12. I am better able to accept the way things work out.
13. I can better appreciate each day.
14. New opportunities are available that wouldn't have been otherwise.
15. I have more compassion for others.
16. I put more effort into my relationships.
17. I am more likely to try to change things that need changing.
18. I have stronger religious faith.
19. I discovered that I'm stronger than I thought I was.
20. I learned a great deal about how wonderful people are.
21. I better accept needing others.

Psychological Well-Being
Posttraumatic Changes Questionnaire

By Stephen Joseph, PhD

Think about how you feel about yourself at the present time. Please read each of the following statements and rate how you have changed as a result of the trauma.

5 = Much more so now
4 = A bit more so now
3 = I feel the same about this as before
2 = A bit less so now
1 = Much less so now

1. I like myself.
2. I have confidence in my opinions.
3. I have a sense of purpose in life.
4. I have strong and close relationships in my life.
5. I feel I am in control of my life.
6. I am open to new experiences that challenge me.
7. I accept who I am, with both my strengths and limitations.
8. I don't worry what other people think of me.
9. My life has meaning.
10. I am a compassionate and giving person.

11. I handle my responsibilities in life well.
12. I am always seeking to learn about myself.
13. I respect myself.
14. I know what is important to me and will stand my ground, even if others disagree.
15. I feel that my life is worthwhile and that I play a valuable role in things.
16. I am grateful to have people in my life who care for me.
17. I am able to cope with what life throws at me.
18. I am hopeful about my future and look forward to new possibilities.

Add up your scores to all eighteen statements. Scores over 54 indicate the presence of positive change. The maximum score is 90. The higher your score, the more positive change you have experienced. You may have changed more in some areas than others: self-acceptance (statements 1, 7, and 13), autonomy (statements 2, 8, and 14), purpose in life (statements 3, 9, and 15), relationships (statements 4, 10, and 16), sense of mastery (statements 5, 11, and 17), and personal growth (statements 6, 12, and 18).

Acknowledgments

Like everything else in life, writing a book is a relational and collaborative project. It requires the collective intention and vision of a group of committed people. I am infinitely grateful to have had people like that along this journey with me.

I want to thank my agent, Jackie Ashton, who believed in me from the start. Jackie, I so appreciate your quiet, behind-the-scenes way of making everything happen with sensitivity and efficiency. I could not have asked for a kinder, more insightful editor than Sarah Pelz at HarperCollins. Thank you, Sarah, for all the ways you encouraged me to dig deeper and for all the insightful, spot-on edits you made. The whole team at HarperCollins has been amazing. Thank you, Emma Peters, for orchestrating the production tasks and keeping us all on track.

Thank you to my dear Linda Sparrowe, whose keen eye and exquisite sensitivity helped make this book come alive. I'm grateful for our collaboration and how you were able to patiently and lovingly guide me to find the right words to convey my message. You have been a true companion on this journey and a real friend.

The idea for this book started more than twenty years ago when I wrote my doctoral dissertation on posttraumatic growth. It took the Universe to align, the kids to grow up, and my practice to build before the book could begin to take shape. In those early days, I was fortunate to learn from and be mentored by some unforgettable teachers. Thank you to Carl Auerbach, whose guidance and belief in me as a young graduate student helped me believe in myself. I'm so grateful that your wisdom, patience, and support have continued unabated over the past twenty-five years. Thank you to Alvin Atkins at Montefiore and social worker Joyce Wong for introducing me to the Cambodian refugee community in the Bronx, a thriving example of posttraumatic growth. And thank you to the Cambodian people for trusting and sharing so openly with me. You taught me so much. Thank you, Kenneth Hardy, for being an amazing mentor. Your courage and unwavering dedication to breaking the cycle of trauma has inspired my own work.

I'm grateful for all the opportunities I have had to work with and learn from Jack Saul. Our time together at the Bellevue Program for Survivors of Torture and the ITSP in New York City was instrumental in both my understanding of trauma and my research into posttraumatic growth. Your insightful, unpretentious advice has continued to be valuable in so many ways. Thank you for your generosity, your willingness to listen, and your decades of friendship.

To Esther Perel, thank you for your friendship and inspiration over the years. I am grateful for the opportunity you gave me to speak to your community and expand on my understanding of collective trauma and collective healing. Many thanks to Laura Maciuika for showing me what it means to be an authentic mentor and introducing me to the foundations of trauma work; to Deborah Munczek, my cherished colleague and friend, for so many great conversations and for sharing your experiences with me; to Carolina Arbelaez, my dear sister, colleague, and writing companion since the beginning of time—the way you weave your wisdom into poetic expression never ceases to touch me; and to Claudia Edwards and all my spiritual mentors and guides, who have taught me how to connect most deeply to my heart.

I am forever grateful to my Happiness tribe: Valerie Freilich, Achim Novak, Juan Jose Reyes. Thank you for always being supportive, seeking the next adventure, expedition, creative exploration, taking us to the next level with shared discussions and new ideas. To Luis Gallardo, the Happiness visionary and conscious leader. Your words of encouragement, unconditional support, and humble mentoring kept me moving forward. Your vision is a true example of collective thinking and being.

Thank you to my splendid office team: The loyalty and dedication of Liliana Orozco, with her growing belly, listening to recordings, making videos, bringing resources, and getting excited about the book. The detailed work of Elizabeth Blanquel, translating hours of transcripts, managing social media, assisting with research. The constant support from Jose Vicente Sevilla, with his cameras and equipment, looking to capture the moment. To Gladys Socha, for taking care of me and my home so I can put all my dedication to the book.

To the brilliant Avi Jorish, thank you for showing me the way and helping with legal questions. To Daniel Orelus St Juste III, for visualizing the dream before it was a reality; you've given me so much strength and care in the process. To Daniza Tobar, editor Ann Sheybani, and Aleyso Bridger, thank you for believing in the early craft and intention of this book, encouraging me to keep going, and for connecting me to the right people at the right time. And to my talented, powerful, and creative friends Tammy, Debbie, and Ivonn, and Rachel and Sylvia: thank you for showing up time and again in so many ways.

This book could never have happened without the incredible teachings I have received from my patients. I'm forever grateful for the trust you have put in me. Your willingness to share your stories of pain and suffering and your commitment to healing and transforming inspires me every day. Witnessing your process keeps me believing that wisdom and growth are indeed possible.

To my family and my ancestors, with infinite gratitude for all you've given me. My grandparents, Lalu and Nana, for their unconditional love and for teaching me what it means to embody wisdom, embrace the hope, and keep it alive. My mom and dad, for always being examples of strength and resilience in life. Thank you for giving me opportunities and privileges that allowed me to nurture my curiosity in life and take risks. To my son, Ariel, for being a teacher, my teacher, a shining light and a constant source of inspiration. You continue to show me what's truly possible by being and living with love and integrity. You are a beacon of light.

My father passed away during the time I was writing this book. There is nothing more painful than losing the ones we love *and* nothing more powerful than the community coming together, feeding each other, hugging, and listening to each other's stories. I had the privilege of healing from pain within the strength and nurturance of such community. I shall forever be indebted to family, childhood friends, and those who came from all over the world to support me and my family. A true testament to the healing power that lies within the center of the collective.

May this book be of benefit, somehow touch the lives of others and alleviate their suffering.

References

CHAPTER 2: THE TRAUMA OF EVERYDAY LIFE

1. For more information on the history of trauma, see Judith Herman's book *Trauma and Recovery* (New York: Basic Books, 1992).

2. Ibid.

3. Lisa Firestone, "Recognizing Complex Trauma," *Psychology Today*, July 31, 2012.

4. David Sack, MD, "8 Reasons It's So Hard to Overcome a Tough Childhood," *Psychology Today*, March 12, 2015.

5. Pauline Boss, *Loss, Trauma, and Resilience* (New York: W. W. Norton, 2006).

6. For more information, see interview with Pauline Boss, "Navigating Loss Without Closure," by Krista Tippett, *On Being*, July 2020, and *Ambiguous Loss: Learning to Live With Unresolved Grief* by Pauline Boss (Harvard University Press, 2000).

7. For more on the benefits of stress, see *The Upside of Stress: Why Stress Is Good for You and How to Get Good at It*, by Kelly McGonigal, PhD (New York: Avery Publications, 2015).

CHAPTER 3: WHAT IS POSTTRAUMATIC GROWTH?

1. Lindsay VanSomeren, "How Do Caterpillars Turn Into Butterflies and Moths Through Metamorphosis?," UntamedScience.com, October 2016.

2. Richard G. Tedeschi et al., *Transformed by Trauma: Stories of Post-traumatic Growth* (self-pub., 2020).

3. Ralph De La Rosa, *Don't Tell Me to Relax* (Boulder, CO: Shambhala, 2020).

4.   Harold S. Kushner, *When Bad Things Happen to Good People* (New York: Anchor Books, 2004).

CHAPTER 4: FLOATING FACTORS

1.   Emmy Werner and Ruth Smith, "The Children of Kauai: Resiliency and Recovery in Adolescence and Adulthood," *Journal of Adolescent Health* 13 (June 1992): 262–68, https://doi.org/10.1016/1054 -139x(92)90157-7.

2.   Namiko Kamijo and Shintaro Yukawa, "The Role of Rumination and Negative Affect in Meaning Making Following Stressful Experiences in a Japanese Sample," *Frontiers in Psychology* 9 (November 28, 2018): 2404, https://doi.org/10.3389/fpsyg.2018.02404.

3.   Ibid.

4.   For more information on fixed and growth mindset, see *Mindset: The New Psychology of Success* by Carol Dweck (New York: Penguin Random House, 2016).

5.   From a panel discussion with Dan Siegel, Dr. Gabor Maté, UCLA researcher and social justice advocate Sará King, and Garrison Institute fellow Angel Acosta, "Building Intergenerational Trauma Sensitivity and Awareness," June 12, 2021, as part of *The Wisdom of Trauma* premiere.

CHAPTER 5: THE INTERGENERATIONAL LEGACY OF TRAUMA

1.   Christian Wolf, "Post-Traumatic Stress Disorder Can Be Contagious," *Scientific American,* October 3, 2018.

2.   Ibid.

3.   Daniel Goleman is quoted in "Relationship Trauma: How Does Emotional Pain from Childhood Get Played Out in Adulthood," by Dr. Tian Dayton, *HuffPost,* July 21, 2008. See also Dr. Dayton's *Emotional Sobriety* (Deerfield Beach, FL: Health Communications, 2007).

4.   Jillian Peterson and James Densley, "How Columbine Became a Blueprint for School Shooters," *The Conversation,* April 17, 2019. Also, see "Thresholds of Violence: How School Shootings Catch On," by Malcolm Gladwell, *The New Yorker* (Oct. 12, 2015)

5.   Youth ALIVE!, "Trauma Is the Virus: Violence as a Public Health Issue," www.youthalive.org, April 19, 2017.

6.   For a more in-depth discussion of this topic see *Teens Who Hurt: Clinical Interventions to Break the Cycle of Teenage Violence* by Kenneth Hardy (New York: Guilford Press, 2005) and his article "Healing the Hidden Wounds of Racial Trauma," *Reclaiming Children and Youth* 22, no. 1 (Spring 2013): 24–28.

7.   Ibram X. Kendi, "Post-Traumatic Slave Syndrome Is a Racist Idea," *Black Perspectives,* www.aaihs.org, June 21, 2016.

8.   Rachel Yehuda's research is explained in "Study of Holocaust Survivors Finds Trauma Passed On to the Children's Genes," by Helen Thomson, *The Guardian,* August 21, 2015.

9.   Patricia Dashorst et al., "Intergenerational Consequences of the Holocaust on Offspring Mental Health: A Systemic Review of Associated Factors and Mechanisms," *European Journal of Psychotraumatology* 10, no. 1 (August 2019): 1654065, https://doi.org/10.108 0/20008198.2019.1654065.

10.   Amrit Shrira, Ravit Menashe, and Moshe Bensimon, "Filial Anxiety and Sense of Obligation among Offspring of Holocaust Survivors," *Aging and Mental Health* 23, no. 6 (June 2019): 752–61, https://doi .org/10.1080/13607863.2018.1448970.

11.   Amy J. Sindler, Nancy S. Wellman, and Oren Baruch Stier, "Holocaust Survivors Report Long-Term Effects on Attitudes toward Food," *Journal of Nutrition Education and Behavior* 36, no. 4 (July–August 2004): 189–96, https://doi.org/10.1016/S1499-4046(06)60233-9.

12.   Irit Felsen, "'The Canary in the Mine': Re-traumatization and Resilience in Offspring of Holocaust Survivors During the Covid-19 Pandemic," *Trauma Psychology News,* November 13, 2020.

13.   Tirzah Firestone, *Wounds into Wisdom: Healing Intergenerational Jewish Trauma* (Rhinebeck, NY: Monkfish, 2019).

14.   Martin Caparrotta, "Dr. Gabor Maté on Childhood Trauma: The Real Cause of Anxiety and Our 'Insane' Culture," HumanMind .com, September 2020.

15.   Peter Nieman, "Shyness Not Necessarily a Lifelong Trait," *Calgary Herald,* December 14, 2017.

16.   Daniel Goleman and Richard Davidson, *Altered Traits: Science Re-*

veals How Meditation Changes Your Mind, Brain, and Body (New York: Avery, 2017).

17. "Epigenetic Patterns Determine If Honeybee Larvae Become Queens or Workers," *Science Daily,* August 22, 2018.

18. Krista Tippett, "How Trauma and Resilience Cross Generations," *On Being,* updated November 2017.

19. Tori Rodriguez, "Descendants of Holocaust Survivors Have Altered Stress Hormones," *Scientific American,* March 1, 2015.

20. Elysia P. Davis and Carl A. Sandman, "The Timing of Prenatal Exposure to Maternal Cortisol and Psychosocial Stress Is Associated with Human Cognitive Development," *Child Devleopment* 81, no. 1 (January/February 2010): 131–48, https://doi.org/10.1111/j.1467 -8624.2009.01385.x.

CHAPTER 6: FROM COLLECTIVE TRAUMA TO COLLECTIVE GROWTH

1. Jonathan Shay, MD, PhD, "Moral Injury," *Psychoanalytic Psychology,* 2014.

2. Diane Silver, "Beyond PTSD: Soldiers Have Injured Souls," *Pacific Standard,* January 2015 (rev).

3. Tirzah Firestone, *Wounds into Wisdom: Healing Intergenerational Jewish Trauma* (Rhinebeck, NY: Monkfish, 2019).

4. Oxiris Barbot, MD, "George Floyd and Our Collective Moral Injury," *American Journal of Public Health,* August 12, 2020.

5. From a panel discussion as part of *The Wisdom of Trauma* premiere entitled "The Wisdom of Trauma: Climate Crisis, Fragmentation, and Collective Trauma," with Dr. Gabor Maté, Eriel Tchekwie, Bayo Akomolafe, and Angaangaq Angaqkkoruaq. (Reprinted at www .indigenousclimateaction.com/entries/climate-crisis-fragmentation -amp-collective-trauma-discussion-with-eriel-deranger-bayo-akomo lafe-angaangaq-angakkorsuaw-and-gabor-mate).

CHAPTER 7: THE STAGE OF AWARENESS: RADICAL ACCEPTANCE

1. Salynn Boyles, "Posttraumatic Stress, Fibromyalgia Linked," WebMD, June 10, 2004.

CHAPTER 8: THE STAGE OF AWAKENING: SAFETY AND PROTECTION

1. "Your Amygdala Gets Bigger If You're Anxious and Depressed," NeuroscienceNews.com, August 5, 2020.
2. Dacher Keltner, "Forget Survival of the Fittest, It's Kindness That Counts," interview by David DiSalvo, *Scientific American,* February 26, 2009.
3. Linda Sparrowe, "Yoga and Cancer: A Healing Journey," *Yoga International,* Fall 2010.
4. Brené Brown, *Dare to Lead: Brave Work, Tough Conversations, Whole Hearts* (New York: Random House, 2018).

CHAPTER 9: THE STAGE OF BECOMING: A NEW NARRATIVE

1. Anne Trafton, "How the Brain Controls Our Habits," *MIT News,* October 29, 2012.

CHAPTER 10: THE STAGE OF BEING: INTEGRATION

1. Joan Borysenko, "Born for These Times," joanborysenko.com, November 17, 2016.
2. Based on the work of Alberto Villoldo and the Four Winds Society, https://thefourwinds.com.

CHAPTER 11: THE STAGE OF TRANSFORMING: WISDOM AND GROWTH

1. For more information, visit https://yodigonomas.com.
2. Yukari Mitsuhashi, "Ikigai: A Japanese Concept to Improve Work and Life," BBC.com, August 7, 2017. For more information, check out *How to Ikigai: Lessons in Finding Happiness and Living Your Purpose,* by Tim Tamashiro (Coral Gables, FL: Mango Publishing Group, 2019).

CHAPTER 12: STAYING ELEVATED

1. Stephen Joseph and P. Alex Linley, "Growth Following Adversity: Theoretical Perspectives and Implications for Clinical Practice,"

Clinical Psychology Review 26, no. 8 (December 2006): 1041–53: https://doi.org/10.1016/j.cpr.2005.12.006.

2. Dean Hamer, *The God Gene: How Faith Is Hardwired into Our Genes* (New York: Anchor Books, 2004).

3. Lisa Miller, Mark Davies, and Steven Greenwald, "Religiosity and Substance Abuse among Adolescents in the National Comorbidity Survey," *Journal of the American Academy of Adolescent and Child Psychiatry* 39, no. 9 (September 2000): 1190–97, https://doi.org/10.1097/00004583-200009000-00020.For a discussion on this and other aspects of Lisa Miller's work on spirituality and depression, see *The Awakened Brain: The New Science of Spirituality and Our Quest for an Inspired Life,* by Dr. Lisa Miller (New York: Random House, 2021).

4. American Psychological Association, "People with a Sense of Oneness Experience Greater Life Satisfaction," ScienceDaily.com, April 11, 2019.

5. Suzanne Simard, "Trees Talk to Each Other: 'Mother-Tree' Ecologist Hears Lessons for People, Too," interview by Dave Davies, *Fresh Air,* May 4, 2021. Further information from *The Hidden Life of Trees* by Peter Wohlleben (London: Allen Lane, 2016) and *Finding the Mother Tree: Discovering the Wisdom of the Forest* by Suzanne Simard (New York: Knopf, 2021).

Index